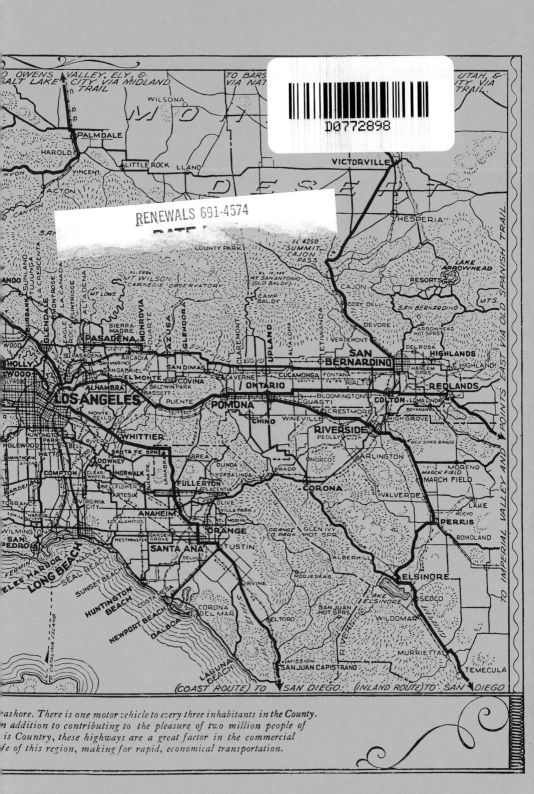

ashore. There is one motor vehicle to every three inhabitants in the County.
 addition to contributing to the pleasure of two million people of
is Country, these highways are a great factor in the commercial
de of this region, making for rapid, economical transportation.

≡

Los Angeles
and the
Automobile

≡

Los Angeles
and the
Automobile

THE MAKING OF THE
MODERN CITY

Scott L. Bottles

UNIVERSITY OF CALIFORNIA PRESS
BERKELEY   LOS ANGELES   LONDON

Frontispiece: Courtesy of Security Pacific National Bank Photograph Collection
Los Angeles Public Library

University of California Press
Berkeley and Los Angeles, California

University of California Press, Ltd.
London, England

Library of Congress Cataloging in Publication Data

Bottles, Scott L.
   Los Angeles and the automobile.

   Includes index.
   1. Transportation, Automotive—California—
Los Angeles.   2. Street-railroads—California—
Los Angeles.   3. Urban transportation—California—
Los Angeles.   4. City planning—California—Los
Angeles.   I. Title.
HE5634.L7B68   1987   388.4'1321'0979494   86–14660
ISBN 0–520–05795–3 (alk. paper)

Printed in the United States of America

1 2 3 4 5 6 7 8 9

To Catherine and Julia

≡ Contents ≡

═ Preface ═

began work on this book several years ago as a graduate student at UCLA. It struck me at the time that few serious historians had examined southern California's rich urban past; although the butt of many jokes, Los Angeles remained a largely under-studied environment. I started examining Los Angeles with the intention of explaining why this city differs so much from many other cities. I found, in fact, that southern California shares many characteristics with other metropolitan areas. Los Angeles, then, is important not because it is a unique city but because its history helps explain the evolution of America's urban development. This work therefore explores not only the history of Los Angeles over the past eighty-five years, but also that of all American urban areas.

Although writing this book was largely a solitary effort, I have accumulated many debts over the last six years. First, I would like to thank the staffs of several libraries who helped uncover much of this city's past, including: the University Research Library of UCLA, the Los Angeles Municipal Research Library, the Los Angeles Public Library, and Special Collections of UCLA. I would especially like to thank Robert Middlekauff, Martin Ridge, and the entire staff of the Henry E. Huntington Library in San Marino. Not only did the Huntington yield important documents for my scrutiny but it also provided me with a halcyon atmosphere in which to write most of my manuscript.

Despite the fact that Los Angeles is often accused of ignoring its past, the city holds within its boundaries several important photographic collections. I would like to thank several of these archives for allowing me to reproduce the photographs that illustrate this book. These include: the Security Pacific National Bank Photograph Collection in the Los Angeles Public Library; the Seaver Center for Western History Research in the Natural History Museum of Los Angeles County; the Los Angeles City Archives; Special Collections of the University Research Library, UCLA; the California Historical Society; the Spence Air Photo Collection at the Department of Geography, UCLA; and the Huntington Library.

Several organizations at UCLA provided me with research funds that enabled me to pursue this project. I would therefore like to thank the Department of History, the Alumni Association, the College of Letters and Science, and the Department of Fellowships and Grants.

Most important, I owe a debt of gratitude to several people who read and criticized this work at various times. Stanley Holwitz at the University of California Press took an early interest in this book and helped guide it through the publication process. David Dexter and Shirley Warren gave my manuscript a thorough reading and saved me from many typographical and grammatical errors. Martin Wachs and Norris Hundley not only read an earlier version of this work but also served on my doctoral committee. Dr. Wachs's knowledge of urban transportation planning was particularly helpful and I thank him for his encouragement. I would also like to thank Jaclyn Greenberg, David Johnson, Kenneth Jackson, Joel Tarr, Roger Lotchin, and Larry Lipin for their careful readings of my manuscript and their suggestions for improvement.

Eric Monkkonen served as a mentor, friend, and eventually as my dissertation chairman. Dr. Monkkonen was a model mentor. He challenged and advised me without interfering with my independence. The fact that I wrote a non-quantitative study alone speaks of Dr. Monkkonen's broad-minded approach to graduate studies.

In reading countless acknowledgment pages of other authors, I am struck by the fact that one's spouse is almost always the last to be thanked. Ironically, I am following in that tradition. Yet I thank Catherine Kelly not for her typing skills, but for her intellectual contributions to this work. A historian in her own right, Catherine has several times put aside her own book manuscript to read and criticize the pages that follow. I therefore thank her for her efforts on my behalf and for her steadfast support while I was struggling to establish myself in a new career.

Introduction

≡

Perhaps no technological in-
novation has affected the character of American cities as
much as the automobile. Until recently, however, few historians ever bothered to examine the impact of cars upon
American society. Those people who did write about the
automobile usually lacked both objectivity and historical insight. This was particularly true during the 1960s when
Americans began to recognize some of the less desirable
aspects of living in a motorized society. The automobile,
critics charged, not only polluted our air but also created
sprawling suburbs, crippled our sense of community, and
blighted inner-city neighborhoods. The 1970s brought new
concerns when the oil crises demonstrated the vulnerability
of a transportation system almost completely dependent
upon the car. Frustrated with the quality of urban life, some
social commentators lashed out at the automobile as the
cause of many contemporary urban problems.[1]

One such critic was Bradford Snell. As a legislative
analyst for the United States Senate, Snell attacked the automobile industry for its role in altering America's urban
transportation system. In his widely quoted report presented
before the Senate Judiciary Committee in 1974, Snell argued
that automobile manufacturers conspired during the forties
to destroy a thriving, efficient system of streetcars in cities
throughout the United States. By purchasing controlling interests in urban railways, the corporations replaced electric

trolleys with diesel motor coaches. The inefficiency of the buses in turn led to the demise of a once healthy public transportation network, and left urban residents with the automobile as their only means of transport. General Motors, Ford, and Chrysler, Snell claimed, had reshaped "American ground transportation to serve corporate wants instead of social needs."[2]

Snell believed that Los Angeles' experience epitomized the malevolent plans of the consortium. "Nowhere," Snell asserted, "was the ruin from GM's motorization program more apparent than in southern California." General Motors and other interested parties, Snell argued, began acquiring transit companies in Los Angeles County during the late thirties. Shortly thereafter began the systematic dismantling of what was once the largest electric interurban system in the world. The new owners replaced the streetcars with motor coaches. "The noisy, foul smelling buses," wrote Snell, "turned earlier patrons of the high-speed rail system away from public transit and, in effect, sold millions of private automobiles." According to Snell, GM's greedy, self-interested actions in southern California turned Los Angeles into an "ecological wasteland."[3]

It is true that General Motors and other automobile-related manufacturers invested in a company that purchased urban streetcar lines. During 1944, the Henry Huntington estate sold the Los Angeles Railway (LARY) to American City Lines, a subsidiary of National City Lines. Minority stockholders in the latter company included General Motors, Standard Oil of California, Firestone Tire and Rubber Company, Phillips Petroleum Company, and Mack Truck. The new management immediately began to replace the railway's streetcars with buses. Two years later, a federal grand jury brought suit against National City Lines for antitrust violations. The government sought to break up the interlocking stock ownership of the company, halt the purchase of equipment without competitive bidding, and abrogate the supplier contracts between National City Lines' operating companies, such as American City Lines, and the oil, rubber, and bus manufacturers. A trial in Chicago later brought both acquittals and convictions; most important, the corporate stockholders of National City Lines divested their holdings of that company before the suit came to trial.[4]

Up to this point, Snell is on safe ground. A company partly owned by automobile-related manufacturers purchased a streetcar line in Los Angeles and converted some of the railway's operations to bus service. It is not surprising that American City Lines purchased its equipment and supplies from some of its shareholders. In doing so, it appears that the company violated various federal statutes concerning the restraint of trade. But Snell assumes that these actions maimed a once healthy and efficient trolley system, leaving Angelenos to rely upon their cars for transportation. Snell therefore implies that the rise in popularity of the automobile in Los Angeles occurred largely because of a General Motors–sponsored conspiracy.

Snell's argument falls apart at this point. First, the decision to remove streetcars in favor of buses had been made years earlier. Traction companies in southern California had begun using motor coaches in suburban areas as early as 1921. Furthermore, the LARY's management had already decided to replace nearly all the company's trolleys with buses four years before American City Lines purchased the network. Only World War II with its rubber and oil shortages prevented the railway from adopting this plan. Consequently, the American City Lines' proposal to do away with the antiquated streetcars was hardly an original one. Nor did the decision to substitute buses for streetcars force commuters into their cars; far more Angelenos at this time used automobiles than public transportation. Several years prior to the sale of the LARY, a study found that 62 percent of the people entering Los Angeles' central business district did so by automobile. This figure was even higher in the suburbs where 86 percent of those traveling to such places as Pomona and Westwood used their cars.

The real irony of Snell's report was that he portrayed the traction companies as virtuous, responsible public utilities trying to provide a public service on the one hand while fighting off the evil designs of the automobile manufacturers on the other. In reality the situation was just the opposite. People in Los Angeles during the first three decades of the century constantly complained about the quality of rail transit. From their point of view the railways sought to benefit at the public's expense. In seeking to operate their business profitably, railway officials, in the minds of many citizens, deliberately ran too few cars, refused to build necessary crosstown lines or tracks into lightly populated areas, ignored the safety of the public, and bribed elected officials for favors. Frustrated by inadequate and inefficient service, Angelenos turned to the automobile manufacturers to supply them with an alternative means of transport. Although Snell portrayed the automobile makers as villains out to destroy the streetcars, Angelenos believed that these corporations could liberate them from the inefficiencies and corruption of the traction companies. Any study of the effect of the automobile on Los Angeles and other American cities must therefore look beyond the post–World War II era and the actions of National City Lines into the early decades of the twentieth century, for it was at that time that American urban dwellers adopted the automobile for urban use.

Los Angeles' close association with the automobile and its sprawling urban form make it a natural case study of twentieth-century urban development. Indeed, many writers have identified Los Angeles as the archetypal modern American city.[5] With the possible exception of Manhattan, which as an island suffers from geographical constraints, all American metropolises now depend heavily on the automobile for urban transportation. Most cities also have experienced substantial suburban development at the expense of their central business districts. It is true that Los Angeles decentralized earlier and to a greater extent than other cities, but that was largely because of the fact that southern California did not emerge as a major urban center until the twentieth century. Older metropolises such as Boston, Chicago, and San Francisco had by that time several layers of urban growth surrounding their downtown commercial districts which exerted strong centralizing forces on the rest of the city. Lacking such prior development, Los Angeles found itself less constricted and hence more easily adaptable to the automobile and a decentralized economy.[6] This should not, however, blind us to the fact that nearly all large American cities have experienced considerable urban sprawl. The difference between Los Angeles and other metropolitan areas is that the former developed much of its present form prior to World War II. Other cities began to decentralize largely after the war.

In order to understand how the spatial transformation of Los Angeles during the twentieth century fits into a general trend in urban development, one must review the structure of American cities prior to the invention of the automobile.[7] Before the advent of mechanized transportation, most people in cities walked. Only the most affluent could afford to keep horses or ride in horse-drawn cabs. This prevailing mode of travel necessarily limited the outward growth of urban areas to a radius of about two miles, the distance most people could walk in half an hour. American cities, however, grew continuously following the Revolution. By the early nineteenth century, large cities such as New York, Philadelphia, and Boston sported residential densities which reached upward of more than 75,000 people per square mile. By way of contrast, New York City in 1980 averaged about 35,000 people per square mile.[8] As the population in cities rose rapidly during the early to mid-nineteenth century, space became an important commodity. Row houses on small lots with tiny front yards became the norm for middle- and upper-class citizens. Members of the working class in the meantime often found themselves living in crowded multiunit apartments. Nor was there much differentiation between the residential and commercial parts of the city. Urban elites sought to avoid lengthy walks and therefore built houses near their workplaces in the urban core. Many white-collar workers, artisans, and skilled workers also lived and worked in the city center, resulting in a broad spatial integration of workplace and residence.

Ironically, the periphery then was the least desirable district within the walking city. The suburbs became the haunt of such objectionable industries as slaughterhouses and tanneries as well as the residence of many poor and unskilled workers who could not afford the high cost of housing closer in. When these suburban residents did find work in the core, they had to walk quite a distance to their place of employment. Their more prosperous neighbors living near the center therefore shunned the suburbs as a place of noisome industry and lowly citizens. One Philadelphian wrote in 1849 that "nine-tenths of those whose rascalities have made Philadelphia so unjustly notorious live in the dens and shanties of the suburb." Fifty years earlier, a Philadelphia newspaper had described the suburb of Southwark as one in which people were "saluted with a great variety of fetid and disgusting smells."[9]

The boisterous, crowded, and largely undifferentiated spatial structure of American urban areas remained typical until the mid-nineteenth century. By that time two factors had encouraged the spatial transformation of the city. First, the rise of an incipient factory system resulted in the separation of residence and workplace for many urban dwellers. Prior to 1830, most master craftsmen lived either above or adjacent to their shops. The distinction between work and residence was further muddled by the structure of the artisanal household. A successful master expected his employees, both journeymen and apprentices, to live in his home where he could exercise patriarchal control over them. Although tension surely must have existed between masters and workers, they nevertheless worked, relaxed, and resided together as a kind of extended family. This system began to break down, however, when an expanding economy encouraged the development of factories emphasizing specialized labor, larger workplaces, and the spatial separation of the manufacturing process from a company's administration.

Cities gradually responded to these changes by assuming a new form. In abandoning the traditional household economy, the factory owners placed both spatial and psychological barriers between themselves and their workers. As the century progressed, proprietors worked alongside their employees with far less frequency. The introduction of standard parts, specialized labor tasks, and later machinery meant that factories could employ semiskilled laborers. No longer did the master craftsman have to teach an apprentice the secrets of his trade. Foremen subsequently came to oversee the manufacturing process while the owner administered the financial, marketing, and planning needs of the company. The breakdown of the apprentice system also meant that workers now lived apart from their bosses. Laborers came to identify with one another and consequently moved into exclusively working-class neighborhoods near the factories. With the influx of semiskilled and unskilled laborers from overseas, these neighborhoods often took on an increasingly foreign character. The factory owners subsequently began to relocate in nicer quarters somewhat removed from the noisy factories and boisterous working-class neighborhoods. The separation of work and residence consequently resulted in the emergence of the central business district exclusively devoted to commercial and industrial enterprise. It also encouraged the rise of residential neighborhoods organized along class lines.[10]

The rapid expansion of urban areas after 1830 also influenced the structure of American cities. Fed by thousands of European immigrants, the population of cities in the United States grew by 92 percent during the 1840s alone. This influx of new residents put tremendous pressure on the already crowded housing stock. Furthermore, the inadequate waste disposal and water delivery systems could not handle the rising population. Cesspools and overflowing sewers leaked into the drinking water of many towns while families regularly tossed their garbage into the streets. All of this made cities during the nineteenth century extremely unhealthful. In addition, the middle class became increasingly uncomfortable living near what it perceived to be unruly and often ethnic working-class neighborhoods. These considerations convinced many middle- and upper-class denizens to look toward the wide open expanses of the countryside as a place of residence. Cities were noisy, crowded, and polluted places where the frequent outbreak of yellow fever, smallpox, tuberculosis, and cholera substantially lowered the life expectancy of its citizens. The rural environment, however, had long held a special place in the American mind. Pastoral and harmonious, the country symbolized healthfulness and virtue. This idealization of nature, combined with a desire to own one's own home and the middle-class dislike of ethnic neighborhoods, encouraged many people to move to the fringe of the city. The development of the suburbs, they hoped, would allow them to enjoy the amenities of the countryside while retaining all of the economic advantages of living in the city. But if one were to reside in the periphery, one needed improved transportation.[11]

The earliest forms of mass transportation in cities appeared prior to the Civil War. Entrepreneurs introduced the omnibus as one solution to the increased demand for public transport. Built as a large carriage drawn by a team of horses, the omnibus typically carried as many as twelve people along a fixed route for a fee of ten cents. Although the cost of riding in the omnibus was beyond the reach of most workers, many middle-class residents eagerly took advantage of this innovation by moving into newly accessible suburbs. Within only a few years, the omnibus had become commonplace in most large cities. As a Baltimore paper explained in 1844, the omnibus allowed "persons to reside at a distance from their places of business in more healthy locations without loss of time and fatigue in walking." This new mode of transport, however, was not without its discomforts. Omnibuses traveled at less than five miles an hour, while the carriages themselves had poor ventilation, uncomfortable seats, and a rough ride.[12] These problems limited its influence in shaping American cities.

The rise of the steam railroad after 1830 also affected the pattern of urban development. Railroad engines started and stopped slowly. They also spewed sparks, ashes, and smoke from their smokestacks, making them unpopular with those living near their tracks. These problems prevented trains from operating effectively within cities. The railroads could, however, connect independent small towns with a regional urban center. Commuter trains therefore created a string of small bedroom communities separated by rural greenbelts. It is not surprising that housing in these suburbs usually surrounded the railroad station. Once again the expense of riding the trains into the city meant that only the more affluent of the middle class could afford this means of transport. Nevertheless, by 1840 Boston, New York, and Philadelphia all had commuter trains serving their suburban districts.[13]

Although the omnibus and steam railroad provided limited urban transportation, it was the streetcar that played the most important role in realigning the American city prior to the twentieth century. Horse-drawn streetcars first appeared in Manhattan in 1832. With tracks laid down the middle of the street, the horse railway provided comfortable rides at a speed of six to eight miles per hour. By the 1850s, streetcars had spread to cities throughout the United States.

Thirty years later, Frank Sprague invented the first practical electric railway. Twice as fast as the horsecar, the electric trolley's advantages were immediately apparent as it opened vast new areas to development.

It is important to note, however, that these transportation innovations by themselves did not inevitably lead to the suburbanization of America. Rather, people invented these new modes of transportation in response to the desire of many city dwellers to live on the periphery of the city. With an efficient alternative to walking, many urban residents left the dense confines of the city. Most of the early transit users came from the middle and upper classes because only they had the time and money to commute between the suburbs and the central business district. Factory hands working twelve hours a day in the nineteenth century did not have time to travel far. Nor did they earn enough to afford the cost of public transport. The availability of mechanized transportation therefore altered both the social and spatial organization of the city. The suburbs, once the retreat of the unskilled and unemployed, suddenly became the preserve of the relatively affluent. At the same time, workers and ethnic immigrants moved into the areas left vacant by those fleeing the inner city. Streetcars, then, turned the walking city inside out, while lowering residential densities and lengthening the journey to work for many.[14]

Although urban railways opened the periphery to extensive development, cities remained highly centralized. People may have lived in the suburbs, but they continued to work and shop in the city center. Most streetcar lines therefore radiated outward from the central business district. The inefficiency of short-haul commercial transport also enhanced this centralized focus. Most goods moved within the city on slow horse-drawn carts. This meant that a city's commercial sector had to remain tightly packed. The decentralization of commerce would have to wait for the arrival of the motor truck.[15]

Electric railways became popular because they offered a solution to many of the nation's most pressing urban problems. Nineteenth-century cities were overcrowded and unhealthful. Government engineers and reformers constantly worried about the inadequacy of urban services such as sewage and refuse collection and the provision of drinking water. The increase in population densities throughout the century only worsened the situation. Streetcars promised to relieve the pressure on these services by dispersing much of the population across the countryside. Removed from the crowded tenements of the inner city, suburban residents could enjoy the amenities of the healthful semirural atmosphere while maintaining easy access to the central business district. The affluent therefore expected the railways not only to provide them with transportation but also to improve the quality of their lives.[16]

Traction companies in cities throughout the United States, however, operated as corporations. Executives of these railways consequently sought to lower costs and maximize income for the stockholders of their firms. This induced them both to build lines only where they might prove profitable and to run as few cars as possible. In addition, streetcar companies in many areas utilized their railways as a means of promoting real estate ventures. After purchasing tracts of land well removed from the city center, traction companies would extend railway lines to their developments and thus increase the value of their holdings. So prevalent was this practice that many urban reformers argued that railway companies designed their transit networks to service their subdivisions rather than the needs of the public. The rapid expansion of many railways also left them financially crippled. Consequently, these companies could not continue to expand their services into new suburbs despite the growing demand for additional housing. Many critics contended that because the trolley companies provided a vital urban service, they should acquiesce to public demands even at the expense of profit. Streetcar users constantly harassed railway executives over such issues as inadequate crosstown lines, overcrowded cars, and high fares.

The fact that streetcar companies along with other public utility companies usually controlled the local political apparatus through a generous use of economic pressure and wholesale bribery raised the public's ire even more. The battle between traction companies and the public therefore contributed to the progressive reform movement during the first two decades of the twentieth century. Although progressivism never existed as a coherent, uniform movement, it did bring together several political factions in an attempt to address various urban problems, including inadequate mass transportation. Ultimately, the fragmented nature of the movement prevented it from radically altering the urban economy. The most lasting legacy of the era was the establishment of government regulatory agencies, which tried to mediate disputes between the utility companies and the public. When these regulatory commissions later failed to solve the problems associated with mass transit, urban dwellers looked elsewhere for an alternative means of transport. They found their answer to these problems in the automobile.[17]

Frustrated by the inadequacies of rail transit, many urban dwellers turned to their automobiles as early as 1910.[18] The automobile provided its owner with unequaled mobility. No longer tied to the railway tracks or a timetable, the motorist could travel whenever and wherever he or she wished. People quickly found, however, that most cities could not accommodate large numbers of automobiles. The narrow, discontinuous streets of most central business districts became horribly congested while parking grew increasingly difficult. Nevertheless, city residents saw in the automobile the solution to their struggle with the streetcar companies and an opportunity to continue their pursuit of the suburban ideal. American urban dwellers therefore did everything they could to facilitate vehicular movement through opening and widening streets and instituting improved traffic regulation. At the same time, most cities did little to subsidize rail transit despite the frequent calls for subway construction. Urban residents believed that the railways should finance transit improvements themselves. The huge costs associated with this proposed construction usually precluded such actions.[19] Consequently, the automobile thrived while mass transit faltered in the congestion of the city core. The postwar inflation, declining patronage, and increased regulation combined to send many streetcar companies into bankruptcy during the twenties and thirties. Few city dwellers wept at the time because the automobile seemed to hold such promise for the future of urban life.

The automobile and truck had a lasting effect on the shape of American cities. Streetcars usually promoted growth only along the immediate vicinity of their tracks leaving large stretches of land vacant. With railways lines radiating from their cores, most cities consequently took on a star-shaped configuration. The automobile, however, facilitated development within the areas lacking rail service. The greater speed of the automobile also encouraged commuters to push suburban boundaries further into the countryside far beyond the reach of the trolleys. This allowed real estate developers to continue building single-family dwellings following World War I.[20]

Automobile traffic initially followed the patterns first established by the streetcar. Autoists lived in the suburbs, but worked and shopped in the central business district. As the number of cars entering the downtown area grew, congestion worsened. The initial attempts to improve vehicular flow through street widening and traffic regulation eased the problem for a few years. But these improvements only encouraged more people to use their autos. As traffic congestion resumed, people looked for new solutions. Businesses discovered that they could avoid the crowded conditions of the city center by moving into the suburbs. Trucks provided an efficient means of transporting goods while the popularity of the automobile ensured an adequate labor force. The central business district which had once contained most of a city's economic activity suddenly became only one of several such centers.[21] The extent and timing of this decentralization varied from city to city. In general, those regions with a long history of urban growth tended to decentralize later than cities such as Los Angeles. New York, Boston, and Philadelphia had built up over the previous two hundred years extensive urban cores, which even today continue to exert a strong influence over the transportation patterns of the surrounding area. These cities consequently experienced most of their economic dispersal following World War II. Other cities such as Houston, Los Angeles, and Phoenix emerged after the invention of the streetcar, automobile, and truck. Because these innovations encouraged residential and economic dispersal, the city centers of these later cities today appear less developed.

Los Angeles led the national trend toward decentralization despite the fact that it did not evolve into a major metropolitan area until after 1900. Founded in 1781, Los Angeles remained an isolated small town until the 1880s when the arrival of the Southern Pacific Railroad linked it with the rest of the country. From that point forward the greater Los Angeles region grew rapidly. By 1910, the city boasted impressive streetcar and interurban systems that allowed much of the population to move into suburban developments outside of the downtown area. Los Angeles therefore never existed as a true walking city. The central business district after 1890, however, dominated the regional economy and Los Angeles retained a centralized urban structure until late in the 1920s.

Los Angeles' suburban residents heavily patronized the streetcars and interurbans operating in the area. Nevertheless, Angelenos were not always satisfied with their transit system. Like urban dwellers throughout the nation, people living in southern California frequently complained about the crowded cars, high fares, and slow service. The railways, along with other public utility companies, tried to shield themselves from the angry public by dominating the local political machine. Sensational revelations of bribery and corruption eventually led to the rise of a reform movement determined to improve the quality of urban services, including mass transportation. When this progressive movement failed to ameliorate the problems associated with rail service in Los Angeles, suburban residents turned to their automobiles.

The adoption of the automobile in Los Angeles, however, did not come easily, as motorists had to fight the railways for the right to use the city streets. Once large numbers of motorists began driving into the downtown area, congestion became severe. The city had long suffered from streetcar congestion in its commercial center. The increasing number of automobiles only exacerbated the situation as autoists competed with the trolleys for precious street space. The City Council finally attempted to resolve this problem by enacting a rigid no-parking law in 1920. The council, in fearing the wrath of the streetcar riders, hoped to rid the town's crowded roads of cars and thereby improve rail service. Its actions engendered a major controversy as it soon became apparent that a majority of Los Angeles' citizens wanted to facilitate rather than restrict vehicular movement. The protest against the ordinance cut across class lines as many working-class commuters opposed the law. Their enmity toward the traction companies and the general perception of the automobile as a democratic piece of urban technology influenced them to support automobile transit as an alternative to the inefficiency and seeming corruption of the railways. The heavy protest and economic pressure applied by the city's residents forced the council to rescind the law. Once more, automobiles freely moved and parked in the downtown area. This crisis over the status of the automobile in Los Angeles provides the historian with a unique window through which to observe the transition from public to private transportation—a process that would later have a profound impact on the spatial organization of the city.

The council's decision to repeal the objectionable legislation sanctioned the automobile's place in the city's transportation system. Nevertheless, the severe congestion that had caused the parking controversy still existed. Indeed, the problem worsened after the council's removal of the parking ban. The heavy traffic in the central business district illustrated an important issue that plagued cities throughout America. Once large numbers of motorists began to use their cars for commuting and shopping, it became apparent that the physical structure of American cities could not readily accommodate the automobile. This was particularly true in Los Angeles where narrow and discontinuous streets, constructed during a different transportation era, could not sufficiently handle the large flow of private vehicles. Once the City Council had accepted the automobile as a legitimate means of transport, it had to find a way to speed its movement. Impatient for a solution, the region's property owners and businessmen took control of the situation themselves. With the approval of the city government, they organized a systematic program to reconstruct the municipal street system. This concerted effort to widen and open the city's roads greatly improved automobile access.

The region's electric streetcars and interurbans did not fare nearly as well. The general outlook for railways throughout the nation looked dim after World War I. Rising labor and material costs, combined with poor management decisions in the past, brought hard times to the industry. Many traction companies in urban areas throughout the United States filed for bankruptcy during the ensuing decade. Most of the survivors were liquidated during the Depression. Los Angeles' streetcar and interurban corporations weathered these adversities. But the prevailing industry environment and their own shaky financial positions prevented them from attracting additional investment capital. Nor could they finance major improvements out of retained earnings. This limited their ability to construct rapid-transit lines that would have segregated their cars from the heavy street congestion. Although the Pacific Electric built a subway in 1926, that by itself did little to ameliorate the overall problem.

The reconstruction of the city's street system succeeded because major elements within society agreed on the automobile's place in the urban transportation network. The same groups could not, however, come to a similar consensus regarding the railways. These differences of opinion were played out in yet another important controversy. What began as a campaign to consolidate the operations of the steam railroads serving the city into a single unified station ended as a referendum regarding public transportation. The issue emerged when the city government asked the state Railroad Commission to order the Southern Pacific, Union Pacific, and Santa Fe railroads to build a jointly owned station to house all of their passenger services. The City Council had hoped that such a terminal would improve railroad access to the city. The carriers steadfastly refused to consider such a project largely because a union station would have opened the burgeoning southern California market to competing railroads. When the Railroad Commission supported the city, the railroads sought an injunction to stay the order. After several years of litigation, the fight reached an impasse. In 1926, the carriers announced a plan which they believed would break the stalemate. They proposed to build a complex system of elevated tracks connecting the existing terminals with each other. In a further attempt to persuade the City Council to drop its complaint with the Railroad Commission, the Southern Pacific Railroad offered to construct a similar set of elevated lines for its subsidiary, the Pacific

Electric. These structures would have reduced the congestion in the city center by removing hundreds of interurban cars from the downtown streets.

This proposition was very attractive to downtown businessmen who feared that heavy traffic on the city's highways would discourage shoppers from entering the central business district. These interests, then, saw the railroad plan as a way to reinforce the region's centralized spatial orientation. Homeowners and some city officials, however, argued that the elevated structures would mar the beauty of the city while lowering property values. They subsequently campaigned for the union station. Citing the irresponsibility of the railroads and traction companies in the past and the failure of elevateds in eastern cities, the union station proponents narrowly prevailed at the polls. Lacking a consensus regarding the nature of rapid transit in Los Angeles, the city could do little to improve mass transportation over the next few years.

The decision to facilitate automobile movement had in the meantime begun to alter the way people thought about the city's physical shape. The electric railways had allowed urban dwellers to move into the suburbs. Still, this dispersal of the population had done little to change the centralized orientation of the city because nearly all of the railways converged on the downtown area. Even the attempt to reconstruct the street system had little initial effect on this pattern because most major highways in Los Angeles radiated from the central business district. But southern California's population growth and automobile usage were booming. The resulting traffic conditions made it difficult for people to drive into the commercial section of the city. Rather than abandon their automobiles, shoppers sought commercial outlets in the suburbs. Many retail stores subsequently established branches in areas well removed from the congestion of downtown. This was the first in a long series of decisions that led to the development of the decentralized city which focused not on the city center, but on many business and industrial districts throughout the county.

People favored this new form of urban development because they felt it offered the possibility of a better life. Earlier in the century Angelenos had expected the railways to resolve many pressing urban problems by distributing residents in low density suburbs throughout the region. Many outlying residents, however, felt betrayed by the traction companies. In addition to reinforcing the centrally focused spatial structure of the region, the railways had failed to provide efficient or even adequate transportation. "Is it inevitable or basically sound or desirable that larger and larger crowds be brought into the city's center; do we want to . . . develop an intensive rather than an extensive city[?]" asked one civic organization.[22] Rather than suffer the crowded conditions found in eastern cities, southern Californians began to espouse the merits of decentralizing many of the urban functions traditionally found in the downtown area. Urban planners agreed as they saw in Los Angeles a chance to design a new type of city which would allow people to live better, more productive lives.[23] Angelenos and planners knew that the automobile would remain the key to developing the ideal city. The railways were tied to their tracks. The automobile, however, could reach any point in the region that had adequate roads. The adoption of the automobile, then, was fueled in part by the desire to restructure Los Angeles' urban space.

Nevertheless, the popularity of the automobile was not without its own problems. As more residents took to their cars, the streets became exceedingly crowded. At first, the congestion only affected the roads leading into the downtown area. But soon traffic became heavy in the newly constructed suburban shopping districts. This situation began to repeat itself with disconcerting frequency. First, city engineers would open or widen new highways to facilitate the flow of vehicles. The improved access would attract heavy usage. Businesses would then move to the new thoroughfare to take advantage of the busy location. Once shoppers began frequenting these stores, traffic movement would slow. This indiscriminate mixing of through and local traffic decreased the efficiency of the roadway as a transportation lane. Motorists subsequently began to look elsewhere to avoid the increasingly crowded conditions. Retail sales would decline in the area and businesses would often close altogether. District after district suffered a similar fate as planners worried that decentralization could lead to a never-ending pattern of falling property values and obsolete shopping centers.

City officials believed they had found the answer to this recurring problem in the much-heralded freeways. In 1938, a federally sponsored traffic survey boldly declared that a system of limited access highways would allow the region to tie its subcenters together. The freeways would once again establish definite transportation routes and thus stabilize land values in business districts spread across the county. Those living in the outlying areas favored the proposal because it promised to speed their daily commute. Downtown business interests also supported the proposition because they felt the new highways would clear the congestion from the streets and once again provide easy access to the central business district. Most important, the users of the system would pay for the cost of its construction themselves.

During the late twenties and thirties, several groups had called for the erection of a subway network. Their plans, however, proved impossible to finance in an equitable manner. Engineers knew that subways would require heavy subsidization because Los Angeles' population density was far too low to make rapid transit self-sufficient.[24] The Los Angeles public had no interest in assessing itself to construct a mass-transit system for the benefit of the traction companies; nor did it want to assume control of the financially failing railways. The freeways, in contrast, would not require subsidies because autoists themselves willingly paid user taxes on gasoline and tires. Furthermore, public transit proponents argued that buses riding along the shoulders of the freeways could provide adequate public transit.

The ready acceptance of the freeways confirmed the belief that the automobile could function as the primary means of transportation in Los Angeles and that a decentralized city form would lead to an improved quality of life. Unfortunately, as Angelenos would later learn, decentralization and the automobile would engender new problems. Nevertheless, it is important to realize that Angelenos freely adopted the automobile as their major means of transportation long before American City Lines purchased one of the city's two major fixed-rail systems. By 1944, the city's streetcar and interurban systems were mere shadows of their former selves. Their decline began with the belief that the automobile could solve pressing urban problems and create a kind of utopia.

⇐ 2 ⇒

The Progressive Response

===

Inside the air was a pestilence; it was heavy with disease and the emanations from many bodies. Anyone leaving this working mass, anyone coming into it . . . forced the people into still closer, still more indecent, still more immoral contact. A bishop embraced a stout grandmother, a tender girl touched limbs with a city sport, refined womens' faces burned with shame and indignation—but there was no relief. Was all this in an oriental prison? Was it in some hall devoted to the pleasures of the habitues of vice? Was it a place of punishment for the wicked? No gentle reader, it was only the result of public stupidity and apathy. It was in a Los Angeles street car on the 9th day of December, in the year of grace 1912; also on any other old day you are a mind to board a city street car between the hours of 5 and 7 in the afternoon.
—Los Angeles *Record*
December 10, 1912

The arrival of the electric railway in American cities brought with it problems as well as promises. People hoped that this technological innovation would improve the quality of urban life by lowering residential densities near the city center. The late nineteenth century saw rapid urban growth throughout the nation. Concerned citizens feared that the influx of new residents would overwhelm the already inadequate infrastructures of most cities. The invention of the streetcar, however, allowed people to move into the suburbs, thereby easing the burden on central business districts. Moreover, the outlying areas offered urban denizens the advantages of homeownership and pastoral beauty. With an efficient transportation system in place, suburbanites could enjoy the benefits of both the city and the countryside. But the traction companies could not always

- 22 -

deliver the kind of services expected of them. Many urban dwellers believed that the railways deliberately ran too few cars, refused to build badly needed crosstown lines, bribed city officials, and abused their franchises in a rapacious attempt to profit at the public's expense. Consequently, railway executives constantly found themselves surrounded by angry patrons demanding improved services and increased government control over public transit.

During the late nineteenth and early twentieth century, public antagonism toward the traction companies contributed to progressive reform movements in cities throughout the United States. Historians writing during the thirties and forties described progressivism as a democratic attempt to rid government of the corrupting influences of monopolistic corporations and trusts. Modern historians, however, no longer see the progressives as a coherent, ideologically uniform assemblage. Rather, many historians believe that reform-minded citizens established numerous pressure groups, each agitating for more control over the political process. Reform to these people meant imposing their own vision of a just political system on the rest of society. Fragmentation occurred because these various interest groups held different ideals regarding urban policymaking. Nevertheless, once several organizations agreed upon a particular set of issues, they could coalesce into a force powerful enough to drive more traditional political machines out of office. Depending on the situation, middle-class professionals, businessmen, workers, labor leaders, and even socialists could come together to reshape American society.[1]

The progressives often succeeded because of the recession of traditional party loyalties. Scandal and corruption in city governments throughout the United States resulted in declining voter turnout and split-ticket voting, which left the ruling party machines vulnerable to the reforming insurgents. "This was the context," writes historian Daniel Rodgers, "within which maverick politicians could vault into office and 'reform' . . . coalitions of all sorts could blossom."[2] But when the factions making up the progressive movement differed over policy or the future of the urban economy, they were left divided and often powerless. Indeed, it was not at all uncommon for workers to support middle-class reform leaders against corrupt machines only to find themselves hopelessly at odds with the new administration over labor's right to strike. These and other confrontations between the supporters of progressivism usually led to the disintegration of their movement and the reemergence of the traditional party leaders.

Although the progressives did not share a uniform set of values and interests, they nevertheless drew upon a related set of ideals regarding urban society.[3] Progressive leaders spent much of their time condemning the power of corporate monopoly. The American distrust of monopoly is deeply rooted in the past, reaching well into the early nineteenth century. The rapid industrialization of the post–Civil War era merely presented monopoly in a new guise—that of the modern corporation. Prior to the turn of the century, those attacking the trend toward economic concentration were outside of the economic and political mainstream. During the progressive era, however, middle-class Republicans began to decry graft, privilege, and corporate political power. These urban dwellers were introduced to the dangers of monopolistic control by public utility companies. Although utilities were not the sole focus of progressive agitation, much of the municipal legislation of the time dealt with the regulation of these economic concerns.

By the late nineteenth century, American urban areas were growing at a rapid rate. The expansion of the city required extensive municipal services, which were, more often than not, supplied by privately operated utility companies. By granting franchises to the utilities, city councils could procure vital urban services without having to finance expensive infrastructures. Although cities often tried to encourage competition by granting franchises to competing companies, efficiency and economies of scale usually required these utilities to operate as monopolies.[4] This left the turn-of-the-century urban dweller vulnerable to economic and political exploitation at the hands of these corporations. In cities throughout the United States, public utility companies controlled local political systems through a cynical use of economic pressure and wholesale bribery. The utilities wielded their political power to lower tax assessments against their properties, grab franchises at cut-rate prices, and avoid having to deliver unprofitable services.

Inspired in part by muckraking journalists and sensational graft trials, loose coalitions of workers, labor leaders, socialists, businessmen, and professionals came together as angry consumers to protest the utilities' inadequate services and corrupt political practices.[5] During their struggle, these consumers became increasingly aware of the need to control their environment. Nineteenth-century cities were notoriously unhealthful places in which to live. By the twentieth century, however, technological advances gave society the opportunity to improve the quality of life through the availability of mechanized transportation, modern sewage treatment, electrical power, telephones, and clean drinking water. The various progressive factions within the cities therefore hoped to unite their fellow citizens in a struggle against the seemingly arbitrary and corrupt power of the monopolies and at the same time create a more harmonious and healthful urban society.

Many middle-class progressives used the modern business organization as a model for a reformed governmental structure since industry placed a premium upon scientific efficiency, rationality, and predictability. This led to the adoption of independent public commissions as a way to control the utilities. By centralizing the regulatory powers of the city in an efficient bureaucracy staffed by experts, reformers hoped to improve and rationalize the delivery of urban services. These agencies seemed effective because they took public policymaking away from the easily corrupted political leader and gave it to the disinterested public servant.[6] In reality these commissions did not necessarily emasculate the power of the corporations or improve the overall quality of urban services. In fact, corporations throughout the United States often welcomed the establishment of regulatory agencies. As historian James Weinstein points out, corporate executives by this time were abandoning their adversarial stance for one of cooperation with government. Business leaders hoped to establish a partnership with government which would lead to a harmonious and efficient economic environment free from the devastating uncertainties of cutthroat competition.[7] The middle-class progressives who staffed the regulatory bodies felt uneasy about attacking the property rights of private capital anyway. These progressives fully accepted the legitimacy of the capitalist system; they merely sought to improve it and make it more equitable by limiting the arbitrary nature of corporations. The utilities therefore often found that they could either control, influence, or co-opt the newly established commissions.

Historian Sam Hays argues that the earlier acts of corruption occurred because the corporate leaders who controlled vast economic power held no acceptable means to influence public policymaking. The business executive's main concern was to encourage the city to aid economic expansion. But machine politics and the ward political structure of most municipalities shut out the new entrepreneurial capitalists. The corporation therefore had to resort to bribery to make its influence felt. The progressive regulatory commissions, however, provided a legitimate public forum where the utility companies could voice their concerns and needs. Consequently, regulation injected a welcome measure of stability into the economic environment.[8] This is not to say that the public utility commissions acceded to every corporate demand. Indeed, many utility companies found it much easier to control regulatory boards at the state rather than local levels and frequently tried to stave off the more radical socialist factions by lobbying for legislation that placed the real power to regulate in the state commissions.

Several historians have argued that the rise of large bureaucracies both in business and government was the outstanding feature of the Progressive Era.[9] Others assert that the progressive reform movement was really a sham because so much of the period's legislation was actually supported by and a benefit to large corporations.[10] Although each of these arguments has some validity, they ignore the democratic thrust behind most of the local progressive campaigns. Although the corporation remained the dominant economic force in America, it could not always forestall legislation it opposed. In addition, these political activists and their supporters were often motivated by a democratic desire to take command of the urban political structure that had been dominated by the corporations for so long. Regardless of the ultimate outcome of progressive reform, these diverse groups of people began their agitation with the hope that they could bring control to their physical and economic environment.

Los Angeles' experience during the Progressive Era clearly supports this last interpretation. Electric streetcars and interurbans brought to the city the possibility of rapid, efficient transportation. Local residents believed that this new form of transport would allow the city to distribute its citizens across the countryside in spacious single-family dwellings. Unfortunately, the operations of the traction companies did not always match local expectations. Rather than create a rational system of transportation, the railway entrepreneurs used their streetcars mainly to speculate in the local real estate market. Saddled with a high debt load from overexpansion, the carriers found that they could not provide the kind of service demanded of them by the local denizens. Joining forces with other utility companies and the Southern

Pacific Railroad, the railways turned to the city's political machine for help. Through bribery and economic pressure, the railroad and utilities came to dominate the City Council and thereby avoid the criticism of angry consumers.

By the early 1900s, a group of middle-class Republicans, disenchanted with party politics, set out to reform the city government. Supported in part by other reform groups, these insurgents eventually captured control of both the mayor's office and the City Council. Once in office, the newly elected officials began instituting changes similar to those put forth by progressive coalitions in cities across the United States, including the creation of a public utilities commission. Shortly after the progressive triumph, however, the uneasy reform alliance fell apart over an outbreak of labor unrest. A socialist bid for the mayor's office temporarily forced the middle-class progressives back into the party fold. Soon thereafter, the reform movement splintered into many divergent causes. As a result, progressivism did little to improve the overall quality of rail service in Los Angeles. Once it became clear that the Board of Public Utilities was either unwilling or unable to effect significant changes in the traction companies' operations, Angelenos began to look for alternative ways of transporting themselves.

Long before the first automobile appeared in southern California, entrepreneurs had already developed mechanized urban transportation for the region. As in most American cities, this mainly consisted of various means of rail transit. Opened in 1874, the first horse-drawn railway line ran for two and a half miles down Spring and Main from the Old Plaza to 6th Street. Later attempts at railway building included cable cars and primitive electric streetcars. Often built by real estate developers to lure prospective buyers to suburban home sites, most of these early railways quickly succumbed to financial and technical difficulties. Frank Sprague's invention of the first practical railway system in the late 1880s, however, sparked something of a streetcar building boom in Los Angeles County. By the turn of the century, several cities in the region boasted modern electric streetcar networks. In addition, several interurban lines ran between Los Angeles and nearby communities. Although popular with the public, these transit systems constantly faced financial crises because electric railway construction was extremely expensive and most of the early systems were undercapitalized. Henry Huntington purchased the controlling stock of one such interurban line following its collapse and thus gained a foothold in southern California's transportation market.[11]

Much has already been written about Huntington and his railway empire.[12] Huntington was the nephew and heir of Southern Pacific Railroad president Collis P. Huntington. Denied the presidency of the Southern Pacific following the death of his uncle in 1900, the younger Huntington turned to real estate and transit development in southern California. He incorporated his famous Pacific Electric Railway Company (the PE) in 1901. During the next nine years, Huntington augmented his railway holdings through an aggressive building program, the incorporation of new railway companies, and the purchase of existing lines.

Like electric streetcar builders throughout the United States, Huntington used his railway system as a way of exploiting his vast real estate developments. After purchasing large tracts of rural land, Huntington would build railway lines to connect his land holdings with downtown Los Angeles. "Railway lines have to keep ahead of the procession [of settlement]," Huntington said in 1904. "It would never do for an electric line to wait until the demand for it came. It must anticipate the growth of communities and be there when the homebuilders arrive—or they are very likely not to arrive at all, but to go to some section already provided with arteries of traffic." Indeed, Huntington anticipated and encouraged the growth of certain communities well enough

LOS ANGELES IMPROVEMENT CO.

33 SOUTH SPRING STREET.

JESSE YARNELL, President.   *E. A. HALL*, Secretary.

PEREMPTORY AUCTION SALE

ON LIBERAL CREDIT!

FOR PARTICULARS APPLY TO

Take these Cable Cars at Corner of Spring and Second Streets, and go to the Property.

Make your Choice and Mark your Catalogue, Before the Day of Sale.

SATURDAY, JAN. 23, 1886,

At 11 o'Clock, A. M.

NEWHALL'S SONS & CO.,

AUCTIONEERS,

225 and 227 Bush Street,   *San Francisco, Cal.*

to make millions of dollars in real estate investments despite the substantial losses of his interurban and streetcar empire. After nine years of railway building and a protracted struggle with the Southern Pacific for control of the PE, Huntington sold much of his traction interests to his rival, the Southern Pacific. Out of this "Great Merger" appeared the two railway companies that would dominate rail transit in the years to come. The "new" PE became a subsidiary of the Southern Pacific Railroad. The PE did operate local streetcar lines, but most of its passenger trains ran as high-speed interurbans on private rights-of-way between Los Angeles and other communities in southern California. At the system's peak, the PE operated 1,164 miles of track in four counties, making it the largest electric railway system in the world. As part of the merger with the Southern Pacific, Huntington received complete control over the Los Angeles Railway Company (the LARY). This narrow-gauge system handled nearly all of the city's streetcar traffic. Local historians have paid much attention to the role of the PE in the Los Angeles transit network, but it was the LARY that carried nearly 90 percent of the city's rail passengers.[13]

The LARY and PE greatly influenced the region's early development. Huntington began building his traction empire at a time when Los Angeles first emerged as a major metropolitan center. Table 1 illustrates the city's remarkable population growth during the late nineteenth and early twentieth century. With such a rapid influx of immigrants, one might have expected the region to develop a densely concentrated city center.[14] Urban regions such as Chicago, Boston, and Philadelphia had experienced substantial expansion during

Plate 1. Los Angeles' railways played an important part in the creation of the city's real estate industry. The connection between streetcars and development is clearly illustrated in this advertisement from the 1880s. (Courtesy of Security Pacific National Bank Photograph Collection/Los Angeles Public Library)

Table 1
Population Growth in Los Angeles City, 1880–1950

	Population	% Increase
1880	11,183	—
1890	50,395	351
1900	102,479	103
1910	319,198	211
1920	576,673	81
1930	1,238,048	115
1940	1,504,277	22
1950	1,970,358	31

Source: U.S. Census

the nineteenth century when horse-drawn carts, omnibuses, and foot traffic served as the major modes of urban transportation. The limitations of such transit forced those cities to develop densely populated urban structures focused upon their central business districts. Although the arrival of the streetcar altered the shape of these cities by encouraging the growth of suburbs, the extensive downtown development continued to exert a powerful influence on the transportation, commercial, and residential patterns of these metropolises.[15]

Los Angeles, in contrast, grew at a time when the railways could spread its residents across the countryside, resulting in much lower urban densities. If eastern cities were characterized by the skyscraper, Los Angeles was symbolically represented by the horizontal sweep of the single-family dwelling. For the moment, Los Angeles retained a highly centralized urban form because its rail lines largely radiated from the downtown district. People may have lived in the suburbs, but they shopped, worked, and conducted business mainly in the city center. Still, southern California's late emergence as a major metropolis meant that its downtown area never developed as fully as those in eastern cities. This would later allow Los Angeles to decentralize earlier than the rest of the country.

It is not surprising, then, that Angelenos relied heavily upon the railways during the early years of the twentieth century. A transportation study completed in 1911 found that city residents averaged one ride per day on the LARY. People living in other cities of comparable sizes averaged only half as many daily rides. Nevertheless, this heavy patronage of the traction companies did not mean that southern Californians were satisfied with rail transit. Despite what nostalgic local historians would have us believe, streetcar riders were frequently frustrated with the railway companies.[16] Their dependence on the streetcars made suburban commuters and shoppers extremely sensitive to the quality of rail service. Caught between their desire to live outside the city center and their dependence on the traction companies, many Angelenos found themselves in a love-hate relationship with the carriers.

Insight into this relationship may be gleaned from a single issue of the Los Angeles *Examiner*. Part One of the August 22, 1911, issue reports that many westside residents favored the LARY's bid for a city franchise to build a sorely needed crosstown line on Vermont Avenue. So desirous were these citizens to obtain the line that they openly petitioned the City Council to grant the franchise. A different article in the same paper, however, found the League of Justice filing a resolution with the council proposing a two-cent fare for those trolley passengers forced to stand in streetcars. The railway, the league claimed, refused to run enough cars to provide seats for every passenger because the company wanted to increase profits. Since the "straphangers did not receive the full value of the fares," the league reasoned that they should not have to pay the entire five-cent fee. "With such an ordinance," the *Examiner* reported, "it is claimed the street railways would operate enough cars to accommodate all passengers." These two articles clearly illustrate the streetcar riders' dilemma. On the one hand, rail transit was absolutely vital to their lives; on the other hand, the railways' monopoly of urban transportation often led to inferior service.[17]

Public antagonism toward the railways began as early as the first decade of the twentieth century. Critics of the traction companies accused railway officials of bribing City Council members, disregarding the public's safety, ignoring the community's needs, abusing their franchise privileges, and profiting at the public's expense. Local newspapers such as the *Record, Examiner,* and *Express* frequently charged that Huntington used his influence with the City Council to secure inexpensive franchises and lower property assessments levied against his companies. "The City has been granting these franchises for years," complained one reform-minded politician. "They have been continuously, willfully and persistently violated to the great injury of the City and the people." Indeed, the PE hauled freight across lines granted solely for passenger trains, refused to pave the roadway in between their rails as required by their franchises, and even laid down tracks on streets before obtaining the city's permission. So blatantly did the traction companies abuse the terms of their franchises that the public voted in 1906 to limit the length of franchise agreements to twenty-one years, far shorter than the city's original grants. The citizenry believed that it could gain some leverage against the railways by threatening to abrogate their contracts at the end of their terms.[18]

Huntington's discrimination against car riders living in areas far removed from his land holdings further outraged the local newspapers. The *Examiner* claimed that the PE and LARY illegally charged higher fares in regions where Huntington held no land "for the purpose of advancing his real estate holdings at the expense of other property." The paper also complained that the history of Huntington's empire would "chronicle a more remarkable modern episode of servitude than the voluntary slavery of the Egyptian race in building pyramids for Pharaoh." Another paper added that Huntington's "clutch is strong and his arrogance unbounded." The city, critics argued, must halt the railways' abuses and formulate a plan to meet the transit needs of the people.[19]

The lack of safety measures on interurbans and streetcars also concerned the local newspapers. Although the number of accidents involving the railways was low compared to the size of the operations, mishaps generated much publicity. Many accidents occurred when impatient passengers disembarked or boarded moving cars. Even more frequently, streetcars ran into unsuspecting pedestrians. Prior to the twenties, the city did not regulate pedestrian movement. With hundreds of people weaving in and out of traffic on the downtown streets, it was not surprising that they often ran afoul of the electric trains. Reformers demanded that the traction companies equip their cars with special fenders that would harmlessly scoop up pedestrians should they carelessly walk in front of a train. The railways resisted these requests and subsequently drew the wrath of many citizens who called on them to stop "the indiscriminate and reckless slaughter and maiming of persons in the streets." Local papers freely criticized railway officials for their lack of concern regarding the public's safety. The Los Angeles *Record* believed that the traction companies' attempts to keep to their schedules forced car operators to drive faster than safety warranted. Railway officials, the paper charged, were more interested in profits than human lives. Other newspapers revealed that the railways often employed drivers with little training or experience.[20]

Angry citizens expressed their frustrations with the railways' policies and services in various ways. Southern Californians voted to establish regulatory agencies, wrote letters to local newspapers, and petitioned public agencies for redress. One of the most direct methods of protest open to the riding public was to try to lower the fares charged by the railways. The LARY was often troubled by critics seeking to reduce its revenues. Although the railway's fee of five cents was consistent with other trolley companies across the United States, many people felt that it produced excessive earnings given the quality of service. Viewing the LARY as a public utility, the leaders of the lower-fare movements argued that the railway should not profit at the public's expense. The *Record* asked during the early part of the century if someone would not step forward to lead the people against the "rich, greedy and venal corporations that so long have been plundering the city treasury?" The paper even accused Huntington of bribing the City Council for favors and a continuation of the five-cent fare. "The people have the Councilmen to blame for creating such creatures as Huntington. They made him by giving him streets; now they aim to keep him in power. He is like the horse-leech, crying 'give! give!' And the Councilmen who created him are trying to deliver the goods."[21]

These early attempts to reduce the LARY's fares failed. Years later in 1926, the railway tried to raise its fees from five to seven cents. A seemingly insignificant amount by modern standards, this represented a substantial 40 percent increase in the price of transportation. The public was outraged even though postwar inflation had sent equipment and labor costs soaring. People could not believe that traction officials had the audacity to ask for increased fares given the inadequacy of their service. When the California Railroad Commission denied the LARY's request, the railway took its case to court where the United States Supreme Court later ruled in its favor. The decision engendered the only serious attempt to municipalize the city's streetcar system. Huntington's death, however, put an end to the negotiations between the company and the city.[22]

The PE's interurbans, which covered far more area

than local streetcars, also fought disenchanted patrons seeking lower fares. The fees collected for interurban travel depended upon the passenger's destination—the longer the ride, the more the user had to pay. Several movements arose during the teens and twenties protesting this fare structure because many citizens did not believe the PE's service warranted fares that totaled as much as one dollar per ride. The PE's history of discouraging or abandoning local traffic further exacerbated the public's animosity. Even the Board of Public Utilities, which usually sympathized with the railway's financial problems, argued that the company's attempt to "discriminate in fares and transfers, to abandon individual local lines, [and] to discourage local business . . . is not in accord with the duty of the company nor the rights and necessities of the public."

Until 1914, when the state Railroad Commission assumed the power to set utility rates, the board would fix what it believed were fair rates for the railways. The City Council, yielding to public pressure, often reduced those fares; the traction companies usually responded with injunctions and restraining orders. The ensuing litigation only increased the public resentment.[23] Citizen groups reacted with popular movements similar to those aimed at the LARY. In the summer of 1913, the Los Angeles Rate Association attacked the PE's existing rate structure. Arguing that railway companies in other parts of the country charged lower fees for longer rides, the organization petitioned the Railroad Commission to lower interurban fares between outlying areas and Los Angeles. The association also held mass meetings and secured the approbation of numerous civic groups. These popular uprisings were hardly spontaneous, for the Los Angeles *Times* noted that the movement to lower car fares was "one which has been agitated each summer for some years."[24]

The attempt to reduce the PE's fares continued for several years. Even court rulings upholding PE rate increases did little to stem the tide of protest. Following World War I, the company requested the Railroad Commission's permission to raise its interurban fares because wartime inflation had greatly increased the railway's operating and equipment costs. Since the PE had operated at a loss for several years prior to the war, it argued quite rightly that it had to raise its ticket prices to remain solvent. The commission agreed with the company and approved the increases. Twenty southern California cities serviced by the railway immediately protested the decision. Arguing that the rate increases were excessive, discriminatory, and a "burden to the public," the cities continued to agitate for relief even after the Railroad Commission reaffirmed its stance. "Every manager knows," a PE official complained, "that the general demand is for improved service as well as improved and more expensive equipment and facilities generally." But if the railways attempted to pay for such services by instituting fare increases, the public revolted. "Let the street railway, or any other railway company, attempt to meet its fast increasing expenses and public demands in the same manner [as any other company], and note 'the tempest in a teapot' that is raised."[25]

The most frequent complaint leveled at the railways concerned the crowded streetcar conditions. People believed that anyone riding a trolley should receive a seat. Yet during the morning and afternoon rush hours, many were forced to stand. Critics of the traction companies assumed that railway officials refused to run more cars because such a move would increase expenses. A Los Angeles judge reported that "on almost every line in the city the cars running, both morning and evening are so crowded that a large proportion of the passengers, many of them women, are compelled to stand crowded together, the women with the men. There is no better excuse for this condition than the desire of the company to make more money." The *Examiner* found the streetcar conditions in the downtown area "little short of

Plate 2. Angelenos frequently complained about crowded street-cars during the rush hours. Taken in 1919 during a LARY employee strike, this photograph illustrates this common problem. (Courtesy of Los Angeles City Archives)

disgraceful."[26] PE and LARY executives argued, however, that they could do little to improve the situation.[27]

Many of the railway's problems resulted from their initial policies of real estate promotion. Rather than develop efficient, rational transportation systems, the LARY and PE had sought to connect subdivisions with the central business district. The *California Outlook*, a progressive reform journal, described Los Angeles' railway system as a "series of radiations from the city's center, lengthened from one real estate tract to another without the slightest consideration of the city's symmetrical and economic development." The traction companies had focused their rail networks upon the downtown district for obvious reasons. Los Angeles at the time was by far the most important commercial center in the region, and only those lines entering the city could attract enough riders to make them self-sufficient. This policy frustrated residents because they could not travel between suburbs without passing through the downtown area. Although politicians and citizens frequently demanded the construction of crosstown lines to serve these regions, the railways refused on the grounds that such routes could not support themselves. The tendency to build outward from the city center reinforced the centralized spatial structure of the area and consolidated Los Angeles' dominance over the regional economy. It also affected settlement patterns because most suburban dwellings were built within easy walking distance of the streetcar tracks. The *California Outlook* reported that in between these lines were "long reaches given up to vacant lots—the home of the billboard, tin can and sheep-sorrel weed."[28]

In their attempts to construct lines to their real estate holdings, the traction companies outstripped their financial capacities. Huntington's aggressive building policies, for instance, saddled the PE with an extremely high debt load. Electric railway construction was very expensive, even more costly than that of steam railroads. In addition, the electric railway industry in America had never shown the favorable returns expected of it. By 1910 the overall debt figures for most companies ran at about 50 percent of their total assets. As a result, Los Angeles' railways, like traction companies throughout the United States, found it increasingly difficult to attract investment capital. Consequently, neither the PE nor the LARY could significantly expand their operations after 1913. The LARY, for example, built only twenty-four miles of track between 1913 and 1925, a period during which the city's population doubled. The high debt ratio also made the railway companies unprofitable because of high interest charges. Between 1912 and 1940 the PE lost large sums of money. During those twenty-nine years the railway averaged annual losses of more than $1.5 million, while turning a profit only three times. The LARY fared a bit better, but it never showed the rates of return expected of it.[29] Given these financial constraints, the PE and LARY could not expand as quickly as the public wanted.

The general outcry against the poor rail service reflected a larger disenchantment with the city's public utility companies. For several years the Southern Pacific Railroad and the utilities had dominated the local Republican and Democratic political machines and therefore the city government itself.[30] The companies used a not so subtle combination of economic pressure and outright bribery to control the mayor and City Council. With a compliant city government in place, the corporations managed to avoid the frequent calls for improved service. By the early 1900s, however, frustrated residents began mobilizing for an electoral assault on the City Council. Concerned citizens realized that the public utility companies offered services that had long since become necessities of urban life. What was to prevent the companies from profiting at the public's expense, asked the reformers. Because the utilities held partial or complete monopolies over their services, individual consumers could do little to protect themselves from exploitation. The time had come, argued many Angelenos, for the municipal authorities to exert greater control over the problems arising from the recent growth of the city.

Despite the general consensus regarding the need for changes, the reform movement in Los Angeles was hardly a unified one. Several groups responded to the political situation by pushing their own particular solutions. One organization, for instance, succeeded in getting the electorate to pass a city charter amendment that established the initiative, referendum, and recall. The city's socialists meanwhile sought to eliminate corruption in government by promoting the municipal ownership of the city's utilities. Middle-class progressives, by way of contrast, wanted to create public regulatory commissions to control the utility companies. The progressives' conscious decision to exclude workers from their organization added to the general lack of unity.[31]

In spite of the movement's fragmentation, the city's reform elements presented a potent political force for a time. In 1906, a nonpartisan slate of progressive candidates won several City Council seats even though the Southern Pacific Railroad's nominee for mayor narrowly defeated his progressive opponent. Following this success, a group of young middle-class professionals formed a Good Government League and City Club to fight machine politics. The later exposure of large-scale corruption in the mayor's office led to a recall election in 1909 and eventually the mayor's resignation. The Good Government candidate, George Alexander, subsequently won the election and the progressives took command of the city government.

But all was not well in the progressive camp, for the socialist candidate for mayor had polled nearly as many votes as Alexander. The split between the two reform factions would later limit the effectiveness of their respective programs. The middle-class professionals comprising the Good Government League believed that they could solve the city's problems merely by introducing an efficient, honest administrative bureaucracy. They turned to the methods of the modern business organization as a model of rational decision making and long-term planning. These middle-class reformers sought to regulate the utilities, not attack them. The socialists, however, proposed that the city purchase these corporations and run them as nonprofit entities. The antagonism between the groups worsened a year later in 1910 when the socialists supported a labor strike against the Los Angeles *Times*. The Good Government administration responded by closing ranks with the more conservative Republican party leaders including *Times* publisher Harrison Gray Otis. Soon after the strike began, the City Council passed an ordinance that forbade picketing. When 400 to 500 laborers were arrested under the new law, someone responded by secretly dynamiting the *Times* building, killing several people in the process. This incident split apart the reform movement once and for all.

A year later during the 1911 primary campaign, the socialist candidate for mayor, Job Harriman, won a startling plurality. Terrified by the prospects of a socialist city government, Alexander allowed the Republican machine to run his final election campaign. The machine used this opportunity to denounce organized labor. With the outcome of the contest in doubt, the machine stepped up its campaign. Four days before election day, two labor organizers stunned the city by confessing to the bombing of the *Times.* This turned the electorate against Harriman who was clearly identified with the striking workers. Alexander won the election but at a price. Labor was permanently alienated from the middle-class Republicans, while the latter had found it difficult to perpetuate themselves without the aid of the regular party leaders. Los Angeles' reform movement subsequently lost its momentum and split into numerous pressure groups.[32]

Los Angeles' experience during the Progressive Era was fairly typical. Throughout the United States, loose co-alitions of socialists, labor leaders, and middle-class professionals worked together to oust corrupt political machines. When focusing upon specific issues such as the inefficiency of mass transportation, these disparate groups could prove a potent political force. Once in power, however, the factions would split apart over divergent ideological differences. They could agree that a problem existed, but not on its solution. Nor was it surprising that the abuses of the railways and other public utilities often sparked reform movements. Not only did people depend upon the utility companies every day but the delivery of urban services necessarily affected the quality of city life.

The impact of the reformers in Los Angeles, however,

was not completely lost. A change from ward to citywide representation crippled the traditional political machines. The city also came to own and operate its own harbor, water supply, and electric company during this period.[33] Finally, the reform City Council members established a number of administrative agencies designed to improve the city government. These regulatory bodies had the most lasting influence on the region. From the moment the progressives had captured control of the City Council, they began pushing for the regulation of the public utilities. No longer would the citizenry allow the monopolies to profit at its expense. The progressives now saw these companies not as money-making concerns but as private contractors providing a public service. Late in 1909 the City Council voted to create a Board of Public Utilities Commissioners. The electorate confirmed this decision in December.[34] In the long run, the board did not do much to improve the quality of rail service in Los Angeles. But during its first few years of existence, the board offered hope to those frustrated with the city's traction companies. In addition to supervising the gas, electric, and telephone companies operating in the city, the commissioners watched over the PE and LARY. Their duties included regulating streetcar and interurban fares and advising the City Council on granting franchises for railway extensions and renewals. The board also investigated complaints about the railways' poor performance.

The board's investigations quickly revealed the validity of the riding public's complaints. In its first few annual reports issued after its formation in 1910, the commissioners complained about severe streetcar congestion in the downtown area. Several years before large numbers of automobiles began entering the central business district, streetcar movement was slow and arduous because narrow roads, poor routing, and a limited number of thoroughfares created numerous bottlenecks. Evening rush-hour conditions were particularly bad as long lines of streetcars backed up on downtown streets. In 1911 the board, in noting the "chaotic" transit situation, stated that "the congestion of street car traffic in the business district at rush hour is indefensible."[35]

The reform-minded City Council responded to the board's investigations by hiring the nationally renowned transportation expert Bion J. Arnold to study the region's traffic problems. Arnold found that while the railways offered good service in the suburbs, they did not perform well in the downtown area. "Fully 40,000 riders on both systems are delayed from five to forty minutes during the rush hours each day," Arnold wrote "and as many more are inconvenienced during the non rush hours, due to the fundamental defects of the transportation arrangements along Main street." "Even a partial list of these defects," Arnold concluded, "makes a formidable catalogue of possibilities for improvements." The basic problem was the mixture of local streetcars and interurban trains on the downtown streets. The PE terminal building was located in the middle of the central business district at 6th and Main. Although the large interurbans ran on private rights-of-way outside of the city, once they reached the downtown area they moved along Main Street to the terminal building, disrupting local streetcar operations. These problems also resulted in overcrowding on many rush-hour lines. "Frequently the delays to the standing patrons become exceedingly tedious," Arnold reported, "and when the car does come there is a general scramble and contest to obtain a seat."[36]

Arnold also complained about various PE and LARY policies. Almost all railway cars operating within the city limits entered the downtown district and thus contributed to traffic congestion. Such a policy made economic sense because only those streetcars and interurbans traveling through the most densely populated areas turned a profit. But this policy was terribly inefficient. Arnold noted as much in his investigation. "Cross connecting lines, which are usually considered as desirable parts of a system of this size,"

– 45 –

Arnold wrote, "have been neglected." To make matters worse, the PE and LARY refused to accept transfers from each other's lines. The PE even refused to issue transfers between its interurban trains and its own local streetcars. In response to this situation, the Board of Public Utilities made several attempts to secure universal transfer privileges between the two systems. However, the board held no legal right to demand such a policy. The railways in turn refused to issue universal transfers for fear of losing revenue. Reporting on these problems in 1911, the commissioners commented that much had to be done to get the railway systems "working adequately for public needs."[37]

In addition to its refusal to issue transfers between interurbans and streetcars, the PE attempted to cut back its local service. While it ran some streetcars in the city, the PE mainly operated interurbans between Los Angeles and suburban communities such as Long Beach and Pasadena. Since it could charge much higher fares on its interurban trains, the PE sought to limit its operation of local lines. Streetcar users within the city of Los Angeles, however, wanted the interurbans running close to their homes to accept local traffic. "The public," the Board of Public Utilities noted, "is in a constant struggle with them for better local service." These citizens eventually petitioned the commissioners to force the interurbans to accept local passengers. Although accepting the PE's contention that this would interfere with its train schedules, the commissioners also argued that "neither the railway nor the suburban public has the right to demand exclusive service over our streets as against the inherent rights of the public who have paid therefor."[38]

The Board of Public Utilities also insisted that interurban cars were too large to operate safely on downtown streets. As early as 1915, the board called for plans to separate these trains from regular street traffic with elevated or subway lines. This issue became even more important in later years because of the increasing number of automobiles on the road. The commissioners additionally reported an extremely high number of accidents involving interurbans and automobiles between 1912 and 1918. Most of these accidents occurred in the downtown area where railway cars and autos shared the streets. Since most of these accidents took place at low speeds, the damage was usually light. Collisions in the outlying areas, however, often ended in death. Freed from the city streets, the powerful interurban trains could develop considerable speed. This was safe as long as the trains did not encounter cross traffic. But as automobile traffic increased throughout the teens, Los Angeles and outlying communities began to install street crossings across PE rights-of-way.

Originally unprotected, these grade crossings became the sites of numerous accidents. Many citizens believed the PE operated its interurbans at unsafe speeds. The traction company, however, accused automobile drivers of incompetence. In response to the public outrage, the Board of Public Utilities ordered the PE to install flagmen and electric warning signals at the most dangerous grade crossings. The public sought more permanent protection. In 1910 civic organizations campaigned to separate street and interurban traffic. The reform-minded Municipal League, "in view of the protests against the dangerous speed of interurban trolley cars over public crossings," requested the Board of Public Utilities to plan "a general campaign for the protection of the important crossings by raising or lowering tracks." The immense capital outlay required to separate the thousands of grade crossings prevented immediate action. In time, the PE did eliminate some of the most dangerous crossings. Nevertheless, this construction did relatively little to improve the overall problem, and the campaign to eliminate grade crossings continued for at least thirty years.[39]

Notwithstanding its attempts to improve rail service in Los Angeles, the Board of Public Utilities ultimately did very little to appease the frustrated streetcar patrons. First, the board could not force the railways to alter their operations. Legislation both at the local and state levels dictated that the body could merely investigate complaints and offer recommendations. Understaffed and lacking adequate funds, the commission found itself overwhelmed by its workload. Finally, the board sympathized with the railways' problems. Mass transit by the second decade of the twentieth century simply was not profitable. High equipment costs, massive debt loads, and rapid inflation did not allow the traction companies to offer extensive improvement in services despite the frequent complaints by the riding public. The board realized this and did little to challenge the railways' overall methods of operation.

The public, however, did not sympathize with the economic plight of the traction companies. Angelenos clearly remembered the earlier corruption and inefficiencies of the railways. They little cared that by 1918 the five-cent fare could no longer support the existing streetcar system let alone expand it. Both the reformers who had first suggested the formation of a public utilities commission and the citizens who had voted to establish the agency grew disenchanted with the body. Some of the more liberal citizens groups began advocating public ownership of certain utilities, a proposal originally suggested by the socialists. Few, however, advocated the municipalization of the railways. First, the estimated cost to purchase the overcapitalized systems was staggeringly high. More important, most citizens did not want the city to take over an unprofitable railway network. Unfamiliar with modern notions of public subsidies, Angelenos refused to consider municipalizing the railways for many years.[40]

This left the individual commuter to fend for himself. While thousands of riders continued to patronize the interurbans and streetcars each year, others began to look elsewhere. Angelenos, then, like urban dwellers elsewhere in the United States, willingly adopted any available alternative to riding crowded streetcars. Once the public began seeking other modes of transport, railway patronage fell dramatically. The PE's ridership, for instance, declined rapidly after 1914 on a per capita basis despite a short respite during the early twenties. The LARY experienced a similar decline from 1913 until 1918, after which time the railway enjoyed a brief resurgence owing to the heavy immigration during the early twenties. From 1924 on, however, the LARY's ridership fell precipitously. Many of the region's residents had turned to other methods of transportation.[41]

One such alternative was the jitney. During the depression year of 1914, automobile owners found that they could subsidize their transportation costs by offering rides to pedestrians at a nickle a lift. Riders found the mobility and speed of the private automobile attractive. Not tied to a set schedule or route, these drivers could drop their charges off anywhere in the city. By late 1914, some enterprising motorists had established the nation's first jitney companies, using oversized automobiles to ply the streets in search of customers. The automobile jitney offered flexibility, convenience, and speed to those disappointed with streetcars. At the same time, motor bus companies began operating interurban lines between Los Angeles and suburban communities. The Board of Public Utilities recognized the experimental nature of these efforts; it wanted to see if motor buses and jitneys would prove more efficient than streetcars. Although continued railway operation seemed essential to the board, the commissioners realized that "should motor buses prove to be more efficient than other means of transportation . . . they would logically in time supersede the present street cars." Though dubious, public officials were willing to accept alternative means of urban transportation.[42]

Although an important factor later during the twenties, interurban buses quickly failed. The poor roads and highways on which they operated made their rides uncomfortable. Jitneys operating in and around the heavily traveled downtown area, however, became popular. Within a year of beginning business, jitneys daily carried nearly 150,000 riders and cut deeply into the railways' patronage and revenues. The LARY vehemently complained to the City Council and Board of Public Utilities about jitney competition because these automobiles lured away their most valuable passenger—the high-volume, short-distance rider. At the same time, jitneys did not have to follow specified routes or timetables, thus giving them an unfair advantage over the railways. The traction company also paid heavy state and local taxes in addition to maintaining the roadway in between its tracks. The jitneys, however, merely paid a nominal licensing fee. Not only did this discriminate against the railways but it also robbed the public of valuable tax receipts. Most important, the railways claimed, the jitneys could ruin the traction companies financially, but could not replace them. "It is apparent that the jitney, as a substitute for the street railway, is impossible," a LARY vice-president wrote. "And as an addition it is little better than a parasite sapping the strength and vitality of the railway service, and giving the public nothing commensurate in return."[43]

City officials agreed. Mayor Henry Rose argued that "the people in the end will be compelled to depend upon the street railways for transportation. Meanwhile, the loss of revenues has affected the whole city." "To dally longer in our present state of irresolution and inaction as regards the 'jitney' bus," Rose concluded, "is to be guilty of gross injustice to the people." The City Council quickly instituted legislation that forced jitney operators to carry insurance, follow regular routes and timetables, and stay out of the congested downtown area. This legislation and the increasing competition among the automobile carriers reduced the jitneys' comparative advantage over the streetcar and effectively ended their operations.[44] Nevertheless, the popularity of the jitney indicated the general dissatisfaction with rail operations in Los Angeles. The jitneys, the Los Angeles *Record* argued, had become popular because the railways failed to respond to the demands of Angelenos for better transit service.[45] It was not until it had become clear that the jitneys could provide only limited mass transportation that city officials moved to protect the streetcars.

The jitney spread to cities throughout the United States with amazing swiftness. Within a year after its introduction in Los Angeles, the jitney had appeared in such diverse towns as San Francisco, Seattle, Denver, and Portland (Maine). By the second quarter of 1915, nearly 62,000 jitneys operated in American urban areas.[46] The popularity of this innovation indicates the deep-seated frustration with local railways. A working-class newspaper in Birmingham, for instance, argued that the jitneys were "cleaner, as safe, . . . more rapid, and a better method than the old way of packing them in like sardines." The people riding the jitneys, the paper continued, were "eagerly accepting the new method of transportation and refusing to be straphangers, and dividend producers for watered stock."[47] Streetcar officials, however, sought protection against the jitneys once it became evident that the latter would cut deeply into the railways' profits. Using arguments pioneered in Los Angeles, the traction companies lobbied their respective city governments for relief. In every situation, local officials responded by severely restricting jitney operations in their municipalities because they feared that they would cripple the more comprehensive streetcar systems.

One of the more conservative aspects of progressivism was the belief that the government had to rationalize the economy by limiting competition. By essentially banning the jitney, American municipalities eliminated an important competitor to the traction companies. City councils, however, could not protect the railways for long. The failure of the traction companies to provide efficient transportation and the inadequacy of the progressive response encouraged urban dwellers to seek new ways of getting around town.

⇐ 3 ⇒

The Democratic Impulse and the Automobile

≡

Gentlemen, Pardon the expression but this d— street car service we are getting these days is something awful and beyond endurance.
— Charles Haines to Los Angeles City Council
September 11, 1919

Is it not about time you took steps to ascertain just why the Pacific Electric gets by with the putrid brand of transportation they are dishing out? Is there no redress for the hundreds of citizens of this community who are forced to pay high fares—to be handled like cattle?
—Venice citizen to Venice Trustees
January 12, 1920

The motor car means rapid transportation for the individual. It is conceded to be one of the greatest conveniences of modern life, and it is unthinkable to virtually bar it from the business district of the city.
—P. S. Albertson
December 25, 1919

everal historians have argued that the Progressive Era was ultimately a conservative one. Rather than challenging the American corporate structure, the reformers accommodated it. These historians assert that corporate leaders in seeking to plan a rational and stable economy free from the debilitating effects of cutthroat competition managed to subvert the progressive movement, particularly at the national level. The corporate world, they noted, needed public regulation to end irresponsible business practices and ensure economic stability. Corporate exec-

- 52 -

utives therefore helped establish regulatory agencies knowing full well that these bodies would be flexible enough to appease middle-class reformers, satisfy their own goal of making America safe for capitalism, and forestall the more radical reform programs of the increasingly popular socialists.[1] Other historians claim that progressivism was an attempt by the middle class to bring order and stability to an ever more complex and confusing society by creating bureaucracies to administer societal needs in an efficient and scientific manner. The progressives, these historians argue, attempted to control, manipulate, and improve the economic structure through enlightened regulation. To these historians, the rhetorical attack on the large corporations and utilities did not amount to much.[2]

It is true that the Progressive Era was ultimately a conservative one. The period did not see the restructuring of the capitalist economy, nor a significant decline in the power and influence of large corporations. But the foregoing arguments ignore the democratic impulse behind the reform movement.[3] The feeble attempts by the public regulatory commissions to improve the quality of utility services in American cities did not satisfy frustrated consumers. Angry citizens felt betrayed by the middle-class progressive reform movement. The fact that the utility commissions could not force the railways and other utilities to expand their services encouraged urban residents to look for other solutions. In the case of urban transportation, city dwellers found a viable alternative in the automobile. Initially, the adoption of the automobile was an individualistic response to the failure of progressive reform. The individual citizen began using his car because the reform movement could not assert its control over the traction companies. The people gave up on the politicians and took reform into their own hands by claiming the right to their own private means of transport. The automobile therefore became a symbol of the democratic impulse that had originally sparked the progressive movement in the first place. By jumping in their cars, urban denizens thumbed their noses at their long-standing antagonist—the railway executive. But however individualistic this reaction may have been in the beginning, it soon evolved into a collective effort to facilitate automobile transit within America's urban areas.

The ultimate challenge to the street railways in Los Angeles came not from the buses or jitneys, but from privately owned automobiles. The public turned to the automobile because the reform movement had failed to solve most of the problems associated with rail transit. Many members of the Good Government League had believed that by regulating the utility companies the city could improve the quality of urban services. They found, however, that the Board of Public Utilities was powerless to effect significant change. This left the individual helpless with regard to the quality of his telephone or natural gas services because he had no substitute for these commodities. But the disgruntled streetcar patron could turn to the automobile as an alternative to the railways. Angelenos no longer needed the public utilities commissioners to mediate their disputes with the seemingly corrupt railways. They could protest the poor quality of rail transit in a much more direct way—they could stop using it altogether. The failure of the middle-class reform program therefore encouraged people in Los Angeles to take to their cars. The automobile became, in part, a symbol of democratic technology and civic reform. Consequently, a large part of the public abandoned its fight with the railways and turned its attention to facilitating automobile movement within the city.

Although automobiles had appeared in southern California as early as the turn of the century, it was not until after 1910 that they came into general usage. During these years, automobile manufacturers made phenomenal progress in automobile design and production techniques, allowing them to offer the public reliable cars at moderate prices. Once the plaything of the wealthy, the car quickly came within the reach of the middle class. By 1917, Henry Ford's sophisticated assembly process enabled him to sell 730,000 Model-Ts annually at the unheard of price of $345 to $360 each. "The day is here when the smallest tradesman, builder, [or] skilled mechanic can own an automobile economically," noted the Los Angeles *Examiner* in 1914. The car, however, largely remained a recreational vehicle until World War I. Some automobile owners used their vehicles for daily transportation; early photos of Los Angeles indicate as much. But for most Angelenos, the family car was used for drives in the country or weekend camping trips.[4]

Sometime during the second decade of the century, an increasing number of automobile owners began using their machines for daily commuting and shopping. The *Examiner* in 1910 cited automobile traffic as a minor cause of streetcar delay in the city center. Two years later the *Times* casually noted that motor cars contributed to the heavy congestion in the central business district. The first official recognition of automobile traffic did not appear until 1918 when the Board of Public Utilities and the Engineering Department commented on the increasing number of vehicles in the downtown area. "Traffic congestion in Los Angeles," the Engineering Department argued, "is relatively more intensified than in any other city commensurate with its size, and the rapid growth of the city in population, coupled with an unusually large proportion of automobiles, will shortly increase the traffic congestion to an alarming degree." Poor streetcar routing, increasing and largely unregulated automobile movement, and a "continuous stream of pedestrians crossing in front of moving street cars" combined to bring downtown traffic to a standstill, particularly during the evening rush hours. Congestion typically became so bad during the afternoon and evening that "street cars accumulate from time to time at such a rate that they often present an unbroken line for over two blocks along Broadway and west Seventh Street." Even with traffic officers stationed at downtown intersections the average transit speed along Broadway was frequently "lower than walking speed."[5]

Congestion in the business district was not unusual; Los Angeles, like most cities, had suffered from it since the turn of the century. In addition, Los Angeles experienced exceedingly large population influxes during the first two decades of the century. By 1920, the city's population had increased by more than five and a half times its 1900 total of 102,000. Yet it was becoming increasingly apparent that this rapid population gain was not solely responsible for the downtown congestion. More people had begun to enter the downtown district every day, and many of them entered with their private automobiles. Automobile commuting made a bad situation worse.

Commuters and shoppers in Los Angeles began using their automobiles because fifteen years of inadequate streetcar and interurban service finally convinced many citizens to seek alternative means of transportation. After 1914, Angelenos purchased automobiles at such a rapid rate that the number of cars per resident rose dramatically. Railway patronage, however, experienced a very different trend. After 1912, per capita ridership on the PE fell precipitously despite a slight resurgence during the early twenties. The LARY showed a similar decline even though it had a stronger revival immediately after World War I. The citizens of Los Angeles had finally found the answer to their frustration with the railways in the motor car. For those already owning a car the switch to automobile commuting must have seemed natural since it provided its passengers with unprecedented mobility and flexibility. No longer tied to the streetcar schedule, the automobile driver could travel whenever and wherever he or she pleased. By the time of World War I, the automobile had become more than a sophisticated means of recreation. The public now saw it as a progressive piece of industrial and urban technology.[6]

Not only were automobiles impressive examples of industrial technology but their design also constantly advanced. Early automobiles were often little more than motorized carriages and most roads were impassable during the winter months. By the time of World War I, both the roads and the automobiles had greatly improved. Manufacturers now produced cheaper and more reliable cars suitable for year-round use. With an increasing number of all-weather roads the industry began switching to enclosed sedans, which even became popular in clement southern California.[7] "There is no question," a Los Angeles automobile dealer boasted, "about the motor car having arrived as an all-year vehicle in the East as well as here." Further improvements, such as electric starters, pneumatic tires, and improved transmissions made the automobile much easier to use. By 1919, the automobile seemed a far cry from the motorized buggies of the early 1900s. "Just how far advanced the motor car of today is over the early type of horseless carriages can be easily visualized by anyone who has the time and does not mind taking a little spin in a modern automobile," one enthusiast remarked. "Stand a present-day Ford alongside its ancient relative," bragged a Ford salesman, "and the contrast is as pronounced as would be a comparison of a modern railway parlor car alongside a prairie schooner."[8]

It is not surprising that the increasing popularity of the automobile as a means of urban transportation coincided with a national "Good Roads" movement. Bicycle enthusiasts had started this campaign during the late nineteenth century. After lagging for several years through want of interest, automobile owners and manufacturers gave the issue new life. American streets at the beginning of the century were notoriously bad. California in 1896, for example, had less than a hundred miles of improved roads, most of which were not only unpaved, but dusty during the summer and impassable during the winter. Motorists, automobile clubs, and car manufacturers lobbied extensively for improvements, arguing that road construction would aid rural communication, recreation, and national defense. They met with success in 1913, when the federal government appropriated $500,000 to ameliorate mail delivery roads. Three years later, the Federal Road Act of 1916 greatly stimulated rural highway improvements by offering states matching construction funds. By 1919, the Los Angeles *Times* estimated that federal, state, and local governments would spend $375,000,000 for road construction and maintenance in that year alone. "Public sentiment," the *Times* noted, "is solidly behind extensive highway building programmes now."[9]

This enthusiasm hit Los Angeles early. In 1913 the chief draftsman for the city's Engineering Department complained that "the people are clamoring for [street] improvements on every side which are necessary and must be made if we would continue to advance." Two years later the city had paved all of its main thoroughfares. The city and county governments also cooperated in an attempt to create countywide traffic arteries. This drive to upgrade highways and thoroughfares facilitated automobile usage in the rural areas of southern California. Once the county had aided highway access, it seemed only natural to begin encouraging automobile transit within the city.[10]

Better city and county highways became especially important for those residents living in newly developed suburbs. As the county's population sharply increased during the first thirty years of the century, real estate developers started opening suburban housing tracts. When the railway companies stopped keeping pace with suburban expansion, outlying residents turned to their automobiles for transportation. The city engineer's field department clearly noted this problem of access in 1917. "As the city grows[,] our work becomes farther away," wrote the field department chief. "It can no longer be handled efficiently by the street cars. An automobile is a necessity for work in much of the outlying districts."[11]

The inability of the streetcars to provide adequate and efficient service and the perception of the automobile as a democratic piece of industrial technology encouraged many Angelenos to adopt the car as a personal means of daily transportation. In the year following World War I, automobile registration nearly doubled. The *Times* remarked that "the demand for cars has increased steadily until now local dealers and distributors are having a continual battle with factories regarding shipments and deliveries." This call for automobiles was not limited to Los Angeles alone. "It is the unprecedented demand for automobiles that comes from almost everywhere in the United States and from many foreign lands that has literally swamped factories with orders," the *Times* reported. The postwar boom was more than merely a reaction to wartime shortages; demand for new automobiles continued to climb throughout the twenties in Los Angeles.[12]

The increasing dependence on the automobile led to major traffic problems in the downtown area. Not only was Los Angeles the fastest growing major city in the nation but it also had an antiquated street system. Initially laid in the eighteenth century, the city's roads tended to be narrow, discontinuous, and confining. The downtown area had always been congested, but once automobiles began entering the business district, traffic became "terrific." The *Times* concluded that there were simply too many cars for the existing street space. The downtown traffic also suffered from the lack of adequate outlets. Streets running north and south provided some relief, but the numbered east-west streets were narrow and infrequently spaced. Bunker Hill to the west aggravated the problem by blocking access in that direction. Los Angeles had a few large highways leading into the city but these were not adequately connected. This exacerbated the downtown congestion since vehicles traveling from one side of the county to another had to pass through the city center.[13]

Eastern visitors to Los Angeles frequently commented on the city's traffic. "At 6 o'clock at night . . . ," a doctor from Cleveland commented, "the situation in Los Angeles becomes intolerable. Apparently every automobile owner in the city suddenly decides to motor through the business section at that time." Some eastern visitors maintained that Los Angeles was "more provincial in its lack of 'snap' in the traffic situation than is justified by the amount of that traffic." The downtown parking situation was particularly bad. "With automobiles parked everywhere, apparently for hours at a time, it becomes practically impossible to make any progress on the cross streets," the same person complained. One outsider commented that western cities might have to alter their parking arrangements to relieve their "antiquated traffic situations." Other visitors cited the exceptionally bad automobile drivers and the dearth of traffic officers in Los Angeles as the cause of the congestion. Many observers also noticed that since streetcars occupied the center part of the streets, pedestrians had to "worm their way through the automobiles" to reach them, "thus holding up the entire movement [of traffic]."[14]

Although the Automobile Club of Southern California had earlier believed that the traffic situation "would automatically adjust itself through the Police Department and other municipal channels," the problem only grew worse. The Board of Public Utilities could regulate streetcars, interurbans, buses, and jitneys, but it held no authority to regulate private automobiles. As vehicular usage continued to increase throughout the teens, local authorities grew exceedingly concerned because continued city growth depended on a solution to the traffic issue. When streetcar and interurban workers struck for higher pay during the summer of 1919,

Plate 3. Prior to 1926, automobile traffic in Los Angeles was largely unregulated. Many visitors to the city during that period argued that poor drivers combined with the lack of traffic officers contributed to the congestion downtown. The photograph above illustrates the problems associated with allowing left turns in the congested central business district. (Courtesy of Los Angeles City Archives)

the public scrambled to purchase even more cars. Although the strike lasted less than a month, congestion during that time reached frightening proportions. This strike finally forced city officials and concerned civic organizations to consider seriously the issue of relieving the chaotic conditions in the city center. "Everyone has agreed for a long time that something ought to be done about the congested traffic conditions on the downtown streets of the city," remarked the

Times. "The unusual number of machines on the streets during the past couple of weeks, due to the strike on the streetcar lines, has simply served to strengthen this conviction."[15]

Several organizations responded by proposing solutions to the mounting automobile congestion. The Chamber of Commerce, which had studied the situation for more than a year, suggested a program of opening, widening, and straightening many of Los Angeles' streets. The chamber also proposed building a boulevard encircling the city to connect the region's major highways and allow crosstown traffic to avoid the business district.[16] Other concerned citizens and organizations offered their opinions. The *Times* feared that the city's traffic threatened its hope for future growth. Looking at the rest of the nation, the paper argued that "cities in the East which have found that motor cars and street cars formed a large, stagnant pool in the business center of the municipality have thrust in the spoon of progress and stirred the stagnant pool to activity." The *Times* argued that other cities such as Cleveland had improved their traffic flow by imposing sophisticated traffic regulations and circulatory systems on their city centers. "Antique methods of parking cars in the business sections, in traffic circulation and in penalties for infringements are going by the board," the paper concluded. Los Angeles needed new methods "which take cognizance of the fact that the motor-driven vehicle is a supreme factor in urban progress" to ameliorate the chaotic traffic conditions.[17]

Those who profited from the rising automobile usage agreed. "Transportation must be cared for," a vice president of a local automobile distributorship argued. "We cannot reduce it or abolish it. We have got to build our roads up to the demands made upon them by the needs of the people. We cannot permit progress to be strangled by inadequate transportation facilities." Other automobile concerns concurred. Wallace Chorn, an executive with a local car dealership, insisted that "the automobile is here to stay and is now regarded as a utility." The city, Chorn contended, could provide traffic relief by constructing thoroughfares and public parking lots. At the same time, the Automobile Club of Southern California sent the City Council several proposals for increasing the flow of vehicles. The club's suggestions included the creation of one-way streets and a ban on freight deliveries in the congested district between 11:00 A.M. and 6:00 P.M.[18]

While the City Council and civic organizations wrestled with possible solutions to the traffic problem, the California Railroad Commission and Los Angeles Board of Public Utilities issued a joint engineering survey of the LARY. The LARY had applied to the Railroad Commission for an increase in its carfare because the inflation following World War I seriously threatened the railway's profits. Labor costs had risen 45 percent in the previous two years, while material expenses had skyrocketed 36 to 150 percent during the same period. The engineering staffs of the Railroad Commission and the Board of Public Utilities agreed to undertake a joint investigation of the company's problems.

The final report concluded that the company could substantially reduce its expenses in several ways. By rerouting existing tracks, purchasing more efficient equipment, and abandoning unprofitable lines, the railway could ease congestion and lower operating costs sufficiently to eliminate the need to increase its fares. The engineers, however, noted that the city's rapid population growth and the "phenomenal increase in the number of automobiles" operating in the downtown area made "expeditious handling of street car traffic practically impossible." The report therefore urged city officials to establish strict parking regulations on its streets to limit the number of automobiles entering the business district. The Board of Public Utilities adopted the engineering recommendations and ordered the LARY to reroute its system to provide more efficient operations. The board also requested the City Council to enact a parking ban on the downtown streets.[19]

The parking situation in the downtown area had long been recognized as a major problem. "There are times," the *Times* reported, "when it is absolutely impossible to obtain parking accommodations for a distance of several blocks from where one desires to make a purchase." Even worse, parked cars blocked the flow of traffic. A row of automobiles parked on either side of an already constricted downtown street effectively narrowed the road by an additional twenty feet; with a double line of streetcars running down the center of the street, there was little room for moving motor vehicles. If automobiles did not have enough space for a lane of their own, they began to interfere with streetcar movement. The resulting traffic conditions threatened to strangle the city's circulation of goods and people.[20]

By late November 1919 the City Council began considering the Railroad Commission's proposal for a ban on downtown parking. Los Angeles already had a law limiting parking in the city center to twenty minutes. Most people, however, chose to ignore the legislation because the police did not have enough personnel to enforce it. One citizen vociferously protested any prohibition against parking because of the indifference toward the present limit. "Flagrant disregard of existing ordinances is responsible for much of [the] present congestion," he argued. The city would not need a parking ban, he insisted, if the police would only enforce the present ordinance.[21]

At about the same time representatives from the Railroad Commission, the Board of Public Utilities, and the LARY met publicly to present their reasons for favoring stringent parking restrictions. Richard Sachse, the chief engineer for the Railroad Commission, indicted the city's automobile users by arguing that excessive parking in the central business district was at the root of the traffic problems. Engineer

Plate 4. By 1920, parked cars on Los Angeles' narrow downtown streets had begun to interfere with both automobile and streetcar traffic. The California Railroad Commission and the Los Angeles Board of Public Utilities used this photograph to support their proposal to ban automobile parking in the city center. (Courtesy of Los Angeles City Archives)

H. Z. Osborne of the Public Utilities Commission insisted that relief of congestion required a complete reorganization of the downtown traffic flow. It would do no good, he argued, to impose changes on the LARY without taking similar action against pedestrians and automobiles. President Edwin Edgerton of the Railroad Commission agreed with Osborne. "The regulation of vehicles and pedestrians," he asserted, "seems necessary as a part of this transportation reform." A representative from the LARY said that his company was willing to alter its operations only on the condition that the city give it "relief from [the] intolerable conditions brought about by automobile traffic." Los Angeles, he concluded, had to abolish automobile parking privileges in order for his company to provide adequate service. Edgerton concurred that the railway had a right to expect the city to do its part in relieving congestion. The City Council quickly responded with a proposed ordinance that would have eliminated parking in the downtown area between 9:00 A.M. and 6:20 P.M. every day except Sunday. In addition, the council promised to institute a one-hour parking limit on the streets surrounding the business district.[22]

Some businessmen favored the proposal because they believed such an ordinance would ease traffic conditions. Most of those presently parking in the downtown area were commuters, they noted. A parking ban would force these people to leave their cars at home and take the trolley. One retailer noted that "many drive back and forth [between home and work], who have little if any use for their cars during the day." The same person believed the ban would encourage property owners to tear down antiquated and unsightly downtown buildings and replace them with parking garages. I. H. Rice, president of the Merchants' and Manufacturers' Association, also favored the law. He believed the city should at least test the ordinance since studies had shown that most cars parked in the downtown area were not used for shopping, but for commuting. The Wholesale Dry Goods Association had been an early proponent of parking restrictions in the downtown area. "The present congested condition of our city streets coupled with ordinances now in force," the Association wrote to the City Council, "make it an absolute impossibility for our wholesale merchants to deliver goods to the retailers and at the same time comply with the law." Even the Automobile Club of Southern California initially favored the proposed ban. A representative of the club admitted that the automobile caused most of the congestion problems downtown. "Our traffic regulations," he said, "are far behind the times. I believe we must eliminate parking in many of the downtown streets."[23]

Despite this initial flurry of support, most downtown

businessmen appeared to denounce the proposed ordinance. Although they generally agreed that the city had to do something about conditions in the business district, they opposed a total ban on parking. Various individuals and organizations consequently launched a furious attack against the council's proposal. The *Times* reported that the "opponents of the stringent no-parking ordinance now before the City Council are organizing and preparing to fight it to the last ditch."[24] Bitter criticism of the ban came from all over the city. Angry opponents of the proposal lashed out at the City Council for its past neglect of the traffic situation. The council, these critics argued, had ignored the deteriorating conditions in the past and now were attempting to solve the entire problem with one piece of legislation. "That this is virtually impossible," wrote the *Times*, "has been the experience of every large city in the United States." Every major urban area, the paper continued, had had traffic problems. Those cities had satisfactorily ameliorated their congestion with the aid of expert traffic commissioners and careful experimentation. Los Angeles, then, should not expect to solve its problems with a panacea. Some relief was certainly needed, the *Times* concluded the next day, but this ordinance would "have very much the effect of a wet blanket cast over the business district of the city." The Motor Car Dealers' Association agreed that the proposed regulations were "too revolutionary and too drastic, and altogether unnecessary." The council, the organization noted, had not even explored other methods of traffic regulation such as one-way streets and restrictions on commercial loading.

A substantial part of the downtown business community concurred with this assessment. It feared that the ban would "simply drive business from the downtown section of the city to the outlying districts." At the heart of this issue was the central business district's attempt to retain control over the local economy. "If this ordinance goes through," one businessman asserted, "Los Angeles might as well wave good-by to all out-of-town trade. People will not come to this city to shop if they are prohibited from using their automobiles." The *Times* believed that a no-parking ordinance would inevitably force retail stores to move outside of the downtown area. "The no-parking ordinance as it now stands," the paper concluded, "is an outrage, and one of the worst blows ever aimed at the business section of Los Angeles."[25]

Opponents of the proposed legislation obviously held little faith in the railways' ability to transport shoppers to the retail district. In fact, the traditional animosity felt by Angelenos toward the traction companies fueled the resentment of many citizens. P. H. Greer, a prominent Los Angeles businessman, believed the no-parking plan had "apparently been offered by the railways and swallowed whole by the City Council." A fellow citizen sarcastically added, "I think this parking ordinance is the greatest thing that ever happened for the Pacific Electric and the Los Angeles Railway. If they can put it over, I'm going to buy stock in both concerns." The Motor Car Dealers' Association assumed that a conspiracy existed when it argued that "it would seem that the traffic regulations proposed by the amendments under consideration would make the Street Railway Companies the sole beneficiaries." While most southern Californians believed that the trolleys had a right to operate on the downtown streets, some argued that streetcars, not automobiles, should be removed from some city streets. "Without any exception," an irate resident claimed, "this no-parking idea is the most absurd proposition ever suggested anywhere. Street cars now occupy every street; why not remove them from one of the downtown streets[?]"[26]

It is not surprising that the Motor Car Dealers' Association, representing nearly all automobile distributorships in Los Angeles, vigorously opposed the proposed ordinance. Yet it would be incorrect to conclude that those fighting the ban did so simply for economic reasons. Opposition to the railways had been building for years. Even before automobiles began clogging downtown streets, citizens complained about the railways' slow and inadequate service. The early popularity of the jitney indicated that Angelenos willingly opted for alternative methods of transit. The City Council had essentially legislated the jitneys off the streets because it did not believe that this form of transportation could replace the city- and countywide rail system. To have allowed continued jitney competition would have threatened the viability of the city's urban transportation system. But the city government had also failed to improve the quality of rail transit in the area despite repeated public complaints. Those who could afford it therefore turned to the automobile as a substitute for streetcars and interurbans.

Private automobiles offered their owners flexibility and efficiency. Traffic jams may have been a nuisance, but it was far better (and faster) to be stuck in one's private automobile than on a crowded streetcar. "The street railway system of our city is and has been for a long period in a very unsatisfactory condition, failing to give prompt and sufficient service," argued a resolution sent to the City Council in December. One angry citizen saw no reason why the city should attempt to protect the failing railways. "When a public utility ceases to be a convenience to the people," he wrote, "its usefulness is at an end and should not be allowed to burden the public with its mismanagement." With the automobile as an alternative, why continue to prop up a burdensome utility, many asked. "If the ordinance is adopted," a commuter lamented, "my machine will be of no use for business purposes. I'll be a straphanger forever."[27]

The automobile, in short, stood as a symbol of urban and industrial progress. It answered an age-old need for rapid, personal transportation. To deny its use seemed absurd to its proponents. "The motor car means rapid transportation for the individual," insisted an automobile dealer. "It is conceded to be one of the greatest conveniences of modern life, and it is unthinkable to virtually bar it from the business district of the city." Why, the opponents of the ban asked, should the City Council ruin the value of such an important technological innovation? Gilbert Woodill, manager of Western Motors, admitted that streetcars had done "a great deal for Los Angeles" in the past, but they had not done as much as the automobile in recent years. To ban the automobile from parking on downtown streets was a backward step as far as he was concerned. A *Times* editorial agreed. "No other innovation has adapted itself so quickly and so universally to the needs of a generation. . . . And any city that endeavors to establish a blockade against the motor car by relegating it to back streets and suburban lanes is making a serious mistake," the paper argued. The automobile, it pointed out, had won its place fairly in the economic and social life of the American people. The 3,000,000 automobiles scheduled for manufacture in the next year alone were incontrovertible proof that the "motor car is a prime necessity of American Life." "As an agent of progress," the *Times* grandiloquently concluded, "it has outstripped the steam engine and telegraphy and stands second only to the printing press."[28]

The motoring public also argued that the new law discriminated against it because the public possessed an inherent right to the use of the roadway. The issue touched the very heart of American individualism. It was the public's prerogative to operate its automobiles in the city streets, the critics claimed. To institute a no-parking ordinance effectively stripped the public of that right. "Why take away the convenient use of uncongested streets from their owners, the people?" asked one citizen.[29]

Not everyone agreed with the automobile proponents, however. The Business Men's Co-Operative Association actively supported the ban. Representing many of the larger business concerns in Los Angeles, this organization even claimed credit for helping to plan the original ordinance. It believed that the proposed legislation would benefit that 90 percent of the population which utilized streetcars. Those opposed to the law, the organization asserted, were a minority of autoists who were not considering the greatest good for the greatest number. The association further believed that those businessmen without "axes to grind" supported the proposal because it would relieve congestion in the downtown area. Some streetcar patrons also supported the ban. "The violent protest of the Auto-Hogs in your city is characteristic of the species," wrote one streetcar rider to the City Council. "Although they are but a small minority of the population they want to retain all-day possession of more than half of all streets in the business center of the city." Arguing that parking in the business district unfairly delayed streetcar patrons, he concluded that "your streets are too narrow to permit this abominable parking nuisance. . . . Cut 'em all out and do away with class privileges. The streets belong to the big public, no[t] to the favored few."[30]

Despite this support for the council's proposed ordinance, the parking ban developed into a major controversy. When large numbers of individuals and representatives from civic organizations appeared before it to protest the ban and offer alternative plans, the council decided to delay a decision by referring the issue back to its Public Safety Committee. The committee announced that it would meet with members of civic organizations to work out a compromise.[31]

Two days after the council returned the proposed no-parking ordinance to the committee, the liberal Los Angeles *Record* began a lengthy exposé on rail transit in the city. "Los Angeles Street Car Service Is Intolerable," ran the first headline. The paper reported that "condemnation of the traction companies of Los Angeles was never so general and bitter as it is today." Reports throughout the city indicated that rail service was "rotten." The streetcar riders' most frequent complaints included crowded car conditions, inexperienced drivers, and poor scheduling.[32]

The crowded conditions and inadequate scheduling of streetcars particularly incensed regular customers. Railway patrons had complained about these conditions for years. Although the traction companies blamed equipment shortages and the crowded streets, many riders believed that the railways deliberately ran too few cars in order to reduce operating costs at the expense of the public's comfort. The classic traction motto, "The dividends are in the straps," held true in Los Angeles, the *Record* reported. The LARY claimed it could maintain its financial footing only if the city cleared up downtown congestion. The *Record*, however, argued that the public "will do well to remember that it is to the pocket book interest of the street car company to operate crowded cars and not to be affected by crocodile company tears shed over their sad plight." The paper concluded that crowded streetcar conditions were outrageous and insulting to the common working man.[33]

The inexperienced operators and conductors added to the problem. Many of these individuals had been hired during the recent strike as scabs. So poorly trained were these workers that they could not even give out adequate information regarding their own runs, let alone other lines. Furthermore, these inexperienced operators, in the minds of many riders, constantly endangered passengers' lives by their inability to operate their cars smoothly. Added to this were the company's attempts to keep impossible schedules, which forced operators to drive at dangerously fast rates, resulting in a twofold increase in accidents since the strike. The LARY and PE argued that the large turnover during the walkout had not caused the increase in collisions. Instead, they held the rising traffic congestion in the downtown area responsible for both the inefficient service and the high accident rate. Despite these assertions, the *Record* averred that "the general public . . . believes firmly that a large share of its troubles are the result of inefficiency and 'green' motormen and conductors." Streetcar patrons also had to endure poor scheduling as railway cars frequently bunched up four or five deep. At other times, riders had to wait quite a long while for a car to arrive. "We are supposed to have eight-minute service," complained one rider. "I have waited a number of times as long as twenty minutes for a car into the city."[34]

The *Record* articles touched off an avalanche of complaints about the poor quality of streetcar service in Los Angeles. The United Improvement Federation, representing many local neighborhood associations, sent a scathing letter to the City Council scoring the LARY for its poor performance. The federation complained that railway service in Los Angeles continued to be "exceedingly bad." Typifying the public's distrust of the railway's complaints about street congestion, the federation argued that it was not convinced that the company could not provide decent service for the existing five-cent fare. Most distressing was the LARY's refusal to supply every patron with a seat. "The long space between average cars precipitates a wild scramble for seats," the federation wrote, "and as there is not nearly enough to go around[,] a large part of the public are compelled to stand for miles at a stretch, often herded together like cattle or sheep in a stock car and often exhibiting the outrageous and illegal condition of hanging all over the steps and outside of cars." The City Council, the organization concluded, should pass a law providing free rides for those forced to stand on cars. Only then might the public receive relief from the railway.[35]

Hundreds of irate streetcar patrons wrote to the *Record* in support of the paper's series. Critics of the railways pointed out that the streets belonged to the public. The streetcar companies held franchises to operate in the streets by the grace of the people. Indeed, the critics believed that the traction companies should be grateful that their representatives had provided them with protection from the jitneys. Yet the public felt that the railways remained indifferent to its needs. "I'm for ripping out all seats on cars used during the rush periods," one angry passenger commented. "What's the use of having seats if more than half the people never get a chance to use them? Let's wipe out this hypocrisy—let's frankly admit that we pay our nickles for the privilege of standing room—and stingy room at that." The LARY argued that the downtown congestion made it useless to schedule more cars as a response to the overcrowding. The *Record*, however, argued that the public remained skeptical: "Ride any street car at any time of the day and you'll become convinced of that."[36]

Only once in this series of articles did the *Record* attack automobile owners for contributing to the downtown traffic conditions.[37] After its initial outburst of indignation, the paper quickly backed away from vilifying the motorists. During the next few weeks, it became increasingly clear that the *Record*'s editors saw the automobile and bus as possible alternatives to the hated traction companies. Instead of antagonizing automobile owners, the *Record* sought an alliance with them. "Twenty years ago influential people rode in street cars," the paper reported. "Today they ride in automobiles." They did so because of Los Angeles' deteriorating transportation system. Unfortunately, these influential middle-class citizens were the only ones who had demonstrated the ability to organize and effect change. "A history of the people's battles with street car corporations in Chicago, Cleveland, Detroit, and other cities of the east would prove conclusively that the most effective fighters for the community in the past were the people of the middle class residence districts," the *Record* continued. These people had organized protests and brandished the threat of public ownership to force the traction companies to improve service. Now the "comfortable" middle-class autoists were "out of the fight and the street car riders are not organizing their protest."[38]

The *Record* soon realized that the motorists were not out of the fight, but embroiled in the middle of the parking controversy. Los Angeles motorists had seen the no-parking law as a ploy by the railways to increase revenues; they responded accordingly by attacking the proposed legislation. The *Record*, while tacitly favoring the ban, was also suspicious of the traction companies. Having favored the municipalization of the street railways for years, the paper particularly wanted to prevent the railroads from continuing to profit at the public's expense. Thus, the paper began advocating alternative means of urban transportation for those forced to rely on the streetcars. Only some form of motorized public transportation offered a possible solution. The paper's editors, then, began to advocate a return to the jitneys and the institution of a municipally owned bus system. Since the automobile provided the technology for possibly breaking the railways' monopoly on urban transportation, the *Record* became far more sympathetic to the concerns of the city's motorists.[39]

The paper first toyed with the idea of resurrecting the jitney. "The revolt against the rotten street car service in Los Angeles is growing," the *Record* asserted. Unless the railways provided some relief, the people might "revive the despised jitney." The paper admitted that the jitney probably would not answer Los Angeles' transportation problems, but an increasing number of people wanted to punish the streetcar companies for their indifference to the public's needs. Citizens outside of Los Angeles agreed. "Is it not about time you took steps to ascertain just why the Pacific Electric gets by with the putrid brand of transportation they are dishing out?" asked a Venice resident of the local board of trustees. "Is there no relief for the hundreds of citizens of this community who are forced to pay high fares—to be handled like cattle?"[40]

The *Record* believed it would find redress for its working-class readers in a municipally owned bus line that could compete with the railways. The paper quoted Lynn Atkinson, a self-proclaimed transportation expert, on the subject.

The streetcar, Atkinson claimed, had outlived its usefulness and its ability to provide adequate passenger-carrying facilities. Streetcars, with their fixed tracks in the middle of the road, actually increased congestion by inhibiting the mobility of other vehicles. Atkinson argued that automobiles and buses were examples of progressive technology. "In the final analysis," wrote Atkinson, "the street car must vacate the streets for it is useless to longer ignore the fact that street car transportation is hopelessly out of date . . . and that these old cumbersome vehicles in their slow, rigid action, are the one big cause of traffic congestion." The automobile and buses with their superior passenger-carrying ability would shortly absorb the entire transportation industry, Atkinson claimed.[41]

By the middle of January, the City Council saw fit once again to bring up the issue of the parking ban. The council invited representatives from the Railroad Commission and the Board of Public Utilities to answer both the motorists' outrage at the institution of a no-parking ordinance and the streetcar riders' accusations against the traction companies. During these meetings it became clear as to why the council had sought such an ordinance in the first place. It had realized that although automobile usage during the previous ten years had sharply increased, most southern Californians continued to enter the business district in streetcars. The Railroad Commission insisted that a ban on automobile parking, combined with newly designed streetcar routes, was absolutely necessary to obviate an increase in the LARY's five-cent fare. The riding public's distrust of the traction companies notwithstanding, the council feared the wrath of the streetcar patrons at the next election. "The majority of the people of Los Angeles use the streetcars and we sincerely trust that the Council will take no action that will open the way for an increase of street-car rates," a railroad commissioner said. Furthermore, at least one council member feared that angry mass-transit users might attempt to pass an initiative prohibiting parking in the downtown area. Such a law could then only be modified by another initiative and would drastically limit the council's flexibility in dealing with the issue at hand. The council, however, could quickly modify one of its own ordinances should conditions warrant such a move.[42]

The council had announced its public meeting with the Railroad Commission and the Board of Public Utilities for two reasons. It wanted to find out how far it could alter the proposed ban without provoking a rate increase. It also wanted the commissioners to comment on the recent controversy concerning the quality of service on the LARY lines. Both bodies readily complied and used these and subsequent meetings both to defend the LARY and to justify their support for a ban. It is clear from their testimony that these public officials did not recognize the automobile as a viable alternative to the railways. As with the jitneys, the commissioners did not believe that private automobiles could replace the streetcar system as a major means of urban transportation. These officials, therefore, argued that they had to protect the traction companies from the encroachment of private "privilege." "Special privileges," President Edgerton of the Railroad Commission insisted, "must give way to the increasing demands and requirements of the general public."[43]

Chief Engineer Osborne pointed out that a parking ban was necessary to keep the downtown streets clear of congestion. Osborne also defended the LARY from the attacks of its critics. Parked cars, not the railway's machinations, had caused the extreme delays in streetcar transit. A delayed car, he noted, picked up far more passengers than it should, thus causing the overcrowded conditions on individual trolleys. Without an improvement in the existing traffic conditions, streetcars would never run on time. Besides, nine people rode streetcars into the downtown district for every one person entering by automobile. A strict parking ordinance, Osborne argued, was necessary to give those not owning automobiles improved transportation service.[44]

In a meeting with the City Council and concerned civic organizations, President Edgerton asserted that the no-parking proposal was not designed to increase the railway's revenues. Rather, it was "prepared and suggested as a step necessary to be taken in the whole programme of street car adjustment." At an earlier meeting, Edgerton claimed that a no-parking ordinance was not "an unreasonable request to make of the City of Los Angeles. It can only be called a sacrifice as to a comparatively few individual interests." Financial difficulties, he pointed out, had forced other cities to raise streetcar fares to as much as twelve cents while cutting back services. Los Angeles, however, "by merely clearing up the congestion on its streets, and adopting rerouting, can obtain the blessing of a fine street car service with the fare remaining at 5 cents." A fellow commissioner argued that Los Angeles had a chance to make its streetcar service the best in the United States. "It is in a position to lead the way," he concluded.[45]

Although the Railroad Commission's chief engineer, Richard Sachse, acknowledged that the present streetcar service was "very bad," he argued that it would greatly improve if the railway would adopt the commission's rerouting plans. This necessitated, however, the removal of automobiles from the business district. "The automobile represents the largest single item of loss in the traffic congestion," Sachse insisted, "and until the automobile is eliminated we will not make much progress in the settlement of the traffic problem." To permit automobile parking in this district disrupted "continuous and regular street car service." "Streets are intended to facilitate business and transportation," Sachse concluded. "The proposition of parking automobiles at the curbs in the business district is preposterous."[46]

The testimony of the Railroad Commission and the

Board of Public Utilities mollified much of the opposition to the ban. Many organizations and individuals previously opposed to the ordinance acquiesced and acknowledged the need for a "betterment of street-car service for the general public and to relieve the intolerable congestion in the downtown district." The public's apparent acceptance of the ban both pleased and surprised members of the City Council and Railroad Commission. The general sentiment at the end of their meetings seemed to be a willingness to give the plan a fair trial; if it proved injurious, the council could modify it accordingly. The *Times* reported that eight out of the nine council members generally approved of the proposed measure.[47]

The *Record* offered the proposed no-parking ordinance cautious support. As a voice of the Los Angeles working class, the paper accepted the ban as a short-term expedient. The paper's commitment to alternative mass transportation and its antagonism towards the traction companies, however, made it withhold complete approbation. The paper's editors argued that the city needed long-range transit plans and immediate traffic relief. In the long run the streetcar would rapidly become an anachronism, the paper argued. "Individual motor-propelled vehicles are replacing it, and seem likely ultimately to entirely banish it." Rail transit, the *Record* continued, was "the slowest and least flexible means of transportation" because it monopolized the center of the street and forced its riders to interrupt traffic while boarding and disembarking. Buses, with greater flexibility and mobility, were quickly taking over the railways' work. Therefore, the city should create its own municipal jitney and bus systems to facilitate the process and prevent another monopoly of transportation by private traction companies. In the short term, however, the city required immediate relief from the intolerable congestion. If it came down to a choice between the streetcar riders and the motorists, the *Record* favored the former. But banning the automobile would prove extreme and impolitic. "That is merely flying in the face of physical [and] mechanical progress," the paper concluded. "But it is fair to restrict their parking, so that that parking will not impede traffic."[48]

There remained, nevertheless, a few outspoken and important opponents of the plan. The Automobile Club of Southern California, the Motorcar Dealers' Association, and the Auto Livery Owners' Association strongly opposed the ban. While agreeing that automobile owners had to make some sacrifices, these groups insisted that motorists had a right to a reasonable use of the streets. They also threatened legal and political action if the council passed the ordinance intact. After a stormy conference between City Council members and various civic organizations, the council agreed to modify the objectionable legislation. This compromise reduced the size of the no-parking area and placed a fifteen-minute limit on the loading and unloading of merchandise and passengers during the no-parking hours of 9:30 A.M. to 6:15 P.M. In addition, the new law forbade commercial deliveries in the congested district between 4:00 and 6:15 P.M. The council later added regulations requiring pedestrians to move in accordance with the directions of traffic officers.[49]

The City Council finally voted unanimously in early February to institute a modified version of the original law. In its final form the new ordinance provided for yet a smaller no-parking area, surrounded by a two-hour parking zone. The council also reduced the daily hours of the ordinance to 11:00 A.M. to 6:15 P.M. Automobiles could stop for two minutes to load and unload passengers in the restricted area, while commercial vehicles could park for fifteen minutes until 4:00 P.M., after which time they could not stop at all. Finally, the ordinance prohibited left turns at some intersections in the congested district. The council scheduled the new ordinance to go into effect on April 10.[50]

Most civic organizations assumed a watchful attitude towards the legislation. The Linen Supply Men's Association, however, circulated a referendum petition against the ban. Complaining that the late afternoon restriction on commercial loading in the no-parking area would impose hardships on its business of supplying clean linen to the downtown hotels, the association hoped to rally enough support to convince the council to repeal the ordinance before April 10. Within three weeks it had gathered the necessary 15,000 signatures to force an election.[51]

The *Times* also vigorously opposed the ordinance. Under the headline, "The Perils of a Parkless Town," the newspaper devoted nearly a full page to denigrating the ban. The new law, the *Times* claimed, would "jam street cars to [an] impossible point and hurt trade." The newspaper reiterated many of its earlier objections to the new legislation. This ban, the paper argued, "will inevitably force the creation of new shopping districts outside the present congested area." Opposed to the idea of decentralization, the paper feared that several smaller retail districts in the outlying areas would threaten the city's business district. According to the *Times*, one eastern merchandiser had plans to build huge retail stores on Wilshire Boulevard in Hollywood to "cater to automobile shoppers." One- and two-story business blocks were already springing up in the suburbs with startling rapidity. This sounded an ominous note for those Los Angeles boosters intent on retaining the downtown district's dominance over rival districts and cities in southern California.[52]

The *Times* also doubted that the railways could handle the extra passenger load expected of them once the ordinance went into effect. The 30,000 cars currently parking in the business district each day carried 82,500 people. Although the LARY announced that it could handle the increase in passengers, the paper claimed that many businessmen doubted this since the railway could not adequately handle the existing passenger load. "To the man familiar with the present congestion on our street cars. . . ," the *Times* noted, "the addition of 80,000 passengers each way is an appalling prospect." Finally, the paper believed that the new law was designed to relieve congestion by limiting the use of progressive technology. There was no question that the ordinance would clear up congestion, "but it will do it on the same principle by which there was no congestion in the Los Angeles streets of 1870."[53]

After venting their anger, the *Times* and other critics remained quiet in the days prior to the ordinance's implementation. The City Council, in the meantime, bought off its last major opponent. Worried about the prospects of a referendum, the council agreed to remove the clause prohibiting late afternoon commercial deliveries on the last day to file referendum petitions against the ordinance; the Linen Supply Men's Association thus decided not to file its petition.[54]

On April 10, 1920, the ordinance finally went into effect. Police that day arrested nearly a thousand violators who were merely given warnings and released. The police announced that after a few days they would begin assessing stiff fines of five and ten dollars for illegal left turns and parking. On the whole, the results of the ban pleased public officials. The city's chief of police remarked that the new law had successfully relieved downtown congestion. Traffic, he noted, moved about 50 percent faster than before the ordinance had gone into effect. H. Z. Osborne of the Public Utilities Commission was particularly pleased. "After spending all morning in touring the no-parking district," he reported, "I am impressed that the new ordinance is a great success. Immediate results have been obtained in relieving congestion." He pointed out that streetcars, which had previously lost forty to sixty minutes on each trip, were finally running on schedule for the first time in years. Automobiles also ran through the downtown area without delay. Osborne reported later in the week that automobile traffic had been speeded up by ten to fifteen minutes during the rush hour, while the number of accidents in the congested area had been reduced dramatically.[55]

The motoring public, however, was not as sanguine. The *Times* reported that thousands of disgruntled autoists parked their cars outside of the no-parking district and walked into the city. The *Examiner* sarcastically reported that "after the first day of the new ordinance everybody seemed satisfied with its operations except the motorists, the professional men, the business houses and the police. . . . One had to walk only one lonely block down Broadway to hear a score of complaints." Meanwhile, shoppers jammed the less fashionable shops on the north side of the congested district. Rather than take streetcars into the city, consumers parked close to the edge of the restricted area and walked to shops on North Spring, North Main, and North Broadway. Merchants in that region recorded their best business in years. Some stores even had to hire extra clerks to handle the rush.

Other motorists planned to test the ordinance in court. Influenced by the many protests of his fellow automobile owners, Earl Anthony set out to challenge the council's authority to enforce the new ordinance. According to Anthony, the first day's trial had brought thousands of complaints from dissatisfied drivers. These citizens argued that they had paid taxes to support road maintenance and construction, yet the ban prohibited them from effectively utilizing those roads.[56]

Initially, motorcar dealers and merchants in the downtown area maintained a "policy of watchful waiting." It did not take long, however, for merchants to feel the effects of the ordinance. Two days after the no-parking ordinance went into effect, retailers issued protests against the ban. Claiming that their businesses had already experienced declining profits, these and other businessmen sent letters of protest to the City Council. As the week wore on, more shoppers avoided downtown shops. "Hundreds have been arrested since the new traffic rules went into effect," the *Times* reported, "but the number dwindles daily as does the motor car traffic on the downtown streets."[57]

Declaring that "dealers in the entire business district have lost tens of thousands of dollars since the law went into effect a week ago," the Business Men's Co-Operative Association called a protest meeting against the parking ban. Over a hundred business representatives attended the gathering held just nine days after the ordinance had gone into effect; several council members also appeared. The law, the representatives agreed, seriously interfered with business. Retail income had fallen dramatically during the preceding week, indicating that "people . . . depend on their motor cars for shopping." Those attending the meeting conceded that the city should not completely eliminate the ordinance, but should alter it so that it "will not cripple business." The councilmen present concurred. "The fact that this ordinance has proved to be too severe is evidence that it must be amended . . . ," one council member acknowledged. "First, last and always, I'm for the protection of the business man, so far as loss is concerned, because we must see to it that he prospers."[58]

The participants appointed a committee to confer with the City Council about possible amendments to the ordinance. Some suggested that the council restrict parking only during the afternoon rush hours because traffic in the morning was never as bad. Two days following the meeting, the committee submitted an amendment to the council for its consideration which called for the elimination of parking restrictions before 10:00 A.M. From that time until 4:30 P.M. the committee suggested a strictly enforced forty-five-minute parking limit on downtown streets. The no-parking law would then go into effect from 4:30 to 6:15 P.M., during which time commercial deliveries would be prohibited. Finally, the committee encouraged the council to allow left turns at Fifth and Hill streets to facilitate traffic circulation.[59]

As the businessmen's committee presented its suggestions to the council, other businessmen stepped up their protest. "We were willing to give the ordinance a fair trial," said one commercial leader. "The actual test has shown that the ordinance has been disasterous [sic] to business, which is the life of our city." Others presented statistics to emphasize their cause. A prominent retailer found that "business men of all kinds in the congested and business districts, and even outside the restricted district, report that their business is dropping off from 25 percent to 35 percent, and some cases 50 percent, as a result of the workings of the ordinance." Realty board representatives claimed that Hill Street cafes were losing $500 a day, while Huntington Rubber Company reported that the tire and rubber dealers' trade was down nearly 50 percent. A bank in the city center asserted that in one day at least forty customers moved their accounts to concerns located outside of the downtown district. Most ominous, a leading businessman predicted that the ordinance, left in its present form, would bankrupt half the city's businesses within three years. The ban, he concluded, was the worst thing to happen to Los Angeles in years.[60]

The three leading newspapers in Los Angeles joined the business leaders in calling for changes to the no-parking ordinance. The *Times* had consistently opposed the ordinance since its inception. The city's largest paper, the *Examiner*, however, had remained largely uninterested in the issue until the law had gone into effect. The consequences of the ban quickly converted the editors. "The people of Los Angeles," an *Examiner* editorial ran, "want traffic and business expedited and not killed. The anti-parking ordinance is being condemned by merchants on the ground that it is ruining trade. If it is, the ordinance should be promptly amended."[61]

Although the reform-minded *Record* had sympathized

with the riding public throughout the parking controversy, the legacy of two decades of poor railway service and the seemingly indifferent attitudes of railway officials had caused the paper to seek alternatives to rail transit. This made the *Record*'s editors far more sympathetic to the motorists' plight. Shortly after the ban began, the paper had urged the city to give the ordinance a fair trial because it had, after all, expedited vehicular traffic. The paper cautioned, however, that the "usefulness of the automobile must not be destroyed." In addition, if the ordinance was "forcing autoists to leave their machines at home . . . and is simply feeding more business into the car company coffers, it is dangerously bad." Once the businessmen's committee petitioned the City Council to alter the ordinance, the *Record* came out strongly in favor of the amendments. Arguing that a proper readjustment of the statute could reconcile the interests of the businessmen, autoists, and streetcar riders, the paper reminded its readers that "nobody wants to cripple trade or turn Los Angeles into a sleepy hollow."[62]

Despite the council's promise for quick relief, business interests and opponents of the ban continued to organize against the offending legislation. Only four days after the Business Men's Co-Operative Association's meeting, hundreds of automobiles paraded through the downtown area displaying banners protesting the ordinance. Gilbert Woodill of the Car Dealers' Association joined the demonstration. He remarked that the council had originally ignored his organization's protests because the politicians had felt that it was merely composed of biased businessmen. Woodill declared, however, that the ground swell of opposition from all over the city clearly indicated the importance of the automobile to urban life. "The day when the automobile was a 'pleasure car' . . . is long since past," Woodill argued. "The motor car is just as much a necessity to business as the street car." The sooner government officials realized that "the hampering of the use of the automobile is hampering the progress of civilization the better off we will all be." According to Woodill, it did not take Los Angeles even twenty-four hours to realize that restricting automobile usage in the downtown area was the same thing as "cutting the throat of business." In Woodill's eyes, the only good thing about the ban was that it finally demonstrated "the extent to which the automobile has become a part of our everyday life." "The vast majority of the people have in a general sort of way," Woodill continued, "felt that the business pulse of Southern California throbbed in unison with the purring motors of its automobiles, but not until the automobiles were practically driven from the downtown streets of Los Angeles by the no-parking ordinance had the fact ever been brought home with such force." The City Council, Woodill concluded, would think twice before restricting automobile usage again.[63]

Such hyperbole might be expected from an automobile salesman economically interested in the outcome of the legislation at hand, but Woodill was basically correct. The city did depend upon the automobile in significant ways. A large segment of the public owned automobiles by this time, with the county of Los Angeles having one car for every five citizens. This meant that there was nearly one automobile for every family living in the county. Denied parking in the downtown district, many of these potential shoppers stayed at home or traveled to other areas rather than ride the streetcars into downtown Los Angeles. Once businessmen felt the financial impact of these decisions, they organized to pressure the City Council to alter the ordinance. The council responded by unanimously voting to amend the offending legislation despite the protests of the Railroad Commission and the Board of Public Utilities, which argued that the city had not given the ordinance a fair trial. The amendment established a forty-five-minute parking limit on the downtown streets from 10:00 A.M. until 4:00 P.M. From then until 6:15 the no-parking restrictions remained intact. The mayor immediately signed the emergency legislation, which went into effect on April 29, just nineteen days after the initial ban had begun. Businessmen applauded the council's actions. The changes were instituted smoothly and caused no noticeable increase in congestion. What little support the original ordinance retained was largely ignored.[64]

The parking crisis was essentially a battle over the use of public space because the ban reduced the effectiveness of the automobile as a means of urban transportation. The City Council, with the support of the state Railroad Commission, implemented the ordinance because it feared that congestion in the central business district would strangle the flow of goods and people within the city.[65] What the council did not realize was that a majority of Los Angeles' citizens wanted to improve rather than restrict automobile movement. The public was fed up with the lack of transportation reform. The traction companies, people argued, were more interested in profits than public service. Furthermore, the inability of the railways to extend their lines into the suburbs restricted Angelenos from moving into newly developed subdivisions. Frustrated car riders consequently turned to the automobile as a democratic alternative to the inadequacy of public transportation.[66] In utilizing their cars, the autoists further asserted that they held an inherent prerogative to use the public streets. To ban the automobile from the city's thoroughfares was to strip them of their rights as individuals and taxpayers. Furthermore, the public did not believe that the railway corporations should retain a virtual monopoly of the road. Indeed, Angelenos had for many years argued just the opposite. The streetcars, they insisted, operated over the streets solely through the grace of the people; the City Council had no right to restrict the use of the public domain for the benefit of the carriers.

The motorists received important support from the city's downtown business interests. These businessmen had long held the reins of the region's economy largely because of the centralized nature of the metropolitan area. In attempting to retain their hegemony, these leaders greatly feared the growth of commercial districts outside of the city center. Although they worried that congestion would discourage shoppers from entering the downtown area, the parking ban proved even worse because automobile owners stopped patronizing their shops altogether. The merchants therefore pressured the council to revoke the law in order to prevent the decentralization of commerce.

The parking crisis in Los Angeles clearly demonstrates that various sectors of urban society could still coalesce into a force powerful enough to impose its will on a recalcitrant city government. Furthermore, the railways found that they could not always hide behind the protection of the regulatory agencies. In this case, the LARY had both the powerful state Railroad Commission and the local Board of Public Utilities fighting its cause. Yet the combined weight of the traction company and the regulatory bodies could not carry out their objectives against a storm of public protest. All of this indicates that the elements that had made up the progressive movement survived the war.[67] Despite their fragmentation, these groups could still rally around individual issues such as the automobile's place in the urban transportation system. Los Angeles was hardly unique in embracing the automobile as a democratic alternative to the railways. Historian Glen Holt has already noted elsewhere that Americans throughout the United States "financed any scheme and tried every available alternative in an attempt to break away from the crowded transit cars and the discipline imposed on personal lifestyle by the necessity of riding a mass carrying system."[68] The inefficiencies of the railways, the long history of corruption on the part of transit officials, and the failure of progressive politics encouraged urban residents to abandon the streetcar in favor of the automobile.

When citizens of other large cities began using their cars, however, they soon faced similar problems to those found in southern California. Shortly after World War I, automobile congestion in downtown Boston became so bad that the city government adopted a no-stopping law reminiscent of the one in Los Angeles. The city later repealed the legislation, however, when shopkeepers vigorously protested that they would lose the carriage trade to the suburbs.[69] Chicago in the meantime toyed with its own parking ban. Various transit interests along with several city officials favored the adoption of a law that would have eliminated all parking within the Loop. Automobile dealers, auto clubs, and businessmen opposed the proposal. The city council eventually passed the ordinance in 1920 only to have it vetoed by the mayor, who noted a storm of protest against the measure by Chicago merchants and the dreadful experience of Los Angeles with its own no-parking legislation.[70] Southern towns also experienced substantial parking problems in their central business districts. Not only did parked cars block traffic lanes, but frustrated drivers would endlessly ply the streets in search of spaces. Only a few short years after the Los Angeles parking crisis, a Nashville business publication lamented that the "lack of parking space causes purchasers to patronize suburban rather than downtown stores."[71] By 1935, only Chicago had instituted a parking ban covering a large section of its city center.[72]

The early acceptance of the automobile in Los Angeles and elsewhere sanctioned the car as a legitimate means of urban transportation. It also highlighted the fact that the narrow and discontinuous streets in most cities could not readily adapt themselves to the increasing number of automobiles.[73] Once city governments accepted the automobile's place within their transportation systems, they had to find new ways to accommodate its presence as the pressure on thoroughfares reached crisis proportions. Somehow these municipalities had to eliminate the stagnation. Los Angeles, along with other cities, eventually came to rely upon an extensive program of street improvements, which, for a time, facilitated the movement of automobiles within its boundaries.

⇐ 4 ⇒

The Power of Consensus

=

The time has arrived for the city to plan a major system of streets radiating from the center of the city to all of the surrounding towns and territory, for we must have adequate facilities for traffic and transportation.

—John Griffin, City Engineer
1921

It is not too much to say that the onward march of Los Angeles towards its place of destiny will be made immeasurably slower unless a solution is found for the traffic problem.

—The Los Angeles Traffic Commission
1922

Los Angeles' dependency on the automobile by the mid-twenties was unusual for American cities. "The place of the automobile in the transportation problem of Los Angeles," wrote the distinguished urban planner and landscape architect Frederick Law Olmsted, Jr., in 1924, "is far more important than in cities of the East." Southern California's favorable climate, "the widely scattered population, and the almost universal housing in detached single-family dwellings" encouraged the widespread use of automobiles.[1] Automobile registration figures bear out the validity of these statements. Table 2 demonstrates that automobile ownership in Los Angeles far outpaced the national average. In 1915, Los Angeles had one car for every eight residents, far more than the national mean of one per forty-three citizens. By 1925, every other Angeleno owned an automobile as opposed to the rest of the country where there was only one car for every six people. Even more

Table 2
Residents Per Automobile

	United States	Los Angeles	Chicago
1915	43.1	8.2	61.0
1920	13.1	3.6	30.0
1925	6.6	1.8	11.0
1930	5.3	1.5	8.0
1935	5.6	1.6	NA
1940	4.8	1.4	NA

Sources: Calculated from information found in the Los Angeles Municipal Research Library card catalogue; Los Angeles County Regional Planning Commission, *A Comprehensive Report on the Masterplan of Highways (1941)*; United States Department of Commerce, *Historical Statistics of the United States: From Colonial Times to 1970* (1975); and Paul Barrett, *The Automobile and Urban Transit.*

NA = Not Available

important, Angelenos used their cars more frequently than did residents of other cities. By 1924, nearly half of all those entering the Los Angeles central business district arrived by automobile. Two years later, a traffic survey in Chicago found that only 33 percent of the people traveling into the Loop did so by car. The contrast was even more striking in Pittsburgh where only 20 percent of all wage earners drove their automobiles to work during the thirties.[2]

Although Angelenos clearly led the way, people in other cities also embraced the automobile enthusiastically following World War I. In 1920, for instance, Chicago had only one automobile for every thirty residents. Ten years later, not only had car ownership increased dramatically, but merchants began to worry about excessive congestion within the Loop. Similarly, surveys in Pittsburgh indicated that automobile traffic in its central business district had risen 587 percent between 1917 and 1927. The automobile became a fixture of urban life even in the South where per capita income fell well below the national norm. A Baltimore newspaper argued in 1924 that people eagerly purchased cars because they allowed the individual to "live in the suburban districts, or a greater distance from his place of employment at a considerable less expense so far as rent is concerned, and [he may] save a considerable amount of car fare by using [his] automobile to and from [his] business." The paper concluded that Americans owned "more automobiles than telephones, and they are increasing year after year, showing conclusively that people want them, and that they are a necessity for business, health, and pleasure." By 1929, a list of American cities with the greatest proportional increase in automobile ownership included not Los Angeles but St. Louis, Memphis, New York City, Cincinnati, Kansas City, and Chicago.[3]

Unfortunately, not one of these cities could easily accommodate large numbers of automobiles within their city centers. The street system of every major city in America was built during an earlier transportation era. The narrow, discontinuous roadways simply could not handle the increased traffic efficiently as streetcars, automobiles, and pedestrians fought over precious street space. This problem affected not just Los Angeles, but all large urban areas in the United States. As early as 1920, an Atlanta newspaper could claim that its city was "confronted with as serious a traffic situation as has existed in any city in the United States." Nor did most observers see congestion as a strictly local issue. The Birmingham *Age-Herald* noted during the twenties that the automobile was "rapidly becoming a serious handicap in downtown business centers."[4] It therefore became imperative for cities to facilitate the flow of traffic. These attempts to ease congestion at least partially succeeded in cities such as Chicago and Los Angeles because a large segment of the population placed great faith in the automobile's ability to provide efficient and equitable urban transportation. The automobile, they believed, could continue the process of residential dispersion favored by homeowners, politicians, and urban planners alike.

The compromise leading to the amended parking restrictions merely served as a temporary solution to Los Angeles' traffic problems. The institution of the forty-five-minute parking limit, the rush-hour ban on parking, and the revamped streetcar routing relieved congestion for a few months, giving the city a much needed respite. The improved conditions, however, encouraged more Angelenos to abandon public transportation in favor of their automobiles. In addition, southern California entered yet another of its periodic real estate booms and population influxes. Thousands of immigrants arrived each month and numerous subdivisions sprang up to accommodate them. With the railways unable to build extensions for financial reasons, the residents of these new suburban areas had to rely upon their automobiles. The initial success of the new parking laws rapidly dissipated with the increased traffic on the city's streets. By accepting the automobile as a major means of transportation, southern Californians soon faced serious vehicular congestion.[5]

The city's rapid population growth following World War I posed difficult engineering problems for city officials. John Griffin, the city engineer, warned the citizens of southern California in 1921 that Los Angeles was no longer the "quiet, peaceful and happy abode of rancheros" and consequently had to plan for its future. "The time has arrived," he concluded, "for the city to plan a major system of streets radiating from the center of the city to all of the surrounding towns and territory, for we must have adequate facilities for traffic and transportation." The existing street system was perfectly adequate for the days of the horse-drawn vehicle, noted one of Griffin's subordinates, but that network of roads was "entirely inadequate for present traffic conditions due to the use of the automobile."[6]

The movement to improve the city's streets was not a new one. Several organizations and individuals had advocated alterations in street design before the parking crisis.[7] Once that issue had resolved itself in favor of the city's motorists, the call for widening existing streets and opening new thoroughfares received renewed support. Indeed, this seemed to be the most direct way to facilitate traffic flow. The width of the city's original roads, a city engineer noted, was completely inadequate for the "auto age." He contended that the city had to begin an extensive campaign of roadway improvement in order to eliminate congestion. The city did not lack roads, he continued. Rather, people had failed to realize the fundamental importance of opening, widening, and permanently paving thoroughfares.

Unfortunately, existing state and city laws made it difficult for the city government to undertake such improvements. A majority of the property owners along any given street, not city officials, normally initiated road construction by petitioning the City Council. The council would then order the Engineering Department to undertake the necessary surveys. After receiving the city's approval, the property owners would hire a private contractor to commence the construction. The council would finally assess the property owners abutting the road for the total cost of the improvements; hence, the property owners essentially taxed themselves for the construction. This method held down the cost of city government, but it made it difficult for local officials to plan a rational system of boulevards. "Our main thoroughfares are so congested that radical steps must be taken for relief," a member of the Engineering Department wrote in 1922. The existing procedure of waiting for property owners to file petitions made it nearly impossible to open and widen the streets "necessary for the future development of the city."[8]

Although some street openings and widenings did take place, the city had no way of coordinating these projects. Frederick Law Olmsted, Jr., commented on these problems when he visited the region in the summer of 1922. Los Angeles, he remarked, had reached a stage in its development where it had to plan a comprehensive park and boulevard system to meet its future traffic needs. Without such a plan, the city would find itself with ridiculously narrow and inadequate streets. While he saw no shortage of roads in the city, Olmsted did note that Los Angeles lacked "big radial channels of communications" because of its haphazard pattern of private real estate development. The developers created severe congestion by providing for local traffic while paying no attention "to the needs of the city as a whole."[9]

Two civic organizations, the Automobile Club of Southern California and the Los Angeles Traffic Commission, addressed this issue during the early twenties. The Automobile Club began a traffic survey of the downtown area shortly after the resolution of the parking crisis. Following two years of study, the club released its findings in the belief that its survey could help remedy "a problem of the utmost importance." By recommending extensive changes in Los Angeles' traffic pattern, the club hoped to serve the needs of the city's business interests, the motoring public, and the public in general. Like Olmsted, the club argued that the congestion in the city arose from the overall pattern of land use in Los Angeles. Subdivisions within the city were planned as private ventures with developers making few attempts to coordinate their layout of streets with neighboring suburbs. The section west of the downtown area fully illustrated this problem. The entire west side suffered from abnormal traffic congestion because Vermont and Western avenues were practically the only thoroughfares in the area.

The City Council, the club proposed, should establish a central authority to coordinate real estate developments and arrange "the continuity of the streets and thus relieve prospective congestion of a similar nature for newer portions of the city." Fortunately, the recently organized City Planning Commission was beginning to assume this authority by reviewing subdivision plats within the city limits and endeavoring to coordinate the new developments with a general highway and street system for the metropolitan area. This, the club believed, would help relieve the city's traffic congestion.[10]

Traffic conditions in the city center concerned the Automobile Club even more. No one, it argued, doubted that "the crowded condition of our streets in our downtown area results in a tremendous loss to business." The club estimated that the traffic delays cost the city's residents thousands of dollars each year in wasted transit time. Congestion in the business district, the club insisted, was largely caused by the fact that Los Angeles had both the highest per capita automobile ownership in America and one of the lowest percentages of land use devoted to street area (see table 3). Although most of the city's development had occurred within the previous twenty years, its downtown streets had been laid in 1781. Not surprisingly, the city's recent intensive growth outstripped the traffic capacity of its roads. The report also noted that pedestrians, "crossing the streets at random, with no regard for the flow of vehicular traffic," inhibited transit, while parked cars, particularly on the narrow east and west streets in the congested area, effectively reduced the width of the already narrow streets. Finally, "the lack of adequate thoroughfares encircling the congested area" greatly contributed to downtown traffic. The absence of such highways forced vehicles attempting to get from one side of town to the other to enter the congested district. The club asserted that the city had to increase the area devoted to streets in the central business district before it could find

Table 3
Area of Central Business District Devoted to Streets, 1924

	Percent
Washington, D.C.	44.0
San Diego	41.0
Cleveland	39.5
Seattle	37.5
San Francisco	34.5
Pittsburgh	34.0
Minneapolis	30.5
Detroit	29.5
Chicago	29.0
Los Angeles	21.5

Source: Olmsted et al., *A Major Traffic Street Plan.*

a satisfactory solution to the traffic situation. It also needed to build adequate thoroughfares to divert the crosstown traffic away from the city center.[11]

The club's report suggested two plans of action to resolve Los Angeles' problems. Citing the recently amended no-parking law as an example of effective legislation, the club argued for further legal action, such as the restriction of pedestrian movement. "The traffic officers questioned regarding this control were emphatic in their statements that vehicular traffic would be improved by the control of pedestrians," the club reported. The club also proposed changes that would both allow right-hand turns regardless of the position of the traffic signal and create one-way streets.[12]

The major advantage of seeking legislative changes to improve traffic flow was that city officials could implement these alterations immediately and at little cost. The club cautioned, however, that "no permanent solution can be found for such relief which does not include construction measures, particularly as regards increasing the street area of Los Angeles." The city's highways were simply too narrow to handle the rise in traffic. One way to correct this deficiency was through an extensive program of reconstruction. The club proposed widening downtown streets by demolishing buildings, constructing underground sidewalks or arcades, and setting back curbs and property lines to allow for future road work. The club also called for a major program to open new streets and extend existing ones. "The City of Los Angeles," the club wrote, "has no broad, diagonal thoroughfares or boulevards. The value of such streets cannot be overestimated." Such streets would allow vehicles to get into or out of the downtown district quickly.[13]

The club's general recommendations for street improvements included a broad traffic quadrangle encircling the congested area, diagonal boulevards leading from the city center to the outlying districts, and a circulatory system of thoroughfares in the suburbs. The report went on to list several specific projects it deemed essential to relieving the region's immediate congestion. Realizing that its proposals might seem prohibitively expensive, the club argued that if the city was to "take its destined place among the great and beautiful cities of the world [it] must eventually make these improvements and the longer the delay the greater the ultimate cost." The club also contended that all road work should fit into a comprehensive master street plan. Such a program would make each local improvement important to the city as a whole. "Consequently, the financial burden for the improvement of such streets as are adopted by the plan should, in a large measure, be widely distributed over the city and the county." No longer could the city leave the street system in the hands of individual groups of property owners. It had to take control of its highways for the good of the whole area. "Without the consummation of such a traffic plan," the club warned, "the city will suffer a loss of millions of dollars annually. Put into operation this loss will be averted, property values will be enhanced, business will be conducted more conveniently and more efficiently and the City of Los Angeles will be enabled to fulfill its destiny as a great world metropolis."[14]

During the latter half of 1921, while the Automobile Club was still conducting its traffic survey, the Board of Public Utilities directed H. Z. Osborne to investigate the traffic situation in Los Angeles. Congestion, Osborne noted, was worsening because of the area's remarkable population growth. After studying the issue in detail, he concluded that "the greatest good can be procured for the city by soliciting the active cooperation of the organizations working on this subject." Osborne's report consequently recommended that representatives from civic and commercial groups interested in traffic meet at a conference to share their ideas. Osborne called for meetings in December and January. Delegates from the traction companies, the leading commercial and civic organizations, and various city commissions attended the conference.[15]

Out of these meetings came the formation of the Los Angeles Traffic Commission. The commission was a voluntary, unofficial advisory body representing most of Los Angeles' business and civic organizations, utility companies, city departments, and newspapers. The commission hoped "to assist the city authorities in solving the traffic problems of Los Angeles." This organization saw itself as a forum where the various interests in the city affected by traffic could arbitrate and compromise divergent viewpoints before presenting remedies to the City Council. The founders insisted that they would not promote any particular interest "be they motorists, pedestrians or car riders." The commission, then, acted as a buffer between the public and the City Council by suggesting needed improvements, circulating petitions, securing deeds for street construction, and aggressively advocating "all measures in the interest of public welfare looking toward the relief of traffic congestion in the City of Los Angeles, and its immediate vicinity."[16]

In speaking as the executive officer of the Traffic Commission, Osborne outlined the issues concerning the organization. If Los Angeles was to resolve its automobile and streetcar congestion, he remarked, it "must provide more streets. Los Angeles must have wide main thoroughfares." Osborne claimed that by spending $23,500 annually, the city could widen 250 to 300 blocks each year. "The plan is perfectly practical," he continued, "but it requires a body like the Traffic Commission to carry out the plan in a successful, intelligent manner." The commission, Osborne hastened to add, would propose to widen streets "mainly through voluntary agreement of the property owners themselves." Finally, Osborne called for a master street plan to coordinate the construction activity. "A comprehensive program ought to be outlined covering a step-by-step plan for a period of fifteen years to eliminate traffic congestion both at the present time and in the future." Osborne, who had previously advocated a total ban on automobile parking, now turned to what he perceived to be the only practical alternative—the reconstruction of the city's street system to accommodate the increasing number of automobiles.[17]

The Traffic Commission's first major effort to tackle congestion was the publication of its own comprehensive street survey. The *Los Angeles Plan* synthesized the commission's research with that of other organizations such as the Automobile Club. "Los Angeles today," the report began, "is the wonder city of the world." Its citizens, however, could not afford "to lose sight of a few obstacles which must be overcome." Los Angeles' narrow streets, narrow sidewalks, and dangerous grade crossings all contributed to the heavy traffic congestion throughout the city. "It is not too much to say," the report warned, "that the onward march of Los Angeles towards its place of destiny will be made immeasurably slower unless a solution is found for the traffic problem." Congestion cost the city's residents thousands of dollars each year, caused countless traffic accidents, and threatened the prosperity of the city itself. "To put off adopting a plan, until the congested district dies of strangulation," the organization cautioned, "means that a new district will spring up elsewhere, leaving depreciation of property value, and disaster in its wake."[18] As late as 1922, then, various civic organizations, businesses, and government officials still believed in the necessity of maintaining a centralized urban structure. The City Council and downtown businessmen had resolved the parking crisis largely because they feared the consequences of decentralization. The Traffic Commission hoped to eliminate this possibility altogether by permanently relieving Los Angeles of its severe traffic congestion.

The commission argued that only a comprehensive and coordinated plan for widening, extending, and opening streets could offer a solution to the problem, for as one engineering journal reported, it was "the common opinion of all visitors to Los Angeles that that busy city is the worst congested in America." The city, however, could expect negligible relief from the further imposition of traffic regulations, the report argued. Los Angeles had finally reached the point where additional regulations merely served as palliatives. "The day of reckoning has arrived and the only logical and permanent relief must come from increased street area," the commission concluded. "The entire city must be embraced in a coordinated system of well defined arteries." Such a plan would have to overcome petty local interests for the good of the entire city. "The average citizen," the commission wrote, "is not far-sighted and unless convinced of the severity of conditions which confront him will not be deeply concerned with traffic plans." Without a complete understanding of the issues, local residents might reject important improvements regardless of the needs of the community as a whole. Concerned citizens, therefore, should formulate a publicity campaign of "sufficient intensity and duration to convince the public mind that the intended plans are for the public good." The commission believed that support for such a street program would be readily forthcoming "once the picture of the Greater Los Angeles is firmly implanted in the minds of the people."[19]

The organization's obsession with community support stemmed from the tremendous estimated financial costs attached to its program. As the situation stood, the property owners abutting each street had to pay the entire expense of any street improvements. The difficulties in coordinating a comprehensive program of road work under such a system were obvious. To plan the opening and widening of major traffic thoroughfares necessitated the cooperation of the majority of the hundreds of property owners along the entire length of each proposed project. Furthermore, such alterations benefited more than just those homeowners living close to the designated streets. The commission consequently believed that it had to persuade the public to share the costs of the program. "Experience has shown," the commission argued, "that [major street improvements] cannot be accomplished without participation of the whole city in their costs." As such, the commission hoped to secure a citywide bond issue to pay for part of each project identified by the master plan. This, the commission argued, was the "only method that will guarantee the necessary impetus to a comprehensive program of street opening and widening." The immediate problem, the organization concluded, was to convince the public to support its efforts. "Let the Los Angeles Traffic Commission resolve itself into a militant group pledged to employ every legitimate means to the carrying out of whatever bond issue may be necessary to cover the city's cost in the program selected."[20]

Despite the commission's specific recommendations for street improvements, little immediate action was forthcoming. The City Council did call for the widening and opening of certain streets, although it admitted that "this piece-meal idea should give way to a wide and comprehensive survey by competent persons." Other cities, the council members noted, had spent millions of dollars to lay out new arterial highways. Los Angeles, on the other hand, might save itself vast sums of money through proper planning. In the meantime, the Community Development Association proposed yet another plan for the widening and opening of specific streets. Although similar to the Automobile Club and Traffic Commission studies, this plan further complicated the matter. Everyone agreed that southern California's population and real estate booms had exacerbated the city's traffic problems by bringing thousands of new residents into the area. "The extraordinary growth of our community," the Public Works Committee of the City Council reported, "and the growth of suburban towns and cities, together with the advent of the automobile and truck, and the enormous increase of our population, make it necessary for us to lay out a comprehensive plan for future development." The Public Works Committee urged the body to appropriate $10,000 to make its own survey before adopting a master city plan for the widening and opening of streets. The council approved the proposal and instructed the city engineer to investigate the feasibility and costs associated with thirty-seven proposed street improvements.[21]

Frustrated by the relative lack of activity on this vital issue, the Traffic Commission finally appointed a special committee of twenty-three men who each contributed $1,000 towards financing a comprehensive highway survey of the region. This Major Highways Committee proceeded to retain the services of three of the nation's most renowned urban planners—Frederick Law Olmsted, Jr., Harland Bartholomew, and Charles H. Cheney—to direct the survey. The planners' reputations and the ample financial resources of the Major Highways Committee enhanced the chances that this street plan would resolve the difficulties of choosing a master list of street improvements.[22]

Olmsted and his colleagues sought to develop a definitive plan "for the reconstruction of the ill-arranged collection of streets of Los Angeles into a well ordered system of traffic arteries." The planners specifically acknowledged the previous plans set forth by the Automobile Club and the Traffic Commission and incorporated many of their proposals into the Major Traffic Street Plan. The planners, however, noted the complete absence of any suitable general outline for an overall system of major thoroughfares. They consequently designed a program to provide "a broad, practical, well balanced scheme for handling traffic toward which the city can advantageously grow."[23] The consultants designed their plan to handle what was then a tremendous flow of vehicular traffic. They warned that the city must implement the plan as a whole for it to provide complete relief of the city's traffic congestion. They further warned that the city could not adopt a rigid, fixed program, but must continually study the problem and make adjustments as necessary. This was why the planners presented a report that focused on major thoroughfares and not individual streets.

Although the study's conclusions regarding Los Angeles' traffic problems were similar to those of earlier surveys, the planners' attempt to study the region's transportation system scientifically gave their report a comprehensive quality unmatched by the earlier proposals. In summarizing their findings, the consultants attempted to isolate the reasons underlying the congestion. They found that the "causes of street congestion in Los Angeles are . . . not unlike those in most other cities," yet they did note that peculiarities within the area tended to intensify these problems. These characteristics were such that "the street traffic congestion problem of Los Angeles is exceeded by no other city."[24]

One of the most important reasons for the traffic problem was Los Angeles' rapidly increasing population, which had nearly doubled between 1910 and 1920. In the four years between the 1920 census and the compilation of the report, the consultants estimated that the number of residents in Los Angeles had again nearly doubled and stood at approximately one million. This inundation was clearly reflected in the county assessor's records of subdivisions and housing activity. Between March 1, 1923, and March 1, 1924, developers subdivided 84,000 new lots and erected 125,000 houses.[25] Automobile traffic, however, had increased even faster than the rise in population. Automobile registration in Los Angeles County alone had increased nearly fourfold between 1918 and 1923 from 110,000 to 430,000. Even more shocking were the traffic figures presented in the report. During the 1920 parking controversy, Richard Sachse estimated that nine streetcar passengers entered the congested district for every motorist. By 1924, nearly as many people reached the downtown area by automobile as did by streetcar. The report noted that during a typical eleven-hour period (7 A.M. to 6 P.M.) automobiles carried 239,202 passengers into the congested district while 261,637 people arrived by streetcars. This almost incredible increase in automobile usage was further reflected in surveys of automobile traffic on certain main thoroughfares in Los Angeles County. Traffic on Long Beach Boulevard, for example, had increased by more than four times between 1918 and 1923.[26]

The heavy vehicular usage exacerbated an already familiar problem—the lack of an adequate street system. Few cities, Olmsted and the others reported, had ample roadways. Los Angeles' problem was particularly bad since its streets comprised a smaller proportion of the total downtown area than any comparable American urban center. The city also lacked an adequate network of thoroughfares, for most streets leading into the city center were far too narrow to serve as major highways. "There are surprisingly few streets of generous width in Los Angeles," noted the consultants. Even worse was the fact that the city's roads formed "a discontinuous and unsystematic arrangement that is the natural result of piecemeal, uncontrolled land subdivision." The city and county planning commissions attempted to remedy this situation by controlling the platting of new housing tracts. Nevertheless, these undermanned commissions spent more time on administrative matters than on controlling real estate promoters.[27] Regulating subdividers alone, the consultants added, would not solve the area's transportation problems. Rather, the city needed to "provide an orderly scheme of thoroughfares, differentiated as to width and arrangement so that the growth of the city and consequent traffic movements might have more of order and less of chaos and confusion."[28]

A further cause of congestion in Los Angeles was the "promiscuous" mixing of different types of traffic on the city's thoroughfares. Because of Los Angeles' narrow streets, truck, automobile, and streetcar traffic were more or less incompatible. The large number of vehicles plying the downtown streets obstructed streetcar movement, while in other areas streetcars restricted the flow of automobiles. The consultants further asserted that the existing streetcar routing in the central business district continued to prove detrimental to the general traffic flow since the trolleys often jogged unnecessarily from street to street. Trucks, on the other hand, interfered with both the streetcars and automobiles. The planners argued that city officials had to segregate these three classes of traffic as much as possible to facilitate the movement of all vehicles concerned.

The consultants recommended several measures to solve the congestion. First, they argued that city officials should institute rigid traffic regulations to speed up traffic. Los Angeles, they noted, already utilized a progressive traffic code as evidenced by the strict parking rules, the elimination of left turns at many downtown intersections, and the use of automated synchronized traffic signals. The city, never-theless, required even more stringent regulation to make the most of the existing street space. The planners recommended extended no-parking hours, a complete ban on automobile parking on certain streets, and the confinement of different types of traffic to specific streets.[29]

The consultants also believed that Los Angeles' great-est immediate need was "the development of an orderly and well-balanced system of thoroughfares throughout the city." Like practically every other major American city, Los Angeles had a street system that had been laid out on the scale of a nineteenth-century "horse-and-buggy town." The city now had to balance and increase its street capacity to improve the flow of traffic. Engineers, the planners remarked, used to lay out every street as a continuous highway. Urban planners soon realized that it was more economical "to provide wider and heavier pavements on a limited number of selected Major Traffic Streets and to keep through traffic off the rest of the streets as far as possible." With the increasing speed of automobiles, this method was both more efficient and safer than attempting to turn every street into a main high-way. Los Angeles and other cities had already begun to designate certain streets as major thoroughfares. The city needed to continue this practice by integrating such streets into a system of highways throughout the region. The plan-ners also argued that the city should build certain streets solely for automobiles in order to segregate vehicles and streetcars and construct crosstown streets to allow suburban traffic to avoid the central business district. Olmsted and his colleagues finally proceeded to describe a Major Traffic Street Plan, which called for the widening, opening, and extending of several hundred miles of streets in the county and city. In sum, the plan delineated 200 separate projects.[30]

Ultimately, the planners concluded, congestion would limit itself. The width and capacity of a city's street system restricted the amount of traffic that could utilize the roads.

Plates 5 and 6. Prior to 1930, Los Angeles lacked an adequate number of thoroughfares leading into the downtown area. Wilshire Boulevard, for instance, could have served as a major boulevard had it not been blocked by Westlake Park (later MacArthur Park).

Even if a city doubled the width of its streets, traffic would eventually rise to its previous level of intensity. Congestion then would "be just as bad as with a smaller limit capacity." It was improbable, the consultants warned, that the city could increase the capacity of the streets beyond the ability of the public to purchase automobiles. Los Angeles might therefore eventually have to distinguish between necessary and unnecessary traffic movement. "The street car, owing to its economy of space and low cost of operation per passenger," the planners argued, "must take precedence over other forms of vehicles in the congested area whenever the traffic capacity of the arteries approaches its limits." The planners also suggested that the city might attempt to separate mass transit from the street traffic by building subways in the

In an effort to provide additional outlets, the city built a bridge across the lake and in the process turned Wilshire into one of Los Angeles' most important traffic arteries. (Courtesy of Los Angeles City Archives)

central business district and by encouraging the decentralization of local retail districts to reduce traffic density.[31]

Representatives from the Traffic Commission formally presented the Major Traffic Street Plan to the City Council in July of 1924. The councilmen enthusiastically received the proposal, calling it the greatest street improvement program ever designed for an American city. The Major Highways Committee of the Traffic Commission urged the council to place the report on the ballot to allow the city's electorate to approve its adoption as the official master street plan. Although this measure would only serve as a straw vote indicating the voters' attitudes toward it, the commission believed such a vote would strengthen its ability to carry out the changes. The Major Highways Committee also proposed fifteen streets for improvement as the first unit of construction and asked the council to place a $5,000,000 bond issue on the ballot to help pay for a part of their construction. The commission argued that a bond issue was perfectly reasonable since the entire city would benefit from the alterations and thus should share the costs with the property owners bordering the improved streets. "Our street traffic problem is the most vital question now before Los Angeles," remarked one member of the Traffic Commission to the council. "It is safe to say that traffic congestion is costing our city $15,000,000 a year." With the first "scientific" street plan ever designed for the city, this same member professed that relief was in sight. "To date," he continued, "our street improvements have been done in hit-and-miss fashion through the initiative of neighborhoods. Now, the city can start underway this systematic improvement program which the survey [sic] of the experts has shown should be done first to bring about relief of traffic."[32]

The next day, the council voted unanimously to put the Major Traffic Street Plan and the $5,000,000 bond issue on the ballot for the approval of the electorate. The Traffic Commission demonstrated its lobbying abilities by actively promoting these two issues in the weeks before the election. Members spoke at numerous functions, while the commission secured the endorsement of more than a hundred civic organizations. Harry Culver, president of a local improvement association on the west side, argued that the failure to pass the bond issue would mean stagnation for the city. "Unless citizens, taxpayers, and business interests heed the warning Los Angeles is doomed. Its growth will be stunted, progress retarded, traffic stopped and streets blocked." Royall Wheeler, president of another improvement association, appealed to the economic interests of the property owners. "It has been the history throughout this city," he proclaimed, "that wherever a street has been widened a splendid development follows, and invariably property values have climbed." Even more important than the support of these local associations was the approbation of every major city newspaper. "The necessity of some such street plan is apparent when one takes into consideration the present inadequate patchwork of narrow streets," the *Times* wrote. The paper believed that the street plan would "receive the support of every voter who is proud of Los Angeles and wants to see it become the world's most beautiful metropolis."[33]

The two measures endorsed by the commission passed by large majorities. The Major Traffic Street Plan and the bond issue were overwhelmingly approved by margins of five-to-one and three-to-one, respectively. Later in the year, the commission secured an additional $1,000,000 from the council to maintain existing street pavement. The organization celebrated its victories. "Perhaps the most encouraging development of the year has been the awakened consciousness on the part of the general public to the vital bearing of traffic on the City's welfare," the commission's president wrote in his annual report. The public now realized that traffic congestion was not a minor inconvenience that could be cured with a little legislation. People finally understood that it was "the most serious problem which confronts the city . . . [and] that millions must be spent to convert our streets into a balanced roadbed capable of handling the enormous and mounting traffic of this modern era."[34]

The favorable reception at the polls, however, did not ensure the completion of the Major Traffic Street Plan. The $5,000,000 raised by the bond issue would only pay for 10 to 20 percent of the construction costs associated with each project. Property owners in the various assessment districts had to foot the rest of the bill. Just as important was the fact that property owners still had to petition the City Council for improvements. The Traffic Commission had offered a program to coordinate the necessary renovations, but its success continued to depend upon the temperament of individual homeowners. Following the election, the *Times* exhorted the city's property owners to pass majority petitions for the projects listed under the first unit because without their support Los Angeles would suffer greatly. "The protestant who will oppose the consummation of the first unit of the Major Traffic Street Plan," contended the paper, "is an enemy to progress in Los Angeles and should be so branded."[35]

Neither the *Times* nor the Traffic Commission had much to fear as property owners throughout the region flooded the city engineer's office with petitions asking for aid. The Major Traffic Street Plan's first unit consisted of only a few improvements for immediate implementation. Homeowners along other designated streets also sought to begin construction. In these cases, the Traffic Commission helped the anxious property owners expedite the proceedings. "Extraordinarily rapid strides have been made in the paving of thoroughfares included in the Major Traffic Street Plan," the commission reported in 1927. The quick response on the part of the city's residents had greatly facilitated the process and thus ensured its success.[36]

City officials interpreted the huge response to their plan as an indication that residents wanted to help relieve Los Angeles of its intolerable traffic congestion. "The people of Los Angeles awoke last year to the situation," concluded the *Times*. The citizens agreed that "more streets must be paved, many of them widened, a number of scores of new streets must be opened to connect with other highways, and jogs and deep cross gutters must be eliminated . . . if Los Angeles was to continue to go ahead at full speed toward achieving its destiny."[37] The Major Traffic Street Plan moved forward so quickly that the Traffic Commission recommended that the City Council impose a temporary property tax to support a second unit of street improvements. The council placed the proposal on the ballot in 1926, just a year and a half after the original bond issue had been approved. The electorate endorsed the plan in an election where all

Plate 7. The authors of the Major Traffic Street Plan noted that the design of many streets in Los Angeles impeded the smooth flow of traffic. Olympic Boulevard, for example, jogged unnecessarily as it crossed Figueroa, making it unsuitable as a thoroughfare. The photograph above illustrates how the Board of Public Works proposed to straighten and widen this street to create a vital traffic artery. (Courtesy of Los Angeles City Archives)

other bond issues on the ballot went down to defeat. Clearly, the voters saw the program to reconstruct the city's street system as a vital issue requiring their support.[38]

In dealing with Los Angeles' complex traffic problems, the commission acted as a facilitator in securing the cooperation of the various city departments, representatives from civic organizations, and the general public. City officials regularly asked the commission for advice on traffic matters and sat in on its meetings. Convinced that its work was "almost indispensable to [the city's] growing needs," the commission expanded the membership of its Major Highways Committee and thereby secured additional funds with which to assist the city Engineering Department.[39] It also strove to enlist downtown commercial interests in its efforts to improve traffic conditions. This was not a difficult task since these businessmen feared that severe congestion would discourage shoppers from entering the central business district. They were more than willing to work with the commission if such cooperation meant clear roads and the continuation of a centrally focused urban structure. Indeed, many of the most prominent commercial figures in the area appeared on the organization's roster.[40]

The commission utilized its considerable influence in other ways. Arguing that the current legal system slowed the process of land condemnation and street widening, the organization lobbied the state legislature for relief. Working with the city attorney and city engineer, the legal counsel for the Major Highways Committee submitted four bills to the state assembly. Once passed, the new laws facilitated work included in the Major Traffic Street Plan. One bill made it possible for the county government to contribute funds to the city treasury for the acquisition of land. This allowed the county and city governments to pool their financial resources and coordinate their highway construction efforts. Another law gave the city the right to overrule majority protests by residents along a major thoroughfare. No longer could intransigent homeowners block vital improvements. Other legislation permitted the city both to create a revolving street construction fund and to commence road work swiftly. The commission's purpose in all of this was to streamline the legal process to the needs of a modern city.[41]

In addition to its efforts to complete the Major Traffic Street Plan, the commission sought to institute a rational set of traffic regulations. Believing that better laws would lead to a more efficient use of the existing street space, the commission retained Miller McClintock of the Harvard University Bureau of Municipal Research to study Los Angeles' traffic statutes. "Los Angeles as you are aware," the commission remarked to the City Council, "has a mass of traffic ordinances which are contradictory—many of them unenforceable, and it is our belief that these should be modified and simplified." The commission subsequently offered McClintock's services to the city free of charge. With the city attorney, the City Council, and the chief of police, McClintock rewrote the city's traffic code. The outcome was a set of laws designed to obtain the maximum use out of the limited street space in the downtown area. Put into action in January of 1925, the McClintock code greatly facilitated automobile movement in the central business district. The commission claimed this as one of its greatest achievements.[42]

The commission's enthusiasm regarding the Major Traffic Street Plan, however, did bring it some difficulties. The organization came close to pushing its designs through faster than the public could pay for them. Subsequently, certain attorneys and politicians attempted to "worm their way into office by attacking the Major Traffic Street Plan." In their bid to win public office, some candidates argued that the street improvement program was financially burdensome to property owners. None of these would-be politicians were voted into office, but the commission thereafter paid more attention to the financial concerns of the city's residents. Still, no street improvement project sponsored by the commission ever experienced anything close to a majority protest during the twenties. An investigation by the Affiliated Improvement Associations of Los Angeles, which represented thousands of homeowners, stood by the commission's efforts. The report argued that the Traffic Commission was comprised of widely divergent interests within the city and that "nothing but good can come to the property owners of the city of Los Angeles through closest cooperation between the Traffic Commission and the Affiliated Improvement Associations, as one representing the business interests and the other the small property owners, makes possible a complete cross-section of public sentiment of the entire city of Los Angeles."[43]

The Traffic Commission, then, managed to bring together many of the most powerful interest groups within the region, including the downtown businessmen, the city's homeowners, traction company officials, and supporters of mass transit. All of these groups believed that the street construction program would benefit them by easing congestion. They also realized that the automobile now played a major role in the region's transportation system. And for a time, their efforts were rewarded with improved conditions as traffic moved more freely and smoothly in the years immediately following the plan's implementation.[44]

The euphoria of success did not last long. Olmsted and his associates had designed the Major Traffic Street Plan to focus upon the central business district. Although the planners recognized the need for some crosstown arteries, most of their thoroughfares marked for improvement carried residents into the downtown area. This was hardly surprising since most urban planners continued to conceive of cities as centralized structures. The dispersal of residents to suburban housing tracts had not greatly altered the area's circulatory patterns. But increasing the traffic capacity of those roads leading into the city center eventually made the existing problem worse. Wider streets eased congestion and encouraged more residents to leave public transportation for their automobiles. A large real estate and population boom in the sections beyond the reach of public transportation also contributed to a sharp increase in automobile transit. By 1930 the Traffic Commission once again despaired that "traffic conditions, particularly in the downtown area, are becoming chaotic, in fact so much so that business interests and the general public are complaining bitterly in many instances."[45]

Plate 8. Although the Major Traffic Street Plan improved traffic for a few years, congestion emerged again during the latter part of the twenties. This photograph shows heavy vehicular and streetcar traffic in the downtown area during the late twenties or early thirties. (Courtesy of Seaver Center for Western Research/Natural History Museum of Los Angeles County)

Nor had the parking problem gone away. The completed portion of the Major Traffic Street Plan forced more cars into the downtown area at a time when the city still could not accommodate their storage needs. The combined congestion and inadequate parking threatened the vitality of the downtown retail districts much to the dismay of merchants in the central business district.

Other cities responded to the increasing automobile traffic in their city centers in much the same way as Los

Angeles had. In the South, urban businessmen welcomed the arrival of the automobile because they believed it would bring more customers downtown while opening up new suburbs to development. As congestion worsened through-out the twenties, the same people began to worry about maintaining easy access to the central business district. Most southern chambers of commerce addressed this problem by encouraging cities to build new roads and widen existing streets. After 1920, no one seemed to suggest limiting the number of automobiles in the urban core.[46]

Chicago responded to the crowded traffic conditions in a manner strikingly similar to that of Los Angeles. Histo-rian Paul Barrett argues that many influential elements in Chicago society sought to accommodate the automobile be-cause congestion in the Loop threatened the central business district's dominance over the regional economy. The Chicago Plan Commission, a body appointed by the city council to study and implement a 1909 beautification program, cited heavy automobile traffic as a justification for street improve-ments. The commission received ample support from the city's business community. The Chicago Association of Com-merce formed a committee on traffic and safety which after 1923 operated much like the Traffic Commission in Los Angeles. The committee became a forum for public dis-cussions concerning traffic and managed to coordinate the efforts of private citizens, businesses, and the city govern-ment to provide traffic relief. In 1925, for instance, the com-mittee joined the city council in hiring Miller McClintock to rewrite the city's traffic regulations. Chicago, like Los Angeles, used the combined efforts of the downtown mer-chants and the city government to improve its street system and institute a rational set of traffic laws. Other cities such as Pittsburgh also saw extensive cooperation between the commercial community and local legislatures, albeit with less success.[47]

Los Angeles and other cities could work effectively

towards solving their traffic problems because most interest groups within urban society agreed upon the automobile's place within their transportation system. Commuters embraced the car as a democratic alternative to mass transit, and planners saw in the automobile a superior agent of residential dispersion. The streetcar companies had started this trend towards deconcentration but could not finish it because their weakened financial conditions prevented them from extending tracks into undeveloped suburbs. Meanwhile, downtown businessmen believed their cities had to maintain unhindered access to the central business district. Urban politicians eventually accepted the importance of traffic relief because it was their responsibility to keep the flow of goods and people moving within the city.[48] By advocating street improvements and modern traffic regulations, these groups successfully fought to facilitate automobile movement within the urban core.[49] They would find it more difficult, however, to ameliorate the problems associated with mass transportation. The same sectors of society that had coalesced around the automobile could not agree on the issue of rapid-transit planning.

The Union Station
Controversy

≡

*No sane person would recomene elevated Railroad Tracts, now-
days, when Subway tracts stops all noise, and stops all darkness to business property, and Subways stops all ecidents in
traffic and makes faster time for railroads entering Citys by
Subways* [sic].

—James Cordray to City Council
February 7, 1926

*Elevated railroads are a curse to any community in which they
have been erected. Chicago more than any other city has felt
their deadly construction, has suffered from their darkening
shadows and their depressive gloom, their dirt and dust,
their interminable ear-splitting screeching and their myriad
dangers.*

Los Angeles *Times*
April 14, 1926

istorians have long won-
dered what happened to the progressive movement during
the 1920s.[1] What little unity the movement once had died
with America's involvement in World War I. The Russian
Revolution and the subsequent withdrawal of the Soviets
from the war discredited the socialists. Indeed, the postwar
era saw a fierce backlash against the Left. Meanwhile, the
general prosperity of the twenties dampened the reform
spirit of the middle class. Although the major objectives
of the middle-class progressives had by this time become
institutionalized in regulatory bodies such as public utility
and planning commissions, urban politics after 1918 became
increasingly fragmented. Factions continued to unite be-

hind various causes, but failed to build a lasting ideological framework.

The adoption of the automobile in cities throughout the United States, however, clearly shows that various elements in urban society could still coalesce into a potent political force. Aided by the general disdain for the traction companies, these coalitions worked effectively to facilitate automobile movement within the central business district. They blocked legislation that threatened to ban curbside parking and agitated for citywide street improvements. Most important, these groups offered acceptable solutions to some of the most pressing problems associated with urbanization. The individual had precipitated the traffic crisis by taking to his automobile in protest. By the twenties this individualistic act had given way to a collective effort to ameliorate the nation's urban transportation system. What emerged from these programs was the public's willingness to tax itself in order to subsidize automobile transit.

These same coalitions, however, split apart over the future of mass transportation. The factions that made up these groups held radically different opinions when faced with the topic of rapid-transit planning. Three basic issues divided the public. First, there was the lingering animosity towards the traction companies. Many people simply found it impossible to support any plan that would have improved the financial conditions of the privately owned railways. This ongoing battle regarding urban-transit companies was related to yet another problem. Rapid transit in the form of subways and elevated railways cost huge sums of money. Not only were such improvements expensive to build, there was little chance that the rapid-transit systems could support themselves without large public subsidies. An already frustrated public saw little reason to subsidize the private sector, particularly when it had antagonized it in the past.

Second, urban dwellers were not particularly enthusiastic about publicly operated rail networks. Any successful mass-transit system would have to coordinate a subway plan with the existing streetcar operations. A city operating its own subway system would therefore most likely have to purchase the local trolley company as well. Unfortunately, most traction companies had vastly overstated the value of their assets, making it all but impossible for municipalities to buy their local streetcar systems.[2] Even were it a possibility, many urban dwellers opposed municipal ownership of unprofitable utilities. This was particularly true once the automobile had begun to provide an alternative means of transportation.

Finally, many suburban residents began to question whether they should support rapid-transit proposals that would encourage further congestion in the central business district. Merchants in the downtown areas of most cities were often the most vociferous proponents of subways and elevateds. They had supported street improvements in the hope that such alterations would facilitate traffic flow into the city center. They argued that the city could further ameliorate crowded traffic conditions by segregating automobiles and streetcars and thus allow the central business district to maintain its domination over the local economy. People and businesses residing in the outlying areas, however, often opposed the continued adherence to a centralized urban structure. The automobile had freed them from the confines of the streetcar tracks. It therefore made perfect sense to these people to patronize businesses in far less crowded suburban shopping areas. Consequently, they saw little reason to support a system of subways that would benefit the core at the expense of the periphery.[3]

These issues left many American cities hopelessly divided over the issue of rapid transit. Unable to build a consensus, most cities allowed their streetcar systems to languish in private hands. Only a handful of municipalities managed to put together the public funds necessary to build a subway system. The fact that these networks could not operate without public subsidies only further discouraged the residents of other metropolises. The automobile, in contrast, won lasting support. User charges in the form of gasoline taxes provided much of the revenue needed to facilitate automobile movement. In addition, the public saw street improvements as democratic. Such changes favored all areas of the city, both suburb and core. Furthermore, these innovations directly benefited the people themselves. The automobile also enhanced the residential dispersal first started by the streetcars and favored by residents and city officials alike. It is therefore not surprising that so many groups could rally around the automobile at the same time they fought over mass-transportation planning.

The parking ban and the Major Traffic Street Plan brought together disparate groups of people seeking to secure the automobile's place within the Los Angeles transportation system. These citizens could work effectively towards that purpose because they agreed upon the future of the automobile as a means of urban transportation. With such a consensus, the electorate willingly taxed and assessed itself to build a new network of streets. The future of rail transit in the metropolitan district, however, was not as certain because serious problems continued to plague the railways in Los Angeles. A public outcry in 1923 had forced the Board of Public Utilities and the City Council to work with the railways to improve their service. Despite the claims of city officials that "a real start has been made toward relieving the deplorable transportation conditions existing in Los Angeles," rail transit remained inadequate. The *Times* reported that streetcars "full of passengers hanging onto straps and clinging to rear fenders" required thirty minutes to move six blocks in the downtown area during the rush hour. With its patience wearing thin, the *Times* told the PE and LARY to "go ahead and make good on your promises to give us adequate transportation facilities."[4]

Still, most people in the city continued to expect that interurbans and streetcars would remain important to the city's transportation needs. The traction companies may have incurred the wrath of an angry public, but they continued to transport millions of people each year. The authors of the Major Traffic Street Plan noted as much in outlining their proposal to facilitate automobile traffic. "The street cars," they wrote, "are the most economical carriers of people and since the street is the only available present right of way for most of this class of traffic its freedom of movement should and must be provided for." Since the crowded traffic conditions in the downtown area resulted from the indiscriminate mixing of automobiles, streetcars, interurbans, and trucks, Olmsted and his partners recommended the increased use of "intensive mass transportation offered by subways or elevated lines."[5]

Beyond this general agreement that public transit was important to the city's transportation needs, the various interest groups in Los Angeles could not agree on how to pay for such improvements, or how to institute them. Without a consensus similar to the one that had led to the reconstruction of the street system, Angelenos could do little to improve their rail facilities. This issue was brought to the forefront of Los Angeles politics by yet another major controversy. For ten years, the City Council had been trying to force the three railroads serving Los Angeles to construct a union passenger station similar to those found in eastern cities. Public officials felt that the city needed such a station both to expand the inadequate passenger terminals and to provide for future growth. The carriers resisted these efforts largely because a union station would allow competing lines to enter the city by making important rights-of-way and station facilities available to the newcomers. In an attempt to stave off the council's suit before the state Railroad Commission, the railroads offered an alternative plan that would link their existing stations together through

a series of elevated railroad tracks. As a further induce-
ment, the railroads offered to share these elevateds with the
PE. This would have removed hundreds of PE interurban
trains from the city's streets each day. The railways hoped
this offer would convince the City Council to drop its petition before the Railroad Commission calling for a union
station. Thus, what began in 1916 as an attempt to improve the city's railroad stations had evolved by 1926 into a
major controversy over the nature of the city's public-transit
system.

The segregation of public-transit lines from private
vehicles through grade separations such as subways and
elevated lines was hardly a new idea. Bion J. Arnold had
suggested these changes as early as 1911, and the Board of
Public Utilities had recommended elevated and subway construction for years.[6] Unfortunately, the city's traction companies had faced serious financial difficulties during these
years. Although the LARY enjoyed a modest profit prior to
1926, it could not attract additional capital with which to
build a segregated transportation system. Similarly, the PE
had continually lost money since 1912. The financial conditions of the railways therefore precluded extensive elevated
or subway construction even though public officials extolled
the virtues of grade separations.

City officials and concerned citizens, however, continued to recommend a segregated transit system as a solution to the downtown traffic problems. J. R. Prince, the
city engineer, believed that the city should coordinate the
county's highway design with future mass-transportation
plans.[7] After touring eastern cities, Los Angeles' chief of
police argued that "the solution of traffic problems in Los
Angeles lies in the building of a subway."[8] Meanwhile, the
Traffic Commission, flushed with the success of its street
plan, proposed that the city and county governments finance
a study of the area's rapid-transit requirements. Such a comprehensive transit survey could serve the city in much the

same manner as the street plan. The report could project the future transit needs for the entire metropolitan area and ensure the coordination of rail facilities with the street and highway improvements currently under construction. This would prevent wasteful, haphazard transit development. "Nothing less than a complete and thorough study by the most competent persons to be found can hope to insure this great community against aggravated and costly errors," the commission wrote. The organization further hoped that those conducting the survey could examine and compare the experiences of other cities with rapid transit as a way of improving Los Angeles' transportation plans.[9]

When the City Council asked the Board of Public Utilities to comment on the Traffic Commission's proposal, E. F. Bogardus, the board's president, responded favorably. He noted that several projects, including the street plan, a citywide grade crossing survey, and the state Railroad Commission's valuation of Los Angeles area street railways, needed coordination. It was absolutely necessary, Bogardus asserted, to secure the services of a transportation expert to study Los Angeles' transportation facilities and recommend a solution to the inefficient public-transit system. "It is conceded by everybody," Bogardus concluded, "that our present conditions as to transportation matters will not brook further delay in arriving at a definite conclusion as to what should be done to remedy the situation." Bogardus consequently urged the council to appropriate $40,000 to pay an expert to conduct a comprehensive survey of transportation in the metropolitan area.[10]

The Board of Public Utilities as a whole strongly recommended R. F. Kelker as an expert worthy of conducting such an investigation. Kelker, in conjunction with his partner Charles De Leuw, had previously developed the Chicago Rapid Transit Plan. With the support of the Traffic Commission, the City Council in February 1924 appropriated $20,000 to hire Kelker, De Leuw & Company to put together a plan for rapid-transit development in Los Angeles. At the same time the council formally requested the County Board of Supervisors to match its funds since "the problem is not one for Los Angeles City only, but to a greater extent effects [sic] the suburban territory." The supervisors concurred and Kelker and De Leuw were hired in the spring of 1924.[11]

The Kelker–De Leuw report, submitted to the City Council in April 1925, presented a general design for a metropolitan transportation system. The Los Angeles electorate had recently approved a city charter amendment that required the city to adopt a master rapid-transit plan before the City Council could authorize any elevated or subway franchises. The authors of this amendment had hoped to prevent the piecemeal development of rapid transit in Los Angeles.[12] The Major Traffic Street Plan had proved a tremendous success; proponents of mass transportation believed the new charter requirement would encourage the design of a similar plan for rail transit. Kelker and De Leuw developed their study to fulfill this covenant. They argued that since much of the area's past development had depended upon the electric railway, it was likely that the county would continue to rely on the interurbans and streetcars to an even greater extent in the future. Besides the necessity of meeting the new charter requirements, the metropolitan area needed a comprehensive transit plan to coordinate its various transportation facilities. "A city plan," the consultants wrote, "is incomplete without a Transit Plan."[13]

Kelker and De Leuw noted that Los Angeles' spatial structure differed from that of other cities. A building height restriction in the central business district, the availability of the automobile, and "the desire of the average citizen to own their own home" had resulted in a widely dispersed population living mostly in single-family dwellings. "Such a condition is very desirable," the engineers remarked, "but it is one of the prime factors which makes the construction of rapid transit lines on a self-sustaining basis, a difficult financial problem." Furthermore, they argued that automobile congestion threatened to ruin the accessibility of the city. The future orderly development of the region therefore required the erection of rapid-transit lines and the extension of existing streetcar and interurban tracks. Only then could Los Angeles keep its unparalleled number of detached houses. "Surely there is nothing which more vitally affects housing conditions and standards of living in cities than does the transit system," they concluded.

Kelker and De Leuw believed that the lack of coordination among streets, streetcars, interurbans, and rapid-transit lines would retard regional development. "Los Angeles has become a large metropolitan center," the consultants noted, "and it is of vital importance, at this time, that transportation facilities be planned upon a scale commensurate with the present and prospective development of the City and County." After all, they continued, a good transportation system greatly benefited the community since it increased and stabilized property values, improved housing conditions and standards of living, encouraged business growth, and ensured orderly urban development. Los Angeles, however, faced a crisis because the recent phenomenal growth in population, industrial activity, and traffic made the construction of rapid-transit lines "not only necessary but imperative if an adequate, quick and convenient means of public transportation is to be provided and traffic conditions are to be improved."[14]

In comparing the Los Angeles area with other cities throughout the United States, the consultants noted that after reaching a certain population level other cities found rapid-transit construction essential to their continued development. They also found Los Angeles' existing interurban and streetcar lines inadequate for the area's recent population influx. Furthermore, the current transportation system allowed all classes of vehicles to operate on the streets. This integration of streetcars, interurban trains, automobiles, and trucks resulted in frequent delays and extensive congestion, particularly on the downtown streets. The street improvement campaign under the auspices of the Major Traffic Street Plan was an excellent and necessary movement, Kelker and De Leuw remarked. Nevertheless, the improved road system merely engendered additional vehicular traffic, which would soon reach a point of saturation. Only through segregating different types of vehicles could the city ultimately resolve this traffic congestion. The city, they insisted, must remove railways from downtown streets and replace them with rapid-transit lines. Freed from the congestion of the street and interference of vehicles and pedestrians, these routes could provide efficient and beneficial service to urban dwellers.[15]

Kelker and De Leuw also sought to delineate and coordinate several kinds of transportation. First, they believed that the city should construct high-speed rapid-transit lines. As the backbone of the proposed transportation system, these limited-stop trains would run along their own rights-of-way connecting the central business district with outlying communities. Kelker and De Leuw also sought to continue the interurban lines currently running between various southern California cities. Street railways would remain vital to the metropolitan transportation system since they provided local service and could act as feeders to the future rapid-transit network. Finally, bus lines could offer local service in sparsely settled or newly developed areas. The consultants argued that a coherent and efficient transportation system depended on close coordination between these four types of public transport. Consequently, they believed that the entire system of rapid-transit lines, interurbans, streetcars, and buses had to be brought under the control of a single management to improve planning efforts and eliminate wasteful duplication of services.[16]

Just as important was the issue of financing this ambitious proposal. The construction of the rapid-transit lines would constitute the major cost in developing the comprehensive transportation network. The builders could place the rapid-rail tracks on elevated structures, in subways, or in open ditches, but somehow they had to segregate them from the street traffic. Kelker and De Leuw clearly favored elevated tracks. Although subways were less obtrusive and quieter, they cost at least two to four times more than elevateds with no appreciable difference in service. Besides, the southern California climate was particularly well suited for elevated construction and recent innovations in elevated design greatly improved their appearance.

Regardless of whether the city favored elevated tracks or subways, someone had to pay for them. The experiences of other cities, Kelker and De Leuw reported, demonstrated that rapid-transit lines could not operate self-sufficiently in the absence of high population densities. Even cities such as New York, Boston, and Philadelphia found it necessary to subsidize their systems. It was doubtful that Los Angeles, with its low population density, could do otherwise. Kelker and De Leuw saw only two choices. The area could have high fares and a limited system, or a subsidized comprehensive network with low fares. If riders, property owners, and the public at large would share the costs of building a rapid-transit system, they could increase the size and scope of the network. The engineers strongly urged the city to allocate tax revenues, issue municipal bonds, and create assessment districts to finance the rapid-rail system, because the entire metropolitan area would "unquestionably benefit" from such a plan. They estimated that the cost of immediate construction projects would amount to $130,000,000.[17]

The initial reaction to the Comprehensive Rapid Transit Plan was generally favorable. The Board of Public Utilities announced that it would cooperate with other public organizations to ensure the eventual completion of the system. "I am sure that everyone in Los Angeles will agree that the city of today and the future require that a start be made

at once toward obtaining additional transportation facilities,"
commented one commissioner.[18] Public interest groups from
the San Fernando Valley and Hollywood actively pursued
the immediate adoption of the Kelker–De Leuw report as the
city's master rapid transit plan. The valley remained largely
isolated from the rest of the city for lack of adequate transportation facilities. Hollywood residents had similar concerns
because their district had emerged as an important regional
center after the major expansion of the PE and LARY. They
had long complained about the poor transit service in their
community. Since the Comprehensive Rapid Transit Plan
proposed extensions into Hollywood and the valley, civic
organizations in both areas strongly favored it.[19]

    This initial support convinced the City Council to fol-
low Kelker and De Leuw's suggestion of forming a citizens'
advisory committee to study and implement the report. After
the success of the Traffic Commission's Major Highways
Committee, this seemed a reasonable strategy. The Traffic
Commission, the reform-minded Municipal League, and
other organizations concurred. At the end of September,
the council established a Citizens' Rapid Transit Committee
composed of council members, other city officials, and representatives from the PE, the LARY, and various civic organizations. At the same time, the Traffic Commission formed
its own committee and pledged its support and cooperation
with the council.[20]

    While these groups sought to convince the City Coun-
cil to adopt the report, others began to express caution and
outright opposition to it. The Municipal League believed the
city's future welfare was "too deeply involved to permit of
haste in the submission, much less the adoption of any
plan." The organization therefore supported the formation
of the rapid-transit committee.[21] City Attorney Jess Stephens
wondered who would pay for the construction costs of the
proposed rapid-transit lines. He estimated that the trains
would require an eight-cent fare if private capital were to

build the project. Stephens feared that Angelenos would oppose this 60 percent increase in the "long-maintained 5-cent fare."[22]

At the first public meeting regarding the rapid-transit proposal in Los Angeles, citizens expressed surprisingly strong opposition to the Comprehensive Rapid Transit Plan. Most of the resistance to the report focused on Kelker and De Leuw's support of elevated construction. Estelle Campbell of the Whittier Boulevard Improvement Association was a vigorous opponent. "In other parts of the city property owners are opposed to elevated lines through their districts," she claimed. "So before you tell us what we are going to have, put the question up to the people who are to help pay the bill." This antagonism quickly quelled the enthusiasm of some City Council members, who assured those present that the council would not "try to thrust any rapid transit plan down [the public's] throat."[23]

As these hearings proceeded, another long-festering issue emerged—the city's attempt to force the three transcontinental railroads serving Los Angeles to build a union station terminal.[24] The Southern Pacific, the Union Pacific, and the Santa Fe railroads each operated separate stations in or near the downtown area. Supporters of the union terminal wanted to consolidate these railroad facilities into a single station. Not only would such a terminal provide more convenient passenger access to the railroads but it would also ensure the city's ability to meet the growing demands of its expanding tourist industry. Furthermore, a union station between the Plaza and the Los Angeles River would eliminate many dangerous grade crossings. Trains entering the Southern Pacific station at Sixth and main ran along Alameda Street. The railroad's use of this major thoroughfare became dangerous and cumbersome once automobile traffic increased near the end of World War I. A station near the Plaza, however, would allow the trains to enter Los Angeles on private rights-of-way parallel to the river. Finally, experts favored the Plaza site because all three of the railroads' tracks converged at this point.

Bion J. Arnold first recommended a union station at the Plaza in 1911 as part of his transit study for the city. After other engineers had confirmed Arnold's recommendations, the City Council in 1916 requested the state Railroad Commission to order the carriers to construct a terminal at the Plaza. The railroads resisted the city's efforts by employing numerous delaying tactics. Over the course of the next ten years, the City Council, the Railroad Commission, and other civic organizations spent more than $50,000 trying to force the railroads to accept their request. The Railroad Commission in 1921 finally ruled in the city's favor and ordered the railroads to construct a union station. Railroad officials took the case to court in an effort to overturn the ruling. The Interstate Commerce Commission (ICC) then entered the fray. After a long investigation, the ICC also ruled in the city's favor. The United States Supreme Court, however, eventually upheld a California Supreme Court decision that concluded that the Railroad Commission could not compel the carriers to build a station. The ICC, while favoring the union terminal, claimed it also lacked the power to force the construction of such a station, but it did recommend that the Railroad Commission hold additional hearings to try to work out some sort of compromise. These hearings were scheduled to begin in March of 1926, shortly after the City Council had begun to consider the Kelker–De Leuw plan.[25]

The City Council approached the hearings with renewed hope. In a resolution unanimously adopted in September of 1925, the council tried to rally popular support to its side. The railroads, it noted, had "combined to fight this necessary public improvement and have pursued every technical avenue to prevent and delay this project so urgently and manifestly needed by the community and have continued such opposition for a period of more than ten (10) years." The ICC, the Railroad Commission, and many engineers had all endorsed the Plaza terminal as the most feasible plan for unifying Los Angeles' railroad facilities, eliminating grade crossings on Alameda, and relieving the presently inadequate passenger facilities. The City Council urged the railroads to accept the ICC ruling and build a union station for the good of the community.[26]

In an attempt to stave off the city's efforts, the railroads jointly offered a new plan in 1926 which would allow them to retain separate stations. Several years prior to the request, the Union Pacific Railroad station suffered a total loss in a fire. The railroad subsequently rented space in the Southern Pacific's Central Station. The railroad proposal would make this arrangement permanent. At the same time, the Santa Fe would construct a larger station at its present location near the Los Angeles River. The Southern Pacific and the Union Pacific would build an extensive system of elevated tracks connecting the Central Station with their rights-of-way near the river. These elevateds would remove steam railroad trains from Alameda Street and eliminate many grade crossings. Not only would the railroad plan separate the trains from street traffic but it would also allow PE interurbans to enter the Southern Pacific station, thus improving passenger access to the steam railroads. The PE trains would also utilize a terminal on the east bank of the Los Angeles River, directly opposite the new Santa Fe station. As an extra incentive, the railroads would construct similar elevated lines leading into the PE terminal building.[27]

In applying for the necessary franchises, the PE noted that the railroad proposal would remove from the streets all of its interurbans entering the downtown area south and east of its terminal. These trains, which currently interfered with both streetcar and automobile traffic, would enter the PE station in the heart of the central business district via elevated tracks. The installation of this system would, the PE contended, "remove many hundred interurban passenger train movements per day from the streets of Los Angeles and will go far towards bettering street surface traffic conditions and will do more to better street traffic conditions than anything that has heretofore been done in the City of Los Angeles." This, the PE argued, would provide faster and more dependable service to thousands of passengers entering Los Angeles every day from the suburbs. The PE, however, insisted that its construction of the new lines was contingent upon the council approving the railroad proposal, because it could not obtain a necessary right-of-way on the east bank of the river unless the Union Pacific was permitted to enter the Central Station over elevated tracks. This bald threat did not fool many. Los Angeles' government officials and the media generally accepted that the railroads offered the city the prospect of improved interurban transit as an incentive for the council to abandon its suit for a union station.[28] What had begun as a controversy over steam railroad access suddenly became largely a fight over urban mass transportation; it even engulfed the Kelker–De Leuw plan, rendering the latter useless. The divisive nature of the issue would leave Los Angeles residents incapable of improving public transit for years to come.

The railroads had garnered support for their proposed solution to the union station controversy even before applying for the necessary franchises. Organized several years earlier by several prominent commercial leaders, the Business Men's Association in 1926 immediately announced its approval of the railroad plan. Claiming that it had always opposed the construction of a union station as unnecessary, the association declared that the carriers' proposal would improve both passenger station facilities and traffic movement. A union station, it insisted, would benefit only those passengers switching trains in Los Angeles. Since the city was a terminus for most people rather than a transfer point, a union station would only serve about 2 percent of the total passenger traffic. The railroads' proposed system of elevated tracks, however, would remove 1200 trains a day from the city's streets. In addition, the railroads would willingly complete the construction within a short period of time. Members of the organization favored the proposal for two reasons. As conservative businessmen, they saw the City Council's suit as an attack on private property. At the same time, the carriers' alternative promised to free the downtown streets of congestion, thus making it easier for suburban shoppers to enter the central business district. Henry S. McKee, president of the association, believed the plan was "the most desirable from any point of view."[29]

Shortly after unveiling their proposition, the railroads themselves tried to turn the city's residents away from the union station plan. F. L. Annable, the general superintendent of the PE, commented to the *Examiner* that "it has been impossible to maintain any regularity in the movement of trains in and out of town due to the increasing vehicular traffic." David W. Pontius, the railway's general manager and vice president, added that there was "no adequate way for the Pacific Electric to serve a union station at the Plaza."[30] The railroads insisted that Los Angeles could not have both a union station and improved transit service; the public would have to choose between one or the other. In this way the railroads and their proponents began transforming the issue of a union station into one focused on rapid transit.

The railroads received a large boost in their campaign against the union station when the board of directors of the Los Angeles Chamber of Commerce adopted a resolution condemning the continued battle to build such a terminal. Following a "lengthy and most careful investigation," the directors decided that immediate solutions to such problems as dangerous grade crossings and traffic congestion were of paramount importance. The union station plan, however, failed to address the issue of PE trains operating on the streets. Since 1916, when the City Council began its suit, the city's population had doubled. "Such increase in population," the directors asserted, "could not possibly be adequately served by a union station at the so-called Plaza site, which we believe would further congest and make increasingly intolerable our already serious traffic condition." The directors subsequently petitioned the City Council to drop its fight with the railroads and seriously consider the carriers' plan.[31] The Board of Public Utilities commissioners, in the meantime, unanimously adopted a resolution condemning the proposed union station at the Plaza site. Without stating its specific objections, the board argued that the project was obsolete, "impractical and contrary to the best interest of the city." In a letter to the City Council, the commissioners urged that body to dismiss its case pending before the Railroad Commission and adopt a comprehensive rapid-transit plan in order to grant new track franchises to the railroads.[32]

Although most of Los Angeles' daily newspapers came to support the railroad proposal, the carriers found their most ready ally in William Randolph Hearst's Los Angeles *Examiner*, the city's largest and most popular daily. It is not completely clear why the paper supported the railroads so strongly, but it did so vigorously. Besides the obvious bias in its regular articles concerning the issue, the paper began a daily series that posed the question "Why do you stand with the Chamber of Commerce in opposition to the Plaza union station plan?" to prominent Los Angeles businessmen. These men responded with the arguments that became the mainstay of the railroad campaign. Jackson Graves, one such business leader, claimed that the proposed terminal at the Plaza site was undesirable since the center of the downtown commercial district had drifted at least a mile away to the south and east. William Lacey, a former president of the Chamber of Commerce, reported that the city's recently approved civic center plan near the Plaza would further congest the already seriously crowded traffic conditions in the area. To build a union station near the Plaza, Lacey insisted, would "produce conditions almost intolerable." In supporting the railroad plan, he argued that "several stations, reasonably near each other, would relieve traffic congestion far better than a union station that would gather all that traffic at one point." Other businessmen insisted the union station was really a real estate scheme to enrich land speculators who owned large plots in the vicinity of the Plaza.[33]

The Business Men's Association also actively cooperated with the railroads in their efforts to stifle support for the union station. In a series of advertisements run in Los Angeles newspapers, the association presented the railroad plan to the public.[34] The advertisements argued that the carriers had designed a solution to the union station controversy "in full realization of their responsibilities to the travelling public, and with a fine spirit of readiness to relieve Los Angeles of traffic congestion and grade crossing hazards, at an early date." The advertisements also noted that business interests needed relief from the severely congested conditions in the central business district. The railroads' system of elevated tracks would ease this traffic problem by daily removing 1200 interurban trains from the city streets. This fact alone, the association asserted, was "a more urgent matter than any union station." Besides, the Southern Pacific and proposed Santa Fe stations with their elevated lines and PE connections would be more accessible than a Plaza station. The association further claimed that the PE could not directly serve a union station.[35]

While the opponents of the union station publicized their alternative, others reminded them of the city charter requirements. A key phrase in the charter prevented the council from issuing any elevated or subway franchises until "after the adoption by the city of a comprehensive elevated railway and subway plan for the development of rapid transit into, out of and through the city."[36] Mayor George Cryer encouraged the City Council to adopt the Kelker–De Leuw study immediately as the city's master rapid transit plan because this would smooth the way for the institution of the railroad's proposal. Cryer preferred this alternative because of the carriers' willingness to spend their own money and begin construction at once. The mayor feared that the railroads would indefinitely delay the development of the union station, leaving the city with inadequate passenger facilities. The City Council–sponsored Rapid Transit Committee agreed, arguing that the adoption of the Kelker–De Leuw report would facilitate railway construction required to relieve crowded traffic conditions.[37]

The Traffic Commission's Rapid Transit Committee avoided any direct comment on the union station controversy. Indeed, the Traffic Commission existed to quiet such disagreements. The committee, however, approved a resolution recommending that the council adopt the general outline of Kelker and De Leuw's report as the official master plan. This would satisfy the city charter requirements while deferring decisions about the structure of the actual tracks until a later time.[38]

Before responding to these requests, the City Council held public hearings to allow residents a chance to express their views on the Kelker–De Leuw report. Several people strongly opposed the plan because of its recommendations favoring elevated tracks. Had the city accepted the study as the master rapid transit plan, the council could have granted forty-year franchises to the railroads for such structures. Many citizens adamantly disapproved of elevated construction for aesthetic reasons. The *Times* described the proposed railways as "four miles of hideous, clattering, dusty, dirty, dangerous, street-darkening overhead trestles."[39]

Other concerned officials and southern Californians believed the future development of the city's transportation facilities was too important to allow the adoption of a transit plan merely because it would help the railroads. Richard Sachse, the former chief engineer for the Railroad Commission and now a private consultant, lamented that the rapid-transit issue had become entangled in the union station controversy. A sound rail system was immensely important to the metropolitan area and required careful consideration. It was most unfortunate, however, that "the far reaching and tremendously important question of a rapid transit plan has now become involved with and beclouded by the separate and distinct steam railroad passenger station question." As a leading member of the Traffic Commission, he further questioned the Rapid Transit Committee's hasty approval of the Kelker–De Leuw study. The extreme expense and importance of the plan necessitated a full investigation before its acceptance, he concluded. Other individuals and organizations joined Sachse in opposing the immediate approval of a master plan. Gordon Whitnall, the city planning director, argued that the rapid-transit problem was "the most important one now facing Los Angeles. It deserves the most serious, careful consideration in all phases before the city commits itself to a rapid-transit plan."[40]

As a long-standing advocate of a union station, the *Times* continued to lobby for the terminal. After the mayor and Board of Public Utilities commissioners came out in favor of the railroads' system, the paper launched a furious attack on the carriers and the elevated network. The *Times* accused the Southern Pacific of using its vast financial power to control the city's other newspapers and the "Boss-controlled" city administration by retaining city officials on its payroll.[41] It also faulted the railroads for making "extraordinary efforts to have the City Council adopt any kind of rapid-transit plan so that [their] franchises can be granted."[42]

The steam railroads, the paper argued, refused to build a union station for fear of losing their monopoly on long-distance passenger traffic into Los Angeles. The city had fewer carriers serving it than any city of comparable size in the United States. The only feasible approach to the central business district lay parallel to the river over land held by the three railroads already serving the area. Three other railroads during the past few years had attempted to enter

Los Angeles but had given up because of the difficulty of obtaining rights-of-way along the river and the expense of building independent stations. A union terminal, however, would provide immediate access to any railroad wanting to serve Los Angeles. Many citizens concurred with this assessment. Local resident E. M. Schwartz wrote the City Council to protest any attempt to abandon the union terminal fight. Schwartz agreed with the *Times* that the carriers' opposition to the union station was "a wholly selfish one on the part of the railroads now here to forever prevent the entrance into this city of any other railroad." To put aside the city's efforts of the past ten years meant "nothing more or less than bowing to a purely selfish motive of the railroads to keep out future development" that would result from the entrance of new railroads into the city.[43]

As the debate over the union station and the future of rapid transit became increasingly heated, the City Council exercised much caution in its public statements even though the *Record* reported bitter fighting between individual council members. Regardless of their personal inclinations, the councilmen admitted feeling tremendous political pressure from proponents of both sides. The *Record* reported that council members realized that "a false move may spell their political finish." Perhaps remembering the political repercussions of the parking ban a few years earlier, Councilman Fred Shaw suggested a resolution placing the issue on the ballot. Such an election would act as a straw vote only; it would not bind the city to any specific action. Near the end of February, the City Council finally agreed to this proposal.

The ultimate decision on the wording of the propositions, however, was anything but peaceful. The *Record* reported that virtual chaos reigned at the council's final session. While most members refused to reveal their opinions publicly, a few strongly favored one side or the other. Two members apparently supported the union terminal because their districts bordered on the Plaza. Others believed the decade-old plan was obsolete. Still another felt a moral obligation to continue the fight against the railroads. "We have fought for the Plaza and won every decision in the courts over the past 10 years," argued this member. "Well, what have you got? Where is the Union Station?" another contentiously queried. Following this heated debate, the council worked out a compromise. It finally agreed that the electorate would vote on two nonbinding propositions. Proposition 8 simply asked, "Shall a Union Railway Passenger Terminal for all steam railroads be established in the City of Los Angeles?" Proposition 9 queried whether the voters wanted a union passenger station located in the Plaza district. Although it took more than two weeks to hammer out the exact wording of the resolution, it became readily apparent to most observers that the council had found a way out of its predicament.[44]

Realizing that the council would eventually put the issue to a vote, the supporters of the rival railroad station proposals launched vigorous campaigns in hope of swaying the public to their side. Their means included a horde of public speakers, advertisements, and newspaper editorials. Although the union station controversy subsumed the rapid-transit plan, one may discern the public attitudes towards the future of electric railway transit in the region largely because the railroads consciously turned this election campaign into a referendum on elevated-rail transit in Los Angeles.

As the City Council worked out the details of the election, the *Examiner* and the Business Men's Association stepped up their campaign. The latter threatened that the carriers' plan was the city's only hope for improved transportation facilities because the railroads could litigate the issue for another ten years. The organization also sought the support of Los Angeles' outlying communities and suburbs by arguing that the proposal would, in effect, bring these areas closer to Los Angeles. This tactic worked well, as at least twenty local chambers endorsed the railroad proposal.[45]

The *Examiner* quoted a federal judge who pointed out that neither the Railroad Commission nor the ICC could force the railroads to build a terminal against their will. The judge, furthermore, favored the railroads' alternative since he could not "escape the feeling that the whole matter grew out of a desire to boost or at least benefit, real estate values in the immediate vicinity [of the Plaza]." Without specifically identifying anyone, the *Examiner* alluded to the fact that certain supporters of the union station held extensive real estate tracts in the area of the Plaza. The charge was directed at Harry Chandler, publisher of the *Times*, who repeatedly denied its implications.[46]

Most of the railroads' support, however, came from those concerned with downtown congestion and rapid transit. One businessman stated that "the paramount question in connection with this railroad terminal issue is, to my mind, the solution of the grade crossing problem and the relief of surface traffic conditions rather than the erection or location of a union station." Thomas Foulkes, the former president of the Board of Public Utilities, agreed. "The important feature is the elimination of grade crossings and the relief of traffic congestion," he argued, "and this would be so thoroughly accomplished by the plan of the railroads that I am an enthusiast for it."[47]

An independent advisory committee appointed by the mayor also favored the railroad proposal because it would give the city some measure of traffic relief within a short time. The area surrounding the Plaza was one of the most congested districts in the city, the committee noted. Not only did several narrow streets converge at this point, there would also be no easy approach to the proposed station. All of this made it an ill-suited location. To build a union station there would "cause serious congestion, intensifying with the growth of the City," which would prove a "serious disadvantage." It would be far better, the committee suggested, to distribute the traffic between two separate stations as was done in New York City.[48]

The mayor's committee also cited the importance of street congestion and the possible elimination of PE grade crossings in its decision. PE trains, it noted, made 18,000 individual grade crossings each day. It was therefore highly desirable "to eliminate the great number of grade crossings involved in their operation because they constantly menace life and limb and seriously obstruct the ordinary vehicular and passenger traffic." Improved and safer transportation of thousands of daily PE passengers was vitally important to the community, the committee concluded. "The actual benefits to be gained thereby far outweigh any possible advantages that would come from a union passenger station" because the PE could eliminate its grade crossings only with the help of the Union Pacific and the Southern Pacific, which were willing to share their proposed facilities with the railway. The committee consequently concluded that a "union terminal station is neither essential to the convenience of the public nor necessary to meet future needs."[49]

Despite these findings, the union station advocates continued to attack the railroads' substitute plan as devious and self-serving. The City Planning Commission and the Municipal League opposed the idea of pushing a rapid-transit plan through the City Council, arguing that the council should forestall any action until the Citizens' Rapid Transit Committee had completed a thorough investigation of Los Angeles' transportation needs.[50] Union station proponents lecturing before civic organizations agreed. Samuel Storrow, a consulting engineer, denounced the railroads in a speech before the City Planning Association, where he accused the PE of trying to jam a makeshift rapid-transit plan through the council. "The railroads," the engineer contended, "are trying to rush through any kind of a plan so that they can get their franchises. You see the scheme?" In speaking before the Monrovia Chamber of Commerce, he queried, "Do we stand for the impartial investigation of a great public question, or do we stand for allowing the railroads to do just as they please, absolutely contrary to the recommendations and orders of every official body which has studied the [issue]?" Storrow concluded that a properly located union station would provide ready access for passengers, eliminate railroad grade crossings, and allow simpler and more economical railroad operation than the present system.[51]

Property owners, who had enthusiastically embraced the Major Traffic Street Plan, also organized in opposition to both the Kelker–De Leuw study and the proposed elevated system. "We shall appeal to the property owners in all parts of the city to join with us in urging the council to consult with property owners before any rapid-transit plan is adopted," exclaimed H. S. Shapiro, president of the Taxpayers' Anti-Elevated League. Shapiro also noted that his organization was "unalterably opposed to the erection of elevated railways on any of our main thoroughfares." Kelker and De Leuw, he argued, had not adequately investigated the adverse effect of elevateds on property values. The league believed that such construction would halve property values within one-half mile of the tracks and mar the beauty of the city. Nor were the league members willing to tax themselves to support a rapid-transit system, because it would be "folly to entertain the thought that the property on main thoroughfares[,] which would have its value depreciated fully one-half[,] should be asked to stand for assessments for the erection of such railways." Besides, the city needed to carefully consider the necessity of building a rapid-transit system "when the auto-stage is making such inroads into the business of all railways." If the carriers wanted to build rapid-transit lines in Los Angeles, the league favored subways.[52]

The Anti-Elevated League was not alone in denigrating the proposed elevateds. Individuals and civic organizations wrote the City Council protesting the erection of elevated tracks anywhere in Los Angeles. James Cordray, a small businessman, wrote that elevateds were outdated, noisy, dark, and harmful to property values. Although hardly eloquent, Cordray's letter to the council captured the essence of those opposed to the elevateds when he wrote, "No sane person would recomene elevated Railroad Tracts, nowdays, when Subway tracts stops all noise, and stops all darkness to business property, and Subways stops all ecidents in traffic, and makes faster time for railroads entering Citys by Subways [*sic*]." Cordray further supported the union station because Los Angeles had already reached a population of one million and would require a terminal large enough to accommodate large numbers of passengers. Besides, Cordray did not trust the railroads after their conduct over the previous ten years.[53]

Many union station advocates attempted to capitalize on suspicions such as these. The animosity expressed towards the electric railways during the previous twenty years remained a powerful issue in Los Angeles, and fifty years of political abuse and economic exploitation on the part of the carriers had imbued many Angelenos with a healthy skepticism of railroad management. After all, the carriers had spent the past ten years in litigation to avoid building a station that the city government, the ICC, and Railroad Commission had recommended. W. H. Workman, an engineer long involved in the union station controversy, saw the issue as one that pitted the people with law and order on their side against the monopolistic railroads, "which propose to do as they please in the face of the orders of the people's commissions, experts and courts." The railroads, he continued, opposed the union station merely to keep other railroads out of Los Angeles. To give up the fight at this point would be an admission that the corporations were stronger than the people. Many citizens agreed. The Los Feliz Improvement

Association, for instance, deplored "the continuous delay and antagonism," and felt that "this attitude upon the part of the Railroads only serves to retard the progressive plans for a greater and better Los Angeles and . . . causes an untold economic loss to the City."[54]

In response to a recommendation by the ICC, the state Railroad Commission held hearings on the union station controversy. A. G. Mott, the commission's chief engineer, argued that the carriers' plan was filled with difficulties. As did the railroads, Mott freely agreed that the controversy involved much more than steam railroad access. "The rapid transit problem in Los Angeles," Mott said, "is a greater, more important problem than that of providing adequate steam road terminals." In contrast to the railroads, however, Mott argued that a union terminal would best solve the city's congestion and grade crossing problems. "Any steam railroad station," he argued, "must be so located as to fit in with this rapid transit plan and with the major traffic highways system. The Plaza union railroad depot location is the only one location that meets all these requirements." Mott also questioned the ability of the PE to provide adequate facilities for handling passengers under the railroads' proposal. Mott asserted that the PE's current system of coordinating its trains was already inadequate; the railroads' alternative would only worsen the congestion at the PE terminal building. Although the PE claimed that the changes under the railroad plan would eliminate fifteen to twenty minutes of travel time per trip, Mott revealed that the existing delays resulted largely from the inadequacies of its own building. "I can see no reason for the Pacific Electric's not having improved its facilities at this station so as to eliminate these delays," Mott testified. Mott further noted that any street obstructions encountered by the PE trains were due to steam railroad and street traffic crossings, which would be eliminated under the union station plan through the use of private rights-of-way.[55]

Richard Sachse also testified in favor of the union station. Sachse had come to the same conclusions reached by nearly every independent engineer examining the problem over the previous twenty years. "A union station on the Plaza site . . . ," Sachse stated, "constitutes the best means for the greatest possible reduction of traffic congestion on Alameda Street, the best plan for serving the public and best for the carriers and at a less cost to them than their own plan." In contrast to the assertions made by the Business Men's Association, Sachse demonstrated that the Plaza area was far more accessible than the Santa Fe and Southern Pacific terminals. "The location of the union railroad passenger station permits ready and convenient access to the existing Pacific Electric system and to any future rapid transit system that may be developed," the engineer concluded.[56]

The supporters of the railroads answered the attacks by stepping up their own campaign. They especially emphasized the grade-crossing issue, while ignoring Mott's testimony. An editorial in the *Examiner* suggested that "the need above all others in this railway problem is to take the trains off our streets, where they are now a menace and a nuisance." Only the railroads' plan could eliminate PE crossings, the paper concluded. City Councilman Ralph Criswell also favored the elevateds. He argued that those who had linked the grade-crossing issue with the union station in the past had only succeeded in delaying the removal of those crossings. "If the people turn down the idea of continuing the fight for the Union Station near the Plaza at the forthcoming election," he remarked, "the way will be clear for carrying out a constructive program for grade crossing elimination."[57]

Opponents of the union terminal also attacked the location of the proposed station. The *Examiner* and others had already claimed that the Plaza area was both too congested and too far removed from the commercial district to serve the city's needs. Less than a month before the election, the paper quoted a staff member of the state attorney general's office who said that the Plaza plan would necessitate extensive street construction in that district to handle the expected increase in traffic. Such improvements would cost the taxpayers thousands of dollars, whereas the railroad plan would not cost the city a penny. As the election drew nearer, the *Examiner* used crude racial images to belittle the Plaza area. "If there is ever to be a union station," an *Examiner* editorial ran, "let it at least not be located between China-town and Little Mexico." Which would the public prefer, the paper asked, a "depot in [the] Chinese district, or no more grade crossings?"[58]

The Traffic Commission had remained silent on the union station issue during the campaign. During the previous six years the commission had created a solid consensus backing street improvements in Los Angeles through its support of judicious traffic studies, its extensive publicity efforts, and its ability to stand aloof from politics. The commission now found itself powerless when confronted with the issue of how best to improve the city's electric railway facilities. Although the commission's Rapid Transit Committee had voted to urge the City Council to adopt a rapid-transit plan, its directors had avoided committing themselves on the union station issue because they found that they were divided into opposing factions. Previously, the organization had worked out such difficulties privately in order to present a solid consensus to the public. It now found it impossible to reconcile differences among its members. Under mounting criticisms that they had sidestepped the controversy, the directors assembled to take a vote on whether to pronounce a recommendation.[59]

D. W. Pontius urged the commission's executive committee to endorse the railroads' elevated system. The PE, he argued, needed the elevateds to facilitate railway movement and improve traffic conditions in the central business district. Although the ballot nominally forced the electorate to vote on the union station issue alone, Pontius insisted that the election was a clear-cut vote between the union station and the elevated system. If the people voted down the Plaza terminal, the council would surely withdraw its petition before the Railroad Commission and allow the PE to build its rapid-transit network.[60] Other directors argued that the commission should remain neutral. J. Hansel Wood noted that the organization was deeply divided over the issue and that "some of our best people and business men are lined up on both sides." To make a recommendation for either side based upon a small majority would sully the commission's reputation and damage its public standing. Richard Sachse agreed. Part of the commission's success in the past was due to its unwillingness to take a stand on a controversy until it had conducted extensive studies. To rush a decision on a politically divisive issue could prove disastrous. Nevertheless, after a heated two-hour debate, the directors voted against the union station and in favor of the elevated system by a margin of eighteen to fourteen.[61]

During the latter half of April, the campaign became even more bitter. The *Times*, for instance, began a series of sensational front-page articles describing the evils of elevated lines in eastern cities. The first story described the problems that confronted Chicago's transportation system after that city had chosen elevated tracks over subways. "Elevated railroads are a curse to any community in which they have been erected," a *Times* reporter wrote. "Chicago more than any other city has felt their deadly construction, has suffered from their darkening shadows and their depressive gloom, their dirt and dust, their interminable ear-splitting screeching and their myriad dangers." The elevateds had slowed progress in Chicago and retarded development in the downtown area, the reporter continued. The tracks had also greatly lowered property values near them, leaving "row after row of dilapidated and antiquated buildings." The president of a traction company in Chicago denounced the use of elevateds to the *Times*, arguing that subways were a far better means of rapid transit.[62]

The *Times* also sent reporters to Boston, New York, and Philadelphia in search of the "truth" about elevateds. A Boston study quoted by the paper argued that had the city realized the impact of elevated lines on property values, noise levels, and public safety it would not have built them. Like Chicago, Bostonian engineers now favored subway construction. A *Times* reporter also interviewed the president of New York's Manhattan Borough, Julius Miller. Miller noted that the city had recently received permission from the state legislature to remove all elevated tracks from Sixth Avenue. "It is the unanimous opinion of those of us who have had to wrestle with traffic problems that elevated lines are inadvisable," Miller cautioned. He warned that Los Angeles was making a big mistake if it allowed "els" in its city. He also described how property values had increased when elevated tracks were banned from certain streets in New York City. In addition, the *Times* ran articles grimly depicting fatal accidents caused by derailed elevated railroads. Anyone undecided about the elevateds, a reporter suggested, should walk down an eastern street covered by such structures. This would convince them that "an elevated is a many-legged and roaring steel serpent and should be shunned by all cities for the machination of the devil it is." The railroad plan, the *Times* claimed, was merely the opening wedge for the more than fifty miles of elevated railways proposed by the Kelker–De Leuw study.[63]

The union station controversy demonstrates how deeply the issue of rapid transit divided the community.[64] The coalition of property owners, civic organizations, newspapers, business societies, and city officials which had worked together to ameliorate the city's inadequate street system dissipated in the face of this fight. Not only did these groups oppose each other, they also experienced internal divisions. The Traffic Commission, for example, had worked effectively and efficiently to improve traffic flow by studying the issues, offering advice and technical assistance to the city government, issuing publicity, and reconciling differences between civic organizations and city officials. When confronted with the union-terminal controversy, however, the commission could offer little more than a weak majority vote recommending that the city adopt the railroads' elevated system.

The city government experienced similar problems when the City Council split over both the issue of a rapid-transit plan and the union station controversy. Some members, seeing an opportunity to eliminate grade crossings quickly and perhaps clear up traffic congestion, favored the carriers' proposal. Others argued that the council had a moral obligation to continue the ten-year-old fight for a union station. Fearing political reprisals from their constituencies, most of the members preferred to delay a decision until the electorate had expressed itself.[65] At the same time, the Board of Public Utilities commissioners, the mayor, and the mayor's advisory committee had unanimously endorsed the railroad proposal, while the city attorney, the head of the City Planning Department, and the Engineering Department opposed it.

The downtown business community displayed a bit more unity. Under the auspices of the Business Men's Association, many downtown businessmen and commercial concerns favored the railroad plan. Composed of prominent bankers, lawyers, and business leaders, the association's members held views similar to those of the railroad officials. Even more important, downtown commercial concerns had long feared that continued traffic congestion in the city center would drive shoppers to the suburbs. Businesses saw the railroads' proposal as a way to bring rapid relief from the crowded traffic conditions. Supporting the Business Men's Association were the directors of the Greater Los Angeles

Chamber of Commerce and the members of more than forty local chambers of commerce. The *Examiner* argued that the area chambers supported the railroads because they believed the claims that the system would save travelers considerable time when riding interurbans bound for Los Angeles.[66]

Not all businessmen and commercial organizations favored the elevateds, however. The Lincoln Heights Commercial and Industrial Association, composed of small suburban businessmen, censured the Board of Public Utilities for opposing the union station. The association wanted the City Council to replace the board with honest persons "who will serve the public and the people and not the corporations."[67] At least one downtown association also opposed the railroads, and many others that had actively participated in the parking controversy remained silent on this issue. Furthermore, not all suburban chambers of commerce supported the elevated system. The railroads lobbied the Harbor District Chambers of Commerce, composed of sixty local chambers, to endorse their cause, but to no avail.[68] The Municipal League, an organization of liberal businessmen, opposed both plans and proposed a third alternative.[69] Still another organization, the City Club, denounced the railroads' plan because it felt that decentralization was the present trend in city planning. The club therefore opposed rapid transit in any form since it forced traffic into the city center.[70]

The city's property owners generally favored the union station over the railroad plan. The most active homeowner group was the Taxpayers' Anti-Elevated Association, which vigorously campaigned against the railroad proposal while promoting the Plaza terminal. Many local homeowner associations also favored the union station; all save one of the improvement associations writing the City Council during this period supported a Plaza terminal. Many opposed the railroads because they feared elevateds would ruin the beauty of the city and lower property values. Others felt the city was obligated to continue its ten-year fight against the railroads. Still others believed the carriers owed the people of Los Angeles a union station in return for their patronage. The *Times* claimed that improvement associations representing two thirds of Los Angeles had endorsed the union station in opposition to the railroads.[71]

Finally, the newspapers in Los Angeles split over whether the city should allow the railroads a free hand in designing the area's transportation system. During the twenties, Los Angeles' newspapers made few pretensions to objectivity as the distinctions between reporting a news item and writing an editorial were blurred. Once a paper's publisher or editors took up a cause, they used their control of the media to pursue their goals relentlessly. When the city's papers all agreed on their objectives, they could be extremely effective—witness the Major Traffic Street Plan. This time the papers opposed each other.

When the controversy finally came to a vote, the union station advocates won. Proposition 8, which asked voters if they wanted a union station for Los Angeles, passed by a margin of 61.3 to 38.7 percent. The electorate also favored the Plaza as the site for the station, albeit by a much smaller majority of 51.1 to 48.9 percent. The 60 percent turnout was the largest to date for a city election in Los Angeles despite the fact that no candidates appeared on the ballot. The *Times* gloated over its success, declaring the vote a "stinging rebuke for the railroads' alternative plan to build elevated roads to their present terminals." City Attorney Stephens claimed the railroads' defeat was "a great victory for the people." The union station victory guaranteed that the City Council would continue to press its case before the Railroad Commission to force the carriers to build a union terminal. At this point, the city's quest for a union station became disassociated from the issue of rapid transit.[72]

The carriers' plan had engendered one of the most acrimonious debates in the history of the city. The various sectors within Los Angeles society which had worked together so amicably to reconstruct the city's street system now bickered among themselves. The issue also caused internal strife within many organizations. The railroads' offer seemed an attractive opportunity to ease traffic congestion in the downtown area. Nevertheless, the old animosities and suspicions towards the railroads and the railways continued to influence many citizens. Many residents also opposed elevated railroad tracks in their city, viewing them as dirty, ugly, and dangerous structures that threatened to mar the aesthetics of the landscape and lower property values. These Angelenos preferred subway construction as an answer to the rapid transit problem. Subways, however, cost a minimum of two to four times as much to construct as elevated tracks. The railroads were unwilling to pay that high of a price to avoid a union station.

When the electorate finally voted down the railroads' proposal, the city was left with the same problems it had before. Downtown traffic was increasing, streetcars and interurbans stalled in the congestion, and the city lacked a plan for improving its public-transit facilities. The voters had declared themselves opposed to elevated tracks in favor of subway construction. The PE, on the other hand, could not afford to build a subway system and Angelenos showed no desire to assess themselves to subsidize a private corporation—especially one that had antagonized them in the past. Thus, Los Angeles society reached an impasse in its attempts to address the issue of improving its public-transit system. The Kelker–De Leuw report was now tainted both because the railroads had adopted it and because it favored elevated railways. The City Council refused to consider the Kelker–De Leuw study after the election and it was soon forgotten. Without a strong consensus favoring public action, the city's denizens did little to save mass transit in Los Angeles, even as they worked feverishly to complete the Major Traffic Street Plan.[73]

A Lack of Consensus

≡

We are now at the crossroads in this city where we must decide in the near future whether Los Angeles will ultimately develop into a metropolitan area primarily decentralized as to its commercial districts, or whether it will still retain the characteristics of other cities which have a dominant central business district surrounded by a group of local commercial centers.
—Donald Baker
1930

he union station campaign in Los Angeles was largely idiosyncratic to that region. The railroads' plan muddled the traditional issues surrounding rapid-transit planning in the rest of the United States. Nevertheless, the controversy displayed all of the divisive forces found elsewhere. The city rejected the railroad proposal and the Kelker–De Leuw report largely because of the public's general distrust of the railroads, the difficulty in financing a subway system, and the growing split between suburban residents and downtown merchants. In the years that followed the union station vote these problems loomed ever larger, making it nearly impossible for Los Angeles or most other American cities to build an effective rapid-transit system.

During the Plaza terminal election, the Los Angeles City Club appointed a committee of its members to study the issue of rapid transit. Although their findings differed substantially from those of others, the committee members were the most prescient observers. They did not believe that anyone could build a self-supporting rapid-transit system in Los Angeles. Southern California, they noted, was an area of single-family dwellings. The resulting low population density made the construction and operation of high-speed rail lines impractical. "The financial problem involved in any such transit program in Los Angeles," they argued, "is . . . well nigh insurmountable."[1] Even more important, the committee members disliked the centralizing effects of rail lines. A rapid-transit system, they argued, would aggravate the existing pedestrian congestion in the central business district, which would in turn adversely affect vehicular traffic. It would also encourage the removal of the building height restrictions in the city center because land values would increase with the rising number of people entering the area. The investigators believed that far from reducing congestion, a rapid-transit program would increase it. The downtown district, they insisted, would always remain congested no matter what plan the city might institute.

The committee also argued that the ultimate solution to the traffic problem lay in decentralization. The telephone, electric power, and the automobile now allowed businesses to move their industrial and commercial facilities outside of the city center. "Banking, industry, commercialized recreation and even retail business are entering upon an era of decentralization," the committee wrote. "Business is pointing the way out of the intolerable congestion situation in downtown areas." Why, it asked, should Los Angeles adopt a rapid-transit plan that would increase congestion in the city center? Instead, Los Angeles should reject the centralized city structure of eastern cities in favor of a "harmoniously developed community of local centers and garden cities."[2]

Many city planners agreed with the committee's conclusions. The well-known planner Clarence Dykstra argued that Los Angeles' downtown business interests sought a rapid-transit system to increase access to the central business district. By bringing large crowds into the area, these businessmen could maintain their commercial control over

the rest of southern California. Dykstra believed that this
"artificial stimulation" of downtown commerce would lead
to many urban problems because "the natural reaction of a
population anywhere is to spread out in sub-centers, to build
up small communities and business districts, to get the advantages of the city without its very apparent disadvan-
tages." Rather than concentrating all of the financial and
professional operations in the city center, Dykstra would
have allowed Los Angeles to develop into a region of small,
self-contained suburban centers. Each area would hold commercial and residential zones, which would allow citizens to
live and work in their own neighborhoods. In such a structure, city life would "not only be tolerable, but delightful."[3]

John Ihdler, manager of the Civic Development Department of the National Chamber of Commerce, agreed
with Dykstra that a rapid-transit system threatened the
promise of the low-density city. "Old time habits of concentrating nearly all the business life of the community [are]
producing conditions that mean constant loss," Ihdler wrote.
"High buildings crowded closely together darken each
other's windows, cut off each other's air, turn streets into
sunless canyons inadequate to carry the traffic demanded by
the abutting population. Rapid transit instead of solving the
problem has intensified it."[4]

Others, especially those connected with the downtown commercial community, worried that decentralization
would render whole areas within the central business district
obsolete. Such a movement away from the city center would
cost investors millions of dollars in lost real estate value
alone. Spokesmen for these interests argued that Los Angeles had to maintain this section of the city as its focus.[5] To
do so meant improving the circulation of traffic within the
downtown area. Business organizations located in the central
business district therefore looked towards rapid transit as a
means of maintaining access to the downtown area and thus
reinforcing their control over Los Angeles' commercial life.

Businessmen became particularly concerned during the late twenties when automobile congestion once again threatened to discourage shoppers from entering the city center. After four years of ignoring the problem, city officials began heeding the commercial community's renewed demands for improved rail service between the downtown and outlying districts.[6]

The City Planning Commission addressed this issue by sponsoring a conference in 1930. Most of those attending the meeting clearly favored the construction of a rapid-transit facility as a way of reinforcing the centralized structure of the city. J. Ogden Marsh, chief engineer of the Board of Public Utilities and Transportation, argued that the "ever increasing street traffic in Los Angeles leaves but little question that sooner or later measures will have to be undertaken for expediting the movement of such traffic." Although he believed that automobile usage had nearly reached a saturation point, Marsh argued that it was "illogical to hope for any curtailment in its use." Marsh accepted the automobile as a legitimate element in the city's transportation network, but foresaw little chance to further improve its movement in traffic because street widening would now have to entail the condemnation and destruction of buildings. Marsh therefore saw the diversion of rail lines above or below the streets as the only solution to congestion.[7]

Others speaking at the conference agreed with Marsh. Donald Baker, president of the City Planning Commission, also spoke in favor of rapid transit. Automobiles entering the central business district, he noted, averaged only slightly more than one person per car, making them extremely inefficient as a means of urban transportation. A rapid-rail network, he claimed, would provide cheap, effective transportation and encourage many to leave their cars at home.[8] D. W. Pontius, now the president of the PE, wanted to see a plan for removing railway lines from the streets of the city center and its surrounding area. Pontius hoped that this would ease congestion and maintain the primacy of the downtown area. Mayor John Porter concurred. Decentralization, he believed, would make business transactions difficult because of the increased distance between establishments. John Bullock, who ironically had been the first department store owner to move a branch store to the suburbs, argued that the health of downtown property values and business activities depended upon efficient transportation. Customers would stop patronizing downtown stores if they could not easily reach the central retail district. This explained why "property owners and business men in the downtown district are concerned in Rapid Transit." Although Bullock accepted the notion of limited decentralization, he continued to espouse the necessity of retaining a strong, concentrated commercial zone in the city center.[9]

Major financial problems, however, faced those favoring rapid-transit construction. Attorney Donald Faries noted that "modern rapid transit system construction is so expensive to construct that private capital cannot possibly bear the burden with any hope of securing an adequate return from the fares to be collected for transportation." There was no chance of obtaining citywide financing either. To garner enough votes for the passage of municipal bonds, the city would have to build subways throughout every one of its districts including those that had no need for them. Besides, state and local laws limited the level of the city's indebtedness to a figure too low to allow for rapid-transit construction. Marsh argued that since mass transit would affect all citizens in Los Angeles, the costs of such a network should be borne by all those who would benefit from it. Baker believed that the city could finance a new railway system in much the same way as street construction; adjoining and adjacent property owners could foot the bill through assessments. Pontius agreed that the local property owners, and not the private traction companies, should pay for the cost of a system, but he doubted whether the city's voters would approve a citywide bond issue.[10]

Many took exception to suggestions that individual property owners should pay for subway construction. Even Richard Sachse, an early proponent of mass transportation and now a consultant to the LARY, doubted the value of a rapid-transit system. He did not oppose rail lines out of hand; rather, he wondered whether it was consistent with recent trends in the city's development and whether the benefits would justify the substantial costs involved. New York City, he observed, had spent about $1 billion on its underground system. Yet it continually lost money and required substantial public subsidies to operate. Furthermore, the subways had failed to lessen congestion in Manhattan. Others concurred that few places in Los Angeles warranted the huge expense necessitated by rapid-transit construction. Property owners in the city were already burdened with high taxes and assessments. It was unlikely that they would accept any additional expenses in the midst of the worst depression of the century. In addition, a Santa Monica planning commissioner pointed out that local interests would prevent any sort of unanimity on the subject. Santa Monicans had turned away from the PE and LARY because the automobile was a far more convenient and faster method of travel. Residents of this region had worked with other communities throughout the county to construct a highway system that provided "a very satisfactory mode of transportation to the city and other points in the metropolitan district." South Bay residents would therefore refuse to contribute to a new rail network for which they had little use.[11]

Sachse and others also wondered whether the centralizing tendencies of rapid-transit lines were appropriate for Los Angeles. Carl Bush of the Hollywood Chamber of Commerce argued that decentralization would continue regardless of the city's actions because satellite business communities had grown in response to public demand. Bush believed that as long as the automobile remained available as a means of urban transportation, rapid transit would do little to stem the process of decentralization. Sachse agreed. Modern cities, he argued, differed greatly from their predecessors of twenty-five or fifty years before because technological changes had allowed them to spread across the countryside. This dispersal lowered densities and allowed "health, light, sunshine, space, and beauty" to rule supremely in the modern metropolis. Quoting from a survey of street railways in Los Angeles, Sachse argued that "the city as a whole is not hurt by decentralization and . . . such decentralization, all things taken into consideration, is deemed desirable." Was it worthwhile from the standpoint of the healthy development of the city, Sachse queried, "to block the tendency of decentralization and to interfere with the building up of outlying business centers?" He thought not and believed that this process would probably continue despite all efforts to prevent it.[12]

Just a few months after the city held this conference, the Planning Commission called for yet another meeting on the issue. Once again city officials, representatives from civic organizations, and business leaders met to discuss the future of the region's transportation system. Several organizations opposed to rapid-rail construction had demanded the second conference as a forum for expressing their views. The presence of Sachse, Faries, and Bush notwithstanding, critics of rapid transit argued that downtown business interests had dominated the first conference. These organizations hoped to redress this perceived bias in the second gathering.[13] Most of the criticism leveled against the proposed railway systems recalled the arguments of the years past. If nothing else, this opposition demonstrated that little consensus existed on the issue.

The president of the Affiliated Improvement Associations, which represented thousands of homeowners in Los

Angeles, expressed his organization's absolute opposition to elevated structures because of their adverse effect upon property values. At the same time, A. J. Samis, a representative of the Anti-Elevated League, issued a strident diatribe against the traction companies. He argued that the rapid-transit issue had been artificially and unnecessarily kept alive by the selfish interests of the railways. The traction companies, he claimed, had offered poor service for years because they had provided transportation to their own suburban developments to the exclusion of others. Whole areas of Los Angeles lay undeveloped only because of their refusal to extend tracks into newly proposed settlements. "This city," Samis lamented, "has already suffered scores of millions of dollars of loss through being forced to put up with a transportation system that is more in the real estate business than it is in the transportation business."[14] Of course, the traction companies had not actively promoted land development for several years and they could not extend their tracks because they lacked the funds to do so. Yet Samis's accusations evoked the memories of thirty years' worth of frustration.

The railway critics also denounced any proposal favoring public support of mass-transit construction. Several speakers particularly opposed the use of assessment districts because they would harm the individual property owners. "The building of a rapid transit system by the direct assessment plan will create a burden that will be impossible to carry and many homes will be sacrificed," claimed a participant. Property owners already carried assessments for street, street lighting, sewer, and sidewalk improvements. With hard times approaching, homeowner representatives argued that they would fight any attempt to add to their financial load. The staggering costs of subway construction and the suggestion that property owners should shoulder those expenses, a real estate broker noted, had already engendered public animosity towards mass transportation.[15]

Others argued that downtown business interests and the traction companies were trying to benefit themselves at the expense of the suburban homeowners. Greely Kolts of the Northwest Civic League accused large commercial concerns in the central business district of "diligently trying to press down upon the people of this city the $135,000,000 Subway and Elevated plan." Speaking on behalf of people and organizations in the northwestern part of the city, Kolts opposed any attempt to force the citizens of Los Angeles County to pay for a subway or elevated network that would benefit the stockholders of the PE or LARY. A system such as the one proposed in the Kelker–De Leuw plan would cost the individual property owner between $300 and $1,100 in assessments. "What has the Pacific Electric and Los Angeles Railways ever done for the people of Los Angeles that the property owners should contribute over a hundred million dollars in the building of subways where the only benefit would be to enable the local traction companies to enjoy a saving in operation each year of hundreds of thousands of dollars[?]" Although Kolts did not believe that Angelenos owed the traction companies anything, he argued that the downtown business organizations and the PE had for the last four years attempted to foist a rail plan on the public. Big business might preach the "glad gospel" that the public must finance a rapid-transit system, he continued, "but we have not heard of the property owners of the city rising up and begging to be permitted to be assessed $150,000,000 for the benefit of the operating street railway companies." The PE and LARY should pay their own way, he concluded. The fact that Los Angeles' new mayor had been elected largely on the strength that he had promised to correct the burdens of overlapping assessments indicated that many agreed with Kolts.[16]

The bitter arguments over the future of rapid transit at these conferences indicate that important elements of Los Angeles society no more agreed on a solution to the city's railway problems in 1930 than they had in 1926. At the heart of the issue now loomed two points of contention. First, there was a philosophical difference. Business leaders and traction officials with major interests in the central business district sought to retain the downtown area as the focus of southern California's commercial life, an endeavor in which they had largely succeeded until the late twenties. The transportation system reflected that hegemony, for all of the major railway lines and highways radiated from the downtown area. At first the dispersal of individual homes across the countryside did little to disrupt this pattern. Suburban dwellers continued to travel into the downtown area every day; they just had to travel a bit further. Later the general acceptance of the automobile engendered severe traffic congestion. By the late twenties, consumers, and later industry itself, began to look elsewhere to conduct their business. Eventually the outlying commercial communities challenged the economic control of the downtown district. Business leaders in the city center subsequently hoped to shore up their domination of the regional economy by building a rapid-transit system that would reinforce the centralized nature of the city.

Businesses, property owners, and civic organizations in the outlying suburbs, however, saw little reason to retain the centrally focused city. They looked upon decentralization as a logical force. It allowed them to continue building single-family dwellings while pursuing the ideal of a healthy, uncrowded urban life. Decentralization also allowed them to utilize fully the advantages of the automobile. This was particularly important since the automobile now served as the only mode of mechanized transport in many areas of the county. These interests, then, opposed rapid-transit construction because they disliked its centralizing tendencies. In addition, many argued that decentralization would continue without regard for the city's best efforts to stop it.

The second area of disagreement, however, eventually assured that the city would not build a rapid-transit system during the next forty years. "The crux of the problem of mass transportation is finance," remarked Donald Baker. "Who shall pay for it?"[17] The fact that the ailing traction companies could not finance a rapid-transit system themselves meant that their supporters had to turn to the public as a whole for help. But residents in the suburbs denounced such measures. With the poor economic situation, property owners could ill afford additional assessments on their homes. Even more important, they saw little reason to support a costly rail network that they would not have used anyway. A majority of the public had already expressed its confidence in the automobile by adopting it for everyday use. Why, then, should the public shoulder the financial responsibility for a rapid-transit system? The fact that rapid-rail lines would operate for the profit of the traction companies only added to its aggravation. By 1930, there was little reason for the average Angeleno to feel kindly disposed toward the railways. Whether the traction companies had actually abused the trust of their patrons in years past, or whether the public expected more of the railways than they could deliver is unimportant. The public had been at odds with the PE and LARY for most of the previous three decades and by now it retained little loyalty towards them. Kolts expressed a common attitude when he said, "We believe that the people of Los Angeles do not owe a single dollar to the Pacific Electric or the Los Angeles Railway Corporations."[18]

With such strident disagreement among Los Angeles' social groups, it was unlikely that much could be done to expedite the erection of rapid-rail lines. The persistent economic depression further assured that no construction would take place during the thirties.[19] The city did make one attempt to secure federal Public Works Administration funding to build a transit system. Business organizations in the central business district asked Donald Baker to draw up plans for such a network as part of the application procedure. Baker complied with a hurriedly drafted study that recommended the construction of four lines extending into the suburbs from the downtown area. The city, however, gave up its quest when the PWA turned down its proposals. Without federal funding, the city could not even afford to finance a traffic study let alone a modern rapid-transit project.[20]

Transportation nevertheless remained an important issue throughout the early thirties. The city had completed a substantial portion of the Major Traffic Street Plan before the onset of the nation's economic difficulties, allowing many more Angelenos to utilize their automobiles as a private means of transportation. The traction companies, however, did not fare well as profits declined precipitously during the decade. The PE, already suffering economically during the twenties, averaged losses of more than $2,000,000 a year from 1931 to 1940. The LARY, which had enjoyed a modest income during the decade following World War I, also suffered significant losses each year of the Depression. As their economic conditions weakened, the railways could ill afford to make capital improvements even on their existing tracks. This led already frustrated transit riders to complain once again about the quality of rail service. "The public is critical and restive," noted city officials in 1935. There was also a rising tide of disapproval for the management practices of the railways. Overcrowding, uneven fare structures, antiquated equipment, and poor routing aroused the public's anger. Crowded cars and a dearth of crosstown lines were long-standing problems with Los Angeles' railways. By the thirties, patrons could also complain about the traction companies' use of obsolete railway cars. On some routes, both the PE and LARY continued to operate open-air trains first utilized thirty years earlier at the turn of the century. Patronage subsequently declined as the decade wore on. The LARY's service was so bad, complained a city councilman in 1933, that the railway was "compelling more and more people to get automobiles to get around in."[21]

Despite the poor quality of the rail service, a considerable number of residents continued to use it. The various rail and bus lines in the county still accepted one million fares a day in 1939. Most of the LARY's streetcar tracks, however, terminated within five miles of the central business district. Naturally, a much higher percentage of those living within this region rode the streetcars into the downtown area than did those living beyond the reaches of the system. Those patrons still utilizing public transit did so because of its availability. A survey conducted in 1939 revealed to no one's surprise that 85 percent of streetcar patrons walked to their boarding place. Of these, 93 percent lived less than five city blocks from the lines. Clearly, the railways attracted mainly Angelenos residing near Los Angeles' original suburban developments.[22]

Nevertheless, even within these areas far more people used automobiles than streetcars. For instance, 25 percent of those living between one-half and two and one-half miles from the city center drove their automobiles into the central business district each day. Only 12 percent of the same population group rode mass transportation into town. This phenomenon had begun during the twenties when the public had eagerly embraced the automobile for urban transportation. The trend continued throughout the thirties despite the Depression. "Surface trams, gasoline buses, and interurban electrics have not proven adequate as to speed, comfort, or convenience," commented a City Planning Department official in 1938. "Hence the typical resident of Los Angeles has his own car." Nor was automobile ownership confined to any geographical area of the city. Per capita car ownership in 1939 was remarkably even throughout the city despite the fact that a substantial number of middle-class families had already begun to flee the inner residential areas for the distant suburbs. City officials further argued that automobile ownership did not vary with economic status.[23]

Even as the various interest groups within the city

bickered over whether to finance a rapid-transit system, Angelenos turned to their cars in increasing numbers. Frustrated with years of broken promises and poor service, the public took to the automobile as a means of efficient transportation. Southern Californians would find, however, that their street system could not support the heavy demands they placed on it. The Major Traffic Street Plan helped some, but even it proved inadequate by the early thirties. As the major highways leading into the central business district became clogged with cars, people again sought an answer to the transportation problem.

Other American cities faced similar issues during the late twenties and early thirties. Congestion continued to plague their central business districts despite their best efforts to widen streets and open new thoroughfares. As automobile traffic worsened, those with economic interests in the urban core feared the loss of business; these same people had originally advocated the street improvements as a way of maintaining access to the downtown area. Once the number of motorists outstripped the capacity of the newly built street systems, merchants again faced the specter of decentralization. Those favoring the city center usually responded with calls for a rapid-transit network. Various organizations in Chicago from 1909 to at least 1930 supported the construction of a subway. They believed that such a system could remove streetcars from the roadways and thereby improve both automobile congestion and mass transportation at the same time. But this plan was far beyond the means of the local traction companies and would thus require municipal support. People in the suburbs, however, began to question the rationale behind the rapid-transit plan. This faction argued that subways would merely enhance the central business district's control over the regional economy. Since the automobile and truck now allowed the dispersal of economic activity into the suburbs, outlying residents saw little reason to lend their financial support to a scheme proposed by the downtown merchants. This inherent belief that mass transportation should sustain its own operations and capital improvements doomed Chicago's streetcar system.[24]

Detroit's rapid-transit plans met a similar fate. In 1923, the city's Rapid Transit Commission unveiled a comprehensive transit plan calling for an integrated system of subways, rapid-rail lines, streetcars, and highways not unlike that proposed by Kelker and De Leuw in Los Angeles. Despite the city government's initial enthusiasm, the plan soon ran into trouble. The costs associated with the proposal precluded anything other than municipal financing. Given the politically sensitive nature of financing such a system, the Detroit City Council refused in 1926 to consider even a scaled-down version of the plan. Three years later, voters overwhelmingly rejected a $54 million bond proposal for subway construction. Property owners denounced the idea of taxing themselves for a rapid-transit system that mostly benefited the merchants in the city center.[25]

The fact that factional politics abounded in American cities following World War I does not explain why these various interest groups could work together to facilitate automobile movement at the same time that they fought bitterly over rapid transit. Historian Paul Barrett suggests that mass transportation planning was by its very nature political, whereas the automobile stood outside the realm of politics.[26] The experience of Los Angeles and other cities indicates otherwise. The attempt to improve vehicular circulation in the nation's cities involved extensive political maneuvering. The automobile's popularity with many urban interest groups does not mean that its adoption occurred outside of the political arena.

Upon further reflection, it appears that the automobile's flexibility allowed it to satisfy several factions at the same time. Urban dwellers initially adopted the automobile because of the failure of railway companies and the progressive reform movement to provide efficient urban transportation. Various sectors of society agreed to facilitate vehicular movement by reconstructing the street system because it met all of their needs. Powerful political and business leaders feared that motorists would shop elsewhere if they did not maintain easy automobile access to the central business district. Suburban interests also favored accommodating the automobile because it opened new areas to residential development while allowing both lateral and radial movement within the city. Initially, the suburban and downtown interests coincided because automotive traffic followed the centrally focused transportation patterns first established by the streetcars. Later, as congestion in the core mounted despite the city's efforts to contain it, a split appeared which pitted those favoring decentralization against others wanting to retain the existing urban structure. As this division came to dominate urban politics, one issue remained clear. The automobile could at least partially satisfy each faction. Downtown interests realized that they had to try to ease automobile congestion, while suburban dwellers understood that the automobile and truck permitted decentralization.[27]

Rapid transit, by way of contrast, appeared to benefit only those interested in keeping the centralized urban form intact. The downtown interests advocated subways and elevateds once street congestion threatened to cut their district off from shoppers. The costs of such a system, however, far exceeded the financial capacity of nearly all privately operated railway companies. Those favoring rail networks consequently argued that cities should subsidize their construction. Nevertheless, many planners and suburban residents had abandoned centralization as an ideal by the mid-twenties. Now that the automobile and the truck permitted easy peripheral movement, numerous people believed that decentralization could solve the age-old problem of crowding at the urban core. Rapid transit, they argued, would only exacerbate the congestion in the city center by bringing more people into the central business district. The dispersal of commercial activities into the suburbs, however, would lessen these concerns. One transportation expert noted in 1925 that central business districts in American cities were "losing their desirability due to modern developments, and business was showing a tendency to migrate to more accessible quarters." "This tendency," he concluded, "should be encouraged." Several years later a Denver planner reported that his city had favored decentralization because it wanted to avoid "the evils of congestion and overcrowding attendant upon excessive use of land."[28] Many suburban businessmen believed that subways represented the downtown interests' latest attempt to maintain their control over the regional economy.

This fundamental disagreement over how American cities should evolve blocked subway construction in all but a handful of cities. The expense involved in building a rapid-transit network required a citywide consensus. But the fragmented nature of urban politics meant that suburban and downtown factions could rarely reach agreement. The automobile proved the exception because its mobility allowed it to win advocates on both sides. Not tied to any tracks, cars could travel either toward the central business district or within the suburbs. Thus, downtown merchants and suburban property owners subsidized street improvements through taxes, assessments, and user charges. Ultimately, this resulted in a victory for those favoring decentralization. As congestion increased on thoroughfares leading into the city center, motorists turned to suburban shopping centers. Employers did likewise as they sought cheap land and ready access to labor. Champion of nearly all segments of society, the automobile especially favored the periphery. In doing so, it brought about a fundamental change in the spatial structure of American cities.

⇐ 7 ⇒

Reshaping the Modern City

≡

Surface trams, gasoline buses, and interurban electrics have not proven adequate as to speed, comfort, or convenience. Hence the typical resident of Los Angeles has his own car.

—City Planning Department
1938

The so-called Central Business District is rapidly becoming just another such center, with few notable characteristics to differentiate it from others.

—E. E. East
1942

The adoption of the automobile for urban transportation had a profound impact on the shape of American cities. The electric streetcar, the horse-drawn railway, and even the omnibus had previously allowed a limited amount of residential dispersion. Thousands of urban dwellers fled to the suburbs with the introduction of these technological advances. Nevertheless, most economic activity within cities remained confined to the central business district. The railways in most urban areas converged upon the downtown area, making it a natural center for theaters, offices, light manufacturing, and department stores. Even heavy industry tended to locate at railroad junctions and along waterways just outside the city center. Steam railroads and barges could effectively move large loads of raw and finished materials long distances. Short-haul transportation, however, continued to rely upon inefficient horse-drawn carts and wagons. The slow, awkward movements of these vehicles required a small tightly packed business center. Consequently, American cities at the turn

– 175 –

of the century retained their highly centralized structures despite the introduction of streetcar suburbs.

At first, the arrival of the automobile did little to disrupt this orientation. Most thoroughfares followed the patterns established by the streetcar, while horsecarts continued to dominate freight deliveries. The automobile may have opened new suburbs, but most people still traveled to the central business district on a daily basis. As congestion increased within the downtown districts and as parking became more difficult, however, shoppers and employers began to look elsewhere to conduct their business. Civic leaders in central cities tried desperately to forestall this decentralization of the economy by rationalizing their street systems. Such actions eased the crowded traffic conditions in the short term but encouraged larger numbers of people to drive their automobiles. Eventually, the increase in automobile usage outstripped the ability of cities to relieve congestion. In addition, the motorized truck quickly caught on as a means of short-haul transportation. With an efficient mode of transport, various economic activities could relocate to the suburbs both to avoid the congestion of the city center and to take advantage of lower land prices. The twenties therefore saw the beginning of economic dispersal in American cities.

The timing of this decentralization differed from place to place depending upon a number of factors, including an area's geographical constraints, the strength of the local economy, its population growth, and the size of the existing central business district. Los Angeles, for instance, decentralized quickly. Not only did southern California have vast tracts of open land, it was the fastest growing metropolis in the nation. Los Angeles' city center, although dominant until the thirties, was relatively small by eastern standards. The region also experienced a major influx of manufacturing during the twenties when automobiles and trucks made it easier to build factories on inexpensive land in the periphery. Finally, Los Angeles never existed as a large walking city. By the time anyone could even point to Los Angeles as a major urban area, it had already established a street railway system. The city's population could therefore spread itself across the countryside more easily than in older eastern and midwestern metropolises. Los Angeles' low population density and weak city center also would later allow it to accommodate the automobile more rapidly than in other parts of the country. As a result, southern California began to emerge during the twenties as a sprawling urban area with huge tracts of suburban housing and several business centers. Los Angeles' downtown district, once the focus of economic activity in the county, deteriorated to the point where it functioned as merely one of several regional centers.

By 1920, Los Angeles had already experienced a substantial amount of residential dispersal. The area's explosive and continuous population growth since the 1880s, combined with its extensive railway network, had encouraged suburban development. The rise of these streetcar suburbs coincided with a building boom in single-family dwellings. As middle-class Anglo-American residents, and later white blue-collar workers, escaped to the edge of the city, they began to seek space and comfort in large yards and detached houses. The desire to live in suburban housing was fueled by long-standing American attitudes towards the countryside and the family. The moral virtue of the country was a theme that had permeated the nineteenth-century American mind. The city, most people agreed, bred not only disease but corruption and avarice. New York social critic John Davenport argued in 1884 that crowded living conditions had resulted "in increasing the poverty and distress of one-half of our inhabitants; has added largely to the number of our drunkards, thieves and other abandoned and dangerous characters; has debauched the morals of our citizens, and, finally has resulted in an increase of disease and death almost unparalleled among civilized people." Seven years later,

Charles Horton Cooley echoed these fears. "No child," Cooley wrote, "has a fair chance in the world who is condemned to grow up in the dirt and confinement, the dreariness, ugliness and vice of the poorer quarters of a great city."[1] Nevertheless, there was something compelling about the nation's cities. From 1840 on, thousands of formerly rural Americans and foreign immigrants descended upon the metropolis seeking opportunity, wealth, and excitement. By 1890, fully one third of the country's population lived in cities. Not surprisingly, this movement created conflict. Most writers claimed that "humanity demands that men should have sunlight, fresh air, the sight of grass and trees." Yet industry demanded that people congregate near factories and centers of commerce. The resolution to this problem lay in the development of suburbs.[2] People living outside the city center could, Americans believed, enjoy both rural and urban amenities.

American attitudes towards the family also spurred suburban growth. The family had always held a place of paramount importance in American society, for it symbolized order and stability. Prior to 1830, most American cities were not only relatively small and homogenous, but displayed a sense of community. The craftsman economy with its apprentice system remained the norm, while the few factories that did exist by this time usually employed fewer than fifteen workers. Although class distinctions certainly existed, people of all ranks had to constantly interact with each other because of the cramped quarters of the walking city. Sixty years later, the United States had emerged as the most important industrial nation in the world. The country's urban areas had also grown extensively with the populations of Chicago, New York, and Philadelphia all reaching the one million mark. As the city became increasingly impersonal, families found that they had to turn inward to maintain their sense of community. They did this by purchasing single-family dwellings on large suburban lots in homogeneous neighborhoods. By doing so, middle-class white natives could avoid what they believed were the undesirable foreign ethnic groups that had begun immigrating to the United States in large numbers. The suburban house also offered status to its owner and the knowledge that he held a permanent and morally correct position in society. "A man is not a whole and complete man," wrote Walt Whitman, "unless he owns a house and the ground it stands on." Years later Lockwood Matthews argued that "a separate house surrounded by a yard is the ideal kind of home."[3]

By the latter half of the nineteenth century, middle-class Anglo-Americans sought to escape the bustling inner-city neighborhoods for the relative calm of the suburbs. Several technological innovations made this exodus possible. Streetcars opened up large sections of relatively cheap land for development and, several decades later, the automobile made even larger tracts available for subdivision. The invention of the balloon frame house in 1833 introduced the mass production of inexpensive houses. Prior to this time, residential construction was both slow and tedious, requiring skilled craftsmen. The new construction techniques, however, relied upon a light wooden frame made up of standard two-by-four studs placed every sixteen inches. This innovation allowed semiskilled workers to erect houses much more rapidly than in the past. Developers could consequently supply thousands of inexpensive houses to those flocking to the suburbs.[4] By 1870, the single-family dwelling had become the prevalent suburban housing unit.

Southern California residents eagerly embraced these new technologies. Since Los Angeles had established itself as a major urban area after the arrival of the horse-drawn streetcar, Angelenos found that they could easily move into the suburbs. By 1930 Donald Baker could argue that southern California's housing stock was largely comprised of detached houses.[5] Most people agreed that the numerous individual homes and consequent low population density was a major attraction of the area. A prominent Los Angeles businessman wrote that the region's large suburban population proved that people moving to California "prefer to live away from the noise and turmoil of the city, and that the five and six room house takes precedent over the flat or apartment." Many argued that continued emigration to the city depended upon the availability of such houses. "Los Angeles' future depends upon the suburban cities surrounding it," wrote yet another businessman. "The ideal life that we have here is the country or home life with your gardens and bungalows." By the late twenties, almost every city official and planner approved of this spatial orientation because such an environment allowed the area to avoid the crowded and unhealthy aspects of eastern urban life. People flocked to Los Angeles, commented one city official, to "escape the discomfort and inconvenience of living in our older cities."[6]

Urban planners throughout the nation encouraged other cities to promote residential dispersion. These professionals initially saw decentralization as an "unmixed blessing" and an answer to the problems of urban congestion. Many planners therefore saw Los Angeles as an ideal urban environment. Unlike the polluted and crowded cities of the East, southern California seemed to offer the advantages of both a small town and a major metropolis. "We in Los Angeles," claimed a local attorney, "realize the value of sunshine, of space and of individual homes as against crowded housing conditions and tenements without proper provision for light, air, yards, lawns, trees, shrubs, flowers, and individual home units." Such a city structure, however, needed efficient transportation. Streetcars and interurbans had provided the original transit requirements for the region, but soon proved inadequate because of their inability to expand into new residential developments. Hence, the automobile became a vital factor in maintaining the single-family dwelling as the region's predominant residential structure. Automobiles were necessarily assimilated into the ideology that preached suburban living and decentralization as the ideal urban form. "The horizontal expansion of the urban community is not due to any new-found desire in urban people," wrote an engineer for the Automobile Club in 1940. Rather, the automobile had made it possible "to satisfy an inherent desire common to all people to find order, space, [and] stability in home neighborhoods, [and] to escape from the noise and confusion of congested living and working quarters." Planners elsewhere generally agreed that cities should accommodate the automobile. Charles Whitnall, a planner in Milwaukee, argued that "the automobile has taught people that they can live as comfortably beyond the city's confines with all the coveted city conveniences and do so with less expense and greater benefits to themselves and their children."[7]

The benefits of home ownership and the suburban dream did not, however, accrue to all of America's residents. Among the rural immigrants flocking to the city between 1880 and 1940 were thousands of blacks, Hispanics, and Asians. The experience of these racial groups in Los Angeles reflected social conditions found in most American metropolises. Prior to 1910, only 2,131 blacks lived in Los Angeles. Accounting for just 2 percent of the region's population, these people found themselves scattered throughout the city. Several years later, immediately before and after World War I, a large migration of southern blacks occurred. This influx into the metropolitan area alarmed the largely midwestern Anglo population and provided an impetus for these whites to move out of older neighborhoods immediately surrounding the central business district. As whites fled to the suburbs, blacks moved into the vacant homes, usually as tenants. Most of the newly arrived blacks found themselves living along Central Avenue in South Central Los Angeles just outside of the downtown area. Whites resisted black expansion into the suburbs through physical intimidation and the use of restrictive covenants forbidding the sale of property to nonwhites. By 1920, 75 percent of all blacks living in Los Angeles resided in three of the city's twelve wards.[8]

Hispanics also suffered from spatial segregation. Between 1910 and 1930, Los Angeles' Hispanic population tripled from 30,000 to more than 90,000. Not only were these Mexicans and Mexican-Americans the largest minority group in southern California but they gave Los Angeles the most concentrated Latino population in the nation. Initially, these people lived near the Plaza, the original center of Los Angeles. The rise in industrial activity, however, pushed the Mexican families into the old Jewish and Eastern European suburbs of Boyle Heights and East Los Angeles. Although many Mexican immigrants chose to live in the barrio for reasons of language, custom, and kinship, white prejudices also prevented the movement of Hispanics into the periphery. Many of the white emigrants living in East Los Angeles moved into the outlying areas once they had attained a bit of affluence. This flight, combined with the heavy Mexican immigration, turned the region into a bustling Hispanic enclave. Railways running into this area allowed its residents to easily commute the two to three miles into the industrial sector of downtown Los Angeles. As Los Angeles' Mexican population rose throughout the twenties, whites successfully increased their efforts to stop Hispanic residential movement into the city's northern and western suburbs. A few isolated Mexican districts sprang up along various PE lines because the railway hired Hispanics to maintain its tracks, but these suburban labor camps remained isolated from their white neighbors.[9]

The southern California landscape soon reflected the middle-class desire to build a suburban metropolis. The area's initial suburban development followed the streetcar and interurban lines. The PE provided ties between Los Angeles and independent communities such as Pasadena, San Bernardino, Long Beach, and Santa Monica. Each of these towns served both as an autonomous city with its own business district and as a bedroom community for Los Angeles. Between these cities stood vast reaches of open land. The PE prior to World War I therefore acted much like the commuter railroads in the East. It allowed people to travel to the Los Angeles central business district while living in a small town. The PE reinforced Los Angeles' regional dominance by running nearly all of its interurban lines through the city.

Suburban expansion also pushed outward from Los Angeles itself. From 1890 until 1930, Los Angeles was the fastest growing metropolitan area in the nation. In 1890, the city held a mere 11,000 people. By the beginning of the Great Depression it had attained a population exceeding 1.2 million. Most of these new residents found themselves living in the suburbs. The early subdivisions on the periphery closely followed the streetcar lines of the LARY. By 1914 the trolleys had opened much of the region within five miles of the downtown area to development. So vital was transportation to these neighborhoods that developers rarely built houses more than four blocks away from a streetcar line.[10] The railways' coverage of this area was fairly comprehensive and helped Los Angeles attract most of the county's new immigrants. Table 4 illustrates the population growth for five different regions within the Los Angeles and Orange County metropolitan area. The central area comprised that portion of Los Angeles served by the LARY. During the first two decades of the twentieth century, far more people moved into this sector than into all of the other regions combined. People lived in this area because the streetcar provided easy access to both the suburbs and the city center.

This pattern of development changed during the twenties with the arrival of the automobile. Freed from the necessity of living near the streetcar lines, Angelenos began moving into those vacant areas in between the tracks. Other residents abandoned the central area altogether and pur-

Table 4

Population Change by District in the Los Angeles Metropolitan Area

	1900–1910		1910–1920		1920–1930		1930–1940		1940–1950	
	N	%	N	%	N	%	N	%	N	%
Central	210,625	206	255,782	82	145,673	26	97,025	14	47,635	6
West	15,981	187	41,387	169	403,458	612	151,329	32	323,541	52
East	48,444	153	52,859	66	133,851	101	82,736	31	228,340	65
Valley	11,770	201	15,253	87	172,900	526	111,281	54	290,650	92
Southeast*	39,559	122	79,035	110	506,559	335	139,902	21	545,385	68

Source: Dudley Pegrum, Residential Population and Urban Transport Facilities. Reprinted by permission of The Regents of the University of California.

N = Number of new residents in the decade

% = Percentage increase during the decade

*Includes Orange County

chased homes well removed from the influence of the LARY. Vacant lots in these districts initially sold for far less than those closer to the central business district because prior to the general adoption of the automobile, these areas remained relatively isolated from the rest of the city. The differential in land prices during the late teens therefore gave automobile owners an incentive to relocate to the outlying regions.[11] In doing so, these Angelenos pushed the boundary of urban development toward those independent communities served by the PE. The open space that separated these small cities from Los Angeles and other communities eventually disappeared and they became indistinguishable from the rest of the suburban sprawl so characteristic of the southern California landscape.

This alteration in Los Angeles' spatial structure worried LARY officials, who responded by constructing a series of maps to study the problem. Each map showed the geographical relationship between the LARY streetcar lines and newly constructed houses. Taken together, they provide valuable insight into the development of southern California.

Several of these maps ended up in the Huntington Library in San Marino when a former LARY employee donated his personal papers to that institution. Three are reproduced here as figures 1 through 3. The first map shows the location of residential construction in the city of Los Angeles during a two-year period ending in November 1920. The parking crisis occurred during this same time, marking it as a transitional period. Most workers at that time commuted by streetcars. An increasing number of residents, however, had begun to turn to their automobiles. All of this is reflected in figure 1. The map itself encompasses an area of only four to five miles surrounding the central business district. By the beginning of the twenties most of the city's development was taking place in the periphery. In the working-class neighborhoods of South Central Los Angeles, developers still built houses close to the railway lines. These residents

Plates 9 and 10. Located several miles west of downtown Los Angeles, Beverly Hills in 1921 existed as an independent town well removed from the suburban sprawl of its larger neighbor.

relied largely upon the streetcars to carry them into town. The more fashionable western and northern parts of the city, however, demonstrated considerable deviation from this pattern. Real estate developers in this sector felt free to build houses in areas well removed from the railway tracks because their middle-class patrons could use their cars for transportation. Subdivisions consequently sprang up both in between and well beyond the reach of the LARY system. Later maps from 1926 and 1930 clearly indicate that by the mid to late twenties, developers had moved far beyond the influence of the streetcars. Table 4 provides further evidence for this point by showing that the central area served by the streetcars fell far behind most of the other sectors of the city in terms of population growth. The LARY and PE tried to tap these markets by extending bus lines into the outlying sections but met with only limited success. The availability of the automobile, not public transportation, now dictated the spatial evolution of Los Angeles.[12]

By 1952, when the photograph in plate 10 was taken, Los Angeles had developed to the point where it had engulfed the open spaces that had once surrounded Beverly Hills. (Courtesy of California Historical Society, Ticor Title Insurance, Los Angeles, and Spence Air Photo Collection, Department of Geography, University of California, Los Angeles)

Compared to its counterparts in the East, Los Angeles was a relatively young metropolis. Table 5 indicates that fully 96 percent of Los Angeles' housing stock was built after the turn of the century. The location of these homes reflected the general trend towards suburbanization. By relying first upon the streetcar and interurban and later the automobile, Angelenos spread themselves across the countryside in detached houses. After 1944, only the older neighborhoods immediately surrounding the city center had densities anywhere close to those found in other large cities. Outside the downtown area, the number of people per acre dropped dramatically.[13]

By 1940, Los Angeles had already experienced tremendous residential dispersion. Unlike any other major city at the time, more than half of its residents lived in single-fam-

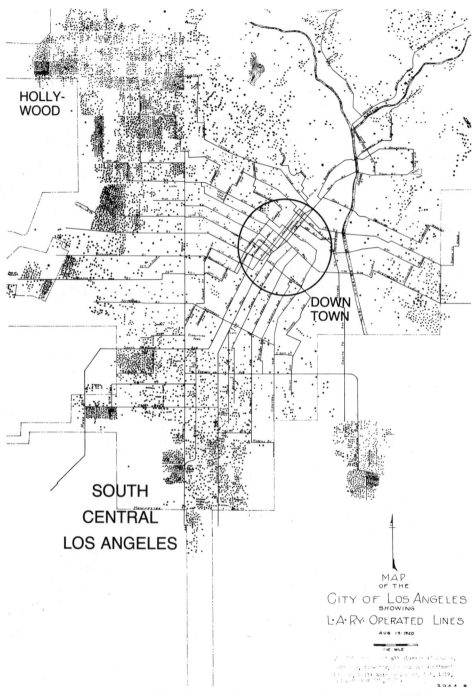

Fig. 1. Location of Residential Construction in Los Angeles, 1919–1920. (Courtesy of Henry E. Huntington Library and Art Gallery)

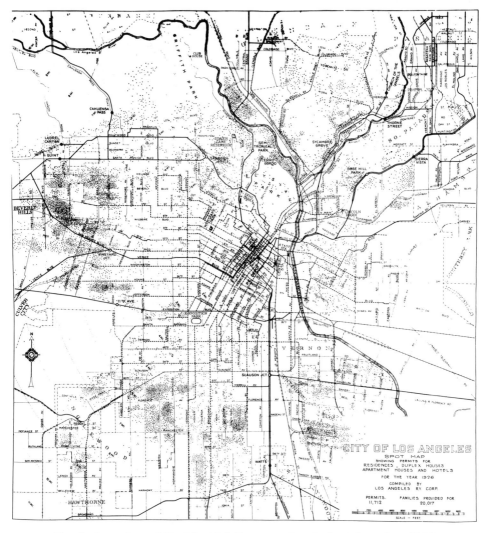

Fig. 2. Location of Residential Construction in Los Angeles, 1926.
(Courtesy of Henry E. Huntington Library and Art Gallery)

ily dwellings. Its nearest rival amongst the three other largest
American metropolises was Chicago with 15.9 percent of its
population residing in detached houses. It is not surprising,
then, that Los Angeles' aggregate poplation density of 3,341
persons per square mile was four to seven times lower than
that of Chicago, Philadelphia, and New York.

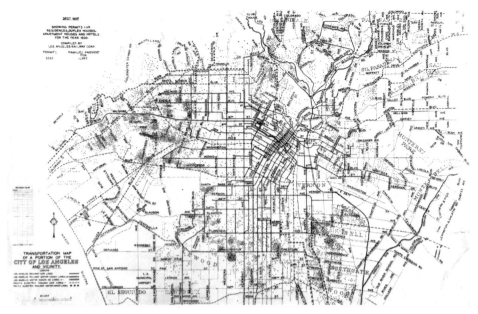

Fig. 3. Location of Residential Construction in Los Angeles, 1930. (Courtesy of Henry E. Huntington Library and Art Gallery)

It would be a mistake, however, to conclude that Los Angeles was wholly unique. Southern California may have led the way in developing automobile suburbs, but other urban areas soon followed. Cities other than Los Angeles enjoyed substantial growth during the twenties and thirties. Residents in those urban areas also used their automobiles to pursue the suburban ideal. During the twenties, for instance, single-family dwellings accounted for 60 percent of all newly constructed residential units in the United States. As a consequence, America's suburban population for the first time grew at a faster rate than that of the core cities. These trends intensified during the late thirties with several northeastern cities actually losing population at the expense of their surrounding suburban communities. Encouraged by a recovery in the general economy and the federal subsidies offered by the Federal Housing Administration, the widespread construction of residential dwellings began again in 1938. From then until the beginning of World War II, 81

Table 5
Age of Dwelling Units as of 1940

| | Percentage of Units Built in Each Interval | | | |
	1899 & before	1900–1919	1920–1929	1930–1940
Los Angeles	3.8	30.8	45.3	19.9
New York	21.6	32.4	34.6	11.5
Chicago	27.1	39.8	30.2	2.9
Philadelphia	38.3	38.8	18.4	4.4

Source: Earl Hanson and Paul Beckett, *Los Angeles: Its People and Its Homes.*

percent of all new American housing units were classified as single-family dwellings. By 1970, the overall population density of American urban areas nearly matched that of Los Angeles in 1940. Los Angeles therefore paved the way for other cities. Because it grew during an era of advanced technology, it could deconcentrate sooner and more fully than other metropolises. Nevertheless, most other urban areas in the United States eventually imitated it at least in part, no matter how much they may wish to deny it.[14]

The expansion of Los Angeles' suburbs lowered residential densities by distributing residents across the countryside. Streetcar and interurban lines first encouraged this process by connecting the central business district with the periphery. As the city grew, so did the suburbs and the number of people entering the downtown district. As the primary economic center in the region, the city center served as a focal point for the entire county. Los Angeles thus remained a highly centralized city despite the booming suburban development. Before 1940, more people traveled between the city center and the suburbs than between the suburbs themselves.

Initially, the adoption of the automobile did not alter these transportation patterns. Cars did allow people to move

Plates 11 and 12. Plate 11 shows that by 1921 building in Los Angeles had reached the Hancock Park area, approximately four miles west of the central business district.

into previously inaccessible areas between the railway tracks and beyond the existing boundaries of the built environment. Nevertheless, the economy continued to revolve around the Los Angeles central business district. Even the Major Traffic Street Plan reflected the region's centralized urban structure with most of its proposed thoroughfares leading into the city's downtown area. At the onset of the twenties, Los Angeles County consisted of a dominant central business district and adjacent industrial area surrounded by satellite cities and extensive residential suburbs.

The automobile and the truck, however, eventually worked together to dramatically change this spatial structure. After 1920 an increasing number of people began to use their cars for daily transportation. In addition, Los Angeles experienced another one of its periodic population booms, leading to heavy congestion in and around the city center.

Plate 12 illustrates how just nine years later Los Angeles had begun to develop its sprawling configuration. A huge population influx during the twenties, the desire of urban residents to live in single-family dwellings, and the availability of the automobile all contributed to the city's spatial orientation. (Courtesy of Spence Air Photo Collection, Department of Geography, University of California, Los Angeles)

Street improvements such as the Major Traffic Street Plan helped at first, but by 1930 traffic once again worsened. Concerned citizens and public officials worried about the consequences of this congestion. As early as 1930, Donald Baker insisted that the central business district had reached a saturation point. He feared that the area was approaching gridlock. E. E. East, an engineer for the Automobile Club of Southern California, agreed. "With per capita use of the automobile increasing," he wrote, "the prospect of future traffic congestion is appalling unless some means are found to develop a genuine, stable system of streets for these automobiles to use."[15]

Although a high proportion of people continued to work in the downtown area during the twenties, it became increasingly difficult to get there because the rapid population growth and increased automobile usage had outstripped the city's ability to open up new thoroughfares. Prior to 1930, for instance, it took only thirty minutes for a PE interurban to travel from Santa Monica to downtown Los Angeles. By 1940, the same trip required an hour by rail and forty minutes by car. Furthermore, the parking issue had never really gone away following the controversy of 1920. People managed to cope with the situation mainly because the owners of obsolete real estate in the central business district had demolished their buildings to open off-street parking lots.[16] Despite the fact that Los Angeles by 1940 had more off-street parking establishments than any other city, the demand for spaces far exceeded the supply. Downtown merchants feared that this lack of parking would turn shoppers away from the central retail district and encourage yet more decentralization. "The failure to provide parking in a business area is to deny access to motor vehicle users," warned a traffic consultant. John Bullock, owner of the Bullock's Department Store, decided in 1928 to locate a major branch of his company on Wilshire Boulevard, a few miles west of the downtown commercial district. Not only was this store close to suburban customers, it was well removed from the congestion of the central business district. Patrons using their automobiles could quickly and easily drive to it. Bullock's Wilshire was therefore constructed facing a large parking lot that provided motorists free automobile storage while shopping. These considerations made the store a favorite with suburban customers.[17]

Bullock's success convinced many department store executives to locate branches in outlying areas to bolster their sales. Within five years, 88 percent of all new retail stores were built in the suburbs. "People couldn't get down town to do business," Donald Baker noted, "so business moved out to meet them." This trend towards commercial decentralization was dramatically reflected in the changing distribution of retail activity within the region. As late as 1929, three-quarters of all department store sales in Los

Plate 13. Congestion on the streets leading into the city center and the rise of modern suburbs encouraged the decentralization of retail establishments. Typical of this movement into the periphery were grocery stores similar to the one illustrated above. This post–World War II shop was located in the San Fernando Valley. (Courtesy of Security Pacific National Bank Photograph Collection/Los Angeles Public Library)

Angeles County occurred inside the city's central business district. Clearly, downtown Los Angeles dominated the local economy. Ten years later, the city center could only claim a 54 percent market share of department store revenue. By this time, many observers reported the pronounced growth of business districts in suburban areas such as the Wilshire District, the San Fernando Valley, Westwood, and Hollywood. The individual freedom afforded by the automobile had "stimulated growth away from the center." Major intersections throughout the metropolitan area now boasted substantial retail centers. "The so-called central business center," E. E. East concluded, "is rapidly becoming just another center, with few notable characteristics to differentiate it from others." Following World War II, the city center's decline steepened. By 1956, downtown department stores could muster only 23 percent of all department store sales in the county.[18]

Another source of economic decentralization came from the industrial sector. Prior to the invention of the truck, businesses in cities throughout the United States built their warehousing and manufacturing facilities close to the central business district. They did so because of the inefficiencies of short-haul freight transportation. The invention of the streetcar provided relatively fast passenger transport and allowed a certain amount of residential dispersion. The movement of goods within the city, however, continued to rely upon antiquated horse-drawn carts. As the population of cities grew, crowding within the downtown districts of these towns increased, resulting in a general rise in land prices in central business districts. Manufacturers of heavy goods could sometimes move their factories to cheaper peripheral land near the intersection of several railroad lines. Such factories relied upon the railroads to deliver bulky raw material and to ship out large quantities of finished goods. Warehouses and distribution centers, however, had to remain near the core because retailers and other companies required local deliveries. The slowness and inefficiencies of the large horse-drawn wagons therefore contributed to the centralized nature of late nineteenth- and early twentieth-century cities, and ensured that economic deconcentration would lag several years behind residential dispersal.[19]

The invention and later refinement of the truck allowed a dramatic alteration in the spatial orientation of economic activity within cities. The first trucks, which appeared sometime around 1910, disappointed many people because of their fragile construction and their solid tires that destroyed the pavement. The invention of the pneumatic tire shortly before World War I, however, made trucks far more attractive for freight delivery. Improvements in design also allowed trucks to carry nearly four times as much as horse-drawn wagons, and at faster speeds. By 1918, it also appeared that companies could operate trucks at about one-half the cost of a horse-drawn cart. Moreover, domestic transportation problems during World War I pressed many trucks into duty with remarkable success. "The value of the motor truck vehicle," wrote the Los Angeles Board of Public Utilities commissioners, "was soon recognized as a cheap and expeditious mode of transportation by not only the merchants and manufacturers of Los Angeles . . . but by the farmer, dairyman, and producer of perishable commodities."[20]

Their success during the war encouraged the widespread use of trucks during the peace that followed. In 1910 there were only 10,100 trucks registered in the United States. Ten years later, that number had increased more than 100 times to 1,107,600. By 1930, nearly 3,675,000 trucks traveled the American highways. The reasons for this phenomenal rise in truck usage seemed obvious to Angelenos. Trucks could service areas previously ignored by the railroads. They could also move goods within the metropolitan area more efficiently than by rail or wagon and at a lower cost. "Motor trucks are solving haulage problems that in the past have been the reason for limited expansion of business, industries and building," noted one Los Angeles businessman in 1919. The Los Angeles *Times* remarked that many freight operators had found it both inexpensive and fast to move goods by truck between Los Angeles and such nearby cities as Pasadena and Burbank. "All night long," reported the newspaper, "long strings of trucks can be seen on any of the local boulevards carrying supplies to every town in the south." As early as 1920, the truck began to dominate local freight transportation. "The railroads are up against a tough proposition," argued a visiting New York salesman in 1920. "All through the country the trucks are taking the shorthauls and as a result the railroads are losing much business. There is no two ways about it, the railroad cannot compete with the truck for short distance hauling."[21]

The adoption of the truck for inner-city transportation came at a propitious time in Los Angeles' history. Prior to World War I, southern California's economy depended almost exclusively on agriculture and tourism. As an industrial area, Los Angeles fell far behind its West Coast rival San Francisco with a meager $68.6 million output of manufactured goods. After 1920, however, the region emerged as the leading industrial center in the West. The booming population growth in the southland, combined with its excellent artificial harbor, transportation facilities, and nearby oil deposits, attracted substantial investment capital. Many midwestern and eastern firms established their West Coast headquarters and factories in Los Angeles during the twenties. Not coincidentally, many automobile- and oil-related companies were among those opening operations in southern California. By 1929, Los Angeles' manufacturing output had risen to $1.3 billion.[22]

Those companies erecting new factories during the twenties often built their facilities on the periphery of the city. The introduction of such mass-production techniques as the continuous assembly line required large one-story structures on an ample parcel of land. Warehouses and distribution centers also found that new material-handling innovations such as the forklift and conveyor belt worked best inside a single-story building. The rise in land prices in the city center by this time prohibited the construction of low-rise plants there. The availability of the automobile and truck, however, encouraged newly arrived companies to locate their plants in the suburbs. Trucks could easily move goods between factories and retail establishments, while the widespread use of the automobile in Los Angeles allowed these businesses to tap a vast labor force. By 1938, 71.7 percent of all employees working in factories outside of the downtown

Plate 14. The development of the truck and automobile allowed many manufacturing firms to build modern one-story plants in the suburbs where inexpensive land was available in large quantities. The photograph above shows an aircraft assembly plant in El Segundo. (Courtesy of Los Angeles City Archives)

area drove their cars to work. Only 20 percent of the laborers used public transportation. The rest walked.[23]

This general trend also held true for oil refineries in Los Angeles and Orange Counties. People had long known that the southern California landscape held large deposits of oil. But it was not until the demand for oil greatly expanded during the first two decades of the twentieth century that oil companies began to actively develop the region's mineral deposits. Cities and refineries sprang up around the petroleum fields and helped establish an important industrial base in the areas outside of the city of Los Angeles. Within a few years, southern California was producing 5 percent of the world petroleum supply. At the turn of the century, refineries in such remote areas as Whittier and Fullerton had to recruit workers from among the local residents settling near the fields. Most of the major production activity, however, occurred after the close of World War I. Refineries built after the war could attract workers from all over the southern California basin because of the automobile.[24]

Figures 4 and 5 dramatically illustrate the realignment of southern California's urban industrial space. The first map shows the location of factories in 1924. By this time, Los Angeles' heavy rail network had developed to the point where manufacturers could build factories outside the city center. The motor truck had also begun to provide short-haul freight transportation. In the meantime, land prices in the central business district had risen to the point where only high-rise office building construction made sense there. Industry consequently had several incentives to migrate away from the downtown area and, by the mid-twenties, manufacturing and distribution facilities had begun to expand into South Central Los Angeles. Nevertheless, figure 4 demonstrates that the city remained highly centralized, with most factories situated in the region immediately surrounding the central business district. The process of economic decentralization had begun, however, and businesses experienced tremendous freedom in locating their facilities.

The impact of these changes may be seen in figure 5. By 1960, the Los Angeles metropolitan area contained several different industrial districts well removed from the downtown district. Trucks by this time provided not only short-haul freight delivery but long-distance transportation. With the exception of heavy industry, manufacturing concerns no longer had to maintain rail access to their buildings. The availability of efficient transportation, the ability of workers to drive their automobiles to suburban industrial centers, and the vast expanses of relatively inexpensive land combined to encourage economic decentralization. This same trend occurred in cities throughout the United States.

LOCATION OF INDUSTRY [1924]

Railroads

Street railways

Plants employing
over 25

Fig. 4. Location of Industrial Plants Employing More than 25 Persons in 1924. *Source*: Dudley Pegrum, *Urban Transport and the Location of Industry in Metropolitan Los Angeles.* (Courtesy of The Regents of the University of California)

Between 1948 and 1963, employment in the twenty-five largest American metropolitan areas grew fastest outside the central city. Suburban communities saw nothing less than an economic boom during this period with manufacturing, trade, and service jobs increasing between 61 and 135 percent.[25]

The decentralization of retail and industrial facilities occurred in part because of the heavy congestion in the central business district. Although a large number of Angelenos continued to work in the city center, it had become increasingly difficult to get there. The Major Traffic Street Plan had widened many streets and opened new thorough-

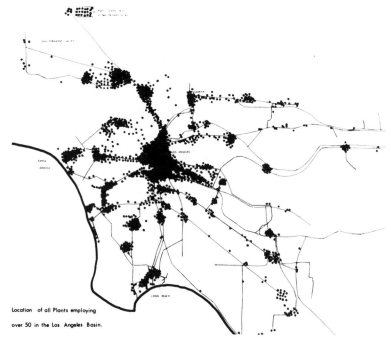

Fig. 5. Location of Industrial Plants Employing More than 50 Persons in 1960. *Source*: Dudley Pegrum, *Urban Transport and the Location of Industry in Metropolitan Los Angeles.* (Courtesy of The Regents of the University of California)

fares. This may have improved access, but it also encouraged more people to abandon the streetcars in favor of their automobiles. As traffic saturation reached alarming proportions, it became doubtful that the roads leading into the downtown area could handle many more vehicles. These problems, together with the other factors discussed earlier, encouraged economic decentralization.[26]

The outward movement of industry and shops in turn altered the transportation patterns within the metropolitan region. Prior to this phenomenon, most vehicular and rail traffic focused on the central business district. People traveled into and out of the city center but did not move between suburbs. Later, the migration of businesses to the outlying districts discouraged this tendency to enter the city center. Table 6 shows the increasing saturation and changing composition of vehicles entering the downtown area between 1923 and 1941. During a typical twelve-hour period in 1923, 605,000 people arrived in the central business district by automobile and streetcar. That constituted 40 percent of the entire metropolitan population, indicating the highly centralized nature of the region. Most of those people reached the downtown district by rail. Eight years later, the total number of residents traveling to the city center had increased only 15.2 percent, at a time when the city's population had nearly doubled. These 697,000 Angelenos who entered the downtown area daily now accounted for only 30 percent of the metropolitan population. By that time, fully 62 percent of those arriving in the city center did so in automobiles. Over the next ten years, the composition of traffic entering the central business district remained the same. In real and relative terms, however, fewer people traveled to the downtown area in 1941 than in 1931.[27]

Although there still existed a significant amount of radial movement into the central business district, this tendency began to weaken during the thirties as traffic increased in the outlying areas. By 1939, those people living in the suburbs traveled downtown far less frequently than those residing near the city center. Nearly 40 percent of all Angelenos located within a radius of 2.5 miles from the central business district entered that district every day. That percentage dropped off quickly thereafter to the point where only 15 percent of those living 7.5 to 10 miles outside of the downtown area bothered to visit that district on a daily basis. Comparable data does not exist for earlier periods, but one would expect that prior to economic decentralization far more people would have made the daily trip into the center of the city. Table 7 provides some support for this argument by showing the increase in traffic in four different

Table 6

Persons Entering the CBD During a Typical Twelve-Hour Weekday: Los Angeles Cordon Count

	1923		1931		1941	
By Rail	315,000	(52%)	262,000	(38%)	246,000	(38%)
By Auto	290,000	(48%)	435,000	(62%)	396,000	(62%)
Total	605,000		697,000		642,000	
Total as a % of County Population		40%		41%		22%

Source: Donald Baker, *Report on Rapid Transit System.*

CBD = Central Business District

Table 7

Increase in Traffic by Zones, 1930–1937

	Increase in Traffic	Actual Number of Vehicles Counted
CBD	7.8%	573,000
Outer Congested District	17.5%	727,000
Residential District	28.2%	854,000
Suburban District	52.9%	464,000

Source: Automobile Club of Southern California, *Survey, Los Angeles Metropolitan Area.*

CBD = Central Business District

zones between 1930 and 1937. The number of persons entering each district increased most dramatically in those furthest from the city center. Traffic, for instance, rose only slightly inside the central business district during this period, whereas congestion in the outermost suburbs increased by more than 50 percent.

Many of the emerging commercial areas developed without adequate railway connections to the central business district, or with each other. Richard Sachse noted that this left commuters and shoppers moving between these suburban business districts wholly dependent upon the automobile for transportation. This accounts for the dramatic rise in suburban automobile traffic.[28] Table 8 clearly illustrates this point by showing that most of the traffic found in suburban business centers was comprised of automobiles. The table shows the composition of traffic in the central business district and three suburban shopping districts. By 1941, slightly more than half of all visitors to the city center arrived by automobile. In the suburbs, the percentage of automobile users rose dramatically to as much as 87 percent. People traveling to regional centers such as Westwood and Pomona depended upon their cars both because congestion in these

Table 8
Traffic Count in Four Business Districts, 1941

	CBD		Long Beach	
By Auto	482,000	(54.9%)	127,000	(63.5%)
By Railway	275,000	(31.4%)	27,000	(13.5%)
By Foot	120,000	(13.7%)	46,000	(23.0%)
Total	877,000		200,000	
	Pomona		Westwood	
By Auto	36,000	(82.5%)	47,360	(87.1%)
By Railway	670	(1.5%)	4,000	(7.4%)
By Foot	7,000	(16.0%)	3,000	(5.5%)
Total	43,670		54,360	

Source: Regional Planning Commission, *Business Districts.*

Note: Data based on a 16-hour traffic count

CBD = Central Business District

areas was relatively light and because they had few alternative means of transport.

The most remarkable alteration in the region's traffic pattern by the late thirties, however, was the now apparently random travel of the city's autoists. No longer did the flow of automobiles and streetcars converge on the central business district. Earlier in the century, the development of suburbs merely meant that commuters and shoppers had to travel a bit farther to reach the city center. Later, the severe traffic congestion on arteries leading into the downtown area, the development of residential and commercial tracts in the suburbs, and the freedom of automobile transit encouraged people to avoid the central business district altogether. Shoppers and commuters now moved freely throughout the metropolitan area creating a mass of confusion. E. E. East described the city's traffic movement as "a million automobiles moving in a million different directions, with their paths of travel conflicting at a million intersections, a million times a day."

An Automobile Club survey in 1937 noted the tangled state of southern California's automobile movement. Figure 6, which originally appeared in the report, dramatically illustrates the new traffic pattern found in 1937 as motorists drove freely between the various subcenters in the area. "The relation which formally existed between the home and place of occupation has almost, if not completely disappeared," the Automobile Club reported. "There are few points of origin and destination common to any appreciable number of vehicles found in any section of the Los Angeles area."[29] This was a radically new departure in the urban structure. Suburbs had appeared in American cities as early as the nineteenth century, but the city center had remained the hub of the region. Los Angeles after 1920, however, began to develop several focal points. It was this transition from the centralized city to the multifocal urban struc-

Plate 15. Westwood Village developed as an important suburban business and residential center during the late twenties. Its wide streets and easy access facilitated automobile traffic to the point where more than 85 percent of those visiting the district arrived by car. The photograph above shows the intersection of Wilshire and Westwood boulevards in 1936. (Courtesy of Security Pacific National Bank Photograph Collection/Los Angeles Public Library)

ture that marked the arrival of the modern decentralized metropolis.

Historian Kenneth Jackson notes that the processes that transformed Los Angeles before World War II also operated elsewhere throughout the United States.[30] Although Angelenos adopted the automobile as their primary means of urban transportation earlier than residents of most other cities, the use of cars for daily commuting was hardly unique to southern California. Workers in Los Angeles did, however, rely upon their cars more heavily than other urban dwellers. Historian Joel Tarr, for instance, has found that in 1934 streetcars carried far more people to work in Pittsburgh than did autos. At a time when 45 percent of all chief wage earners in that city owned a car, 49 percent rode the trolleys to work, 28 percent walked, and only 20 percent drove their own vehicles.[31] Jackson cites a 1933 study of sixty-eight urban areas which generally confirms Tarr's conclusions. Still, a significant number of commuters in cities other than Los Angeles drove to their places of employment. This trend increased following the Depression. Once the housing industry got back on its feet during the late thirties, nearly all new residential construction took place in the periphery. Only World War II with its various shortages forestalled this building pattern. Later during the fifties, the inner-city population began to fall in many cities while the suburbs experienced booming population rises. Coinciding with this rush to the suburbs was an increasingly heavy dependence on the automobile. By 1970, 81.4 percent of all American urban households owned an automobile.[32] Los Angeles may have led the way in automobile usage, but the rest of the country soon followed.

In his recent book, *Crabgrass Frontier*, Jackson sought to explain the underlying reasons behind this nation's remarkable suburban growth. Jackson concluded that America's adherence to the suburban ideal and its rapid urban population growth set the stage for residential dispersion, whereas various economic and social conditions actually caused it. Americans, he argued, had long searched for a balance between the tranquillity of the countryside and the economic necessities provided by the city. At the same time, a continuous influx of new residents badly strained the delivery of urban services. These factors created a desire on the part of many residents to move into the less-congested suburbs.

The actual impetus for this movement resulted from racial prejudice and technological innovation. A flood of rural blacks, Hispanics, and foreign immigrants throughout the nineteenth and twentieth centuries convinced many Anglos to flee the inner city for independent suburban communities. Once there, these citizens pursued both the suburban ideal and racial exclusion. These residents could do so because of

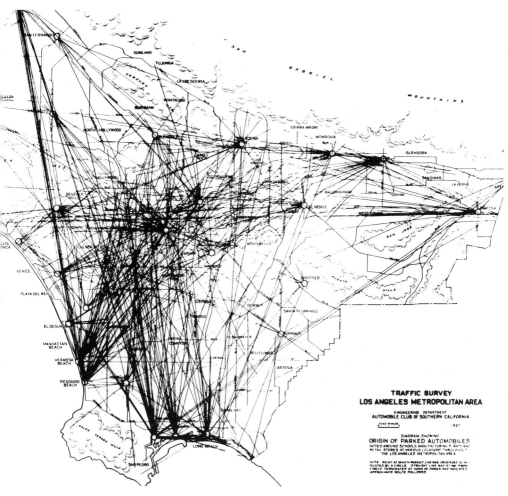

Fig. 6. Origin of Parked Automobiles in Southern California, 1937. *Source*: Automobile Club of Southern California, *Traffic Survey, Los Angeles Metropolitan Area, 1937*. (Courtesy of Automobile Club of Southern California)

various economic factors including the availability of inexpensive land and housing as well as technological inventions such as the streetcar and automobile.[33] These transportation innovations became the means by which middle-class Americans could satisfy their desire to live on the periphery. One should add to this analysis the importance of the truck in shaping the modern American city. Businesses now could move their factories, warehouses, and retail shops to the suburbs. There they could take advantage of low land prices, efficient one-story industrial building designs, and an increasingly mobile labor force. It was, in fact, the movement of economic activity to the suburbs which completed the decentralization of the modern urban structure.

The Road to Autopia

=

If the street cars were to stop, life would go on about as usual. But if automobiles were to suddenly cease to function, the whole economic and social structure would be disrupted.
—Ed Ainsworth
1938

Shall we subsidize, at great and continuing expense to the public treasury, rapid transit rail facilities affording comparatively low-grade and unprofitable mass transportation? Or shall we, out of public funds made available by the generous contributions of street users themselves, provide adequate, safe, efficient, and modern traffic facilities so that automobile users will provide their own transportation of a high character at their own operating costs?
—Miller McClintock
1937

y the late twenties, most American urban planners embraced the automobile as a positive force in society. The automobile, they believed, could once and for all change the spatial organization of the metropolis. No longer would urban dwellers have to suffer from the crowded and unhealthful conditions of the walking city. Streetcars had given Americans a glimpse of the suburban ideal. Now it appeared that the automobile could fulfill the promise of residential dispersion. Furthermore, by opening subdivisions well removed from the city center, the automobile could lower population densities at the core and thus ease the burden on the urban infrastructure. The automobile therefore seemed to offer a solution to many of the problems facing city planning commissions at the time. Given the enthusiastic response to the automobile, it is not surprising that the profession sought to facilitate its use. "The future city will be spread out," reasoned Cambridge planner John Nolen. "It will be regional, it will be the natural product of the automobile, the good road, electricity, the telephone, and the radio, combined with the growing desire to live a more natural, biological life under pleasanter and more natural conditions."[1]

Ten years later, some planners began to sense that something had gone wrong. Although decentralization had taken place as planned, it left behind it the signs of urban decay. Planners who had earlier championed the benefits of dispersion now worried about the effect of deconcentration on the central business district. The flight of industry and retail stores to the suburbs, when combined with the deleterious impact of the Depression, left many city centers blighted and crippled. Automobile congestion in downtown areas further contributed to these problems by slowing the flow of goods and people within cities. By 1932, Harland Bartholomew, who had once preached the gospel of decentralization, began to argue that America needed "a real effort to prevent [the] endless spread of population with its concomitant disintegration of the larger central areas of cities." Even more distressing was the appearance of traffic congestion in suburban shopping centers. Poor highway planning and commercial zoning encouraged the development of crowded regional centers, which soon experienced their own transportation problems. By 1929, real estate developer Jesse Nichols could argue that "throughout the land the present-day congestion problem of our central business areas is being repeated in scores of outlying places throughout every large city." Once these centers became too crowded, shoppers began searching for new developments. An area that had fallen into disfavor quickly declined. A Los Angeles civil engineer warned in 1937 that "each of the *outlying* centers, whether large or small, also had its little ring of blight or potential blight."[2]

It had become apparent by the late thirties that street widening alone could no longer provide adequate relief from the mounting congestion. Planners, government officials, and others therefore turned to expressways as a solution to their traffic problems. Limited access highways proved popular in large cities throughout the United States because they satisfied the apparent needs of the most powerful segments of society. Downtown business interests favored freeways because they believed that the new roadways would improve access to the central business district and thus halt its decline. Suburban property owners supported expressways because they promised to ease congestion in both outlying shopping centers and in the city center. Planners, moreover, argued that these superhighways would allow sensible city planning by reestablishing distinct traffic patterns and forestalling the further deterioration of older business districts. Finally, the availability of public funds from user charges such as gasoline taxes made the freeways extremely attractive to city officials. They saw the expressway as a practical solution to the issue of congestion and seized upon it as a panacea for many of their cities' most pressing concerns. By the late forties, American metropolitan areas such as New York, Chicago, Detroit, and Los Angeles had made important strides in constructing expressway systems.[3]

The economic and residential dispersion prevalent in Los Angeles after 1920 greatly altered traffic patterns within the county. Unfortunately, these changes also led to even worse automobile congestion. Crosstown traffic now tried to move on a system of streets that radiated from the city center. Even though the Major Traffic Street Plan had opened some lateral highways, they could not handle the increasing vehicular movement in the suburbs. Even more alarming was the rise in congestion in business districts outside of the downtown area. Recently opened thoroughfares would attract autoists seeking uncrowded routes. At the same time, homeowners along these streets would sell out to commercial interests because families did not want to live near the noise and pollution of busy streets, while businessmen sought to open retail shops on major arteries. Once businesses sprang up along the new streets, local shopping traffic mixed with through traffic. Vehicles constantly slowed as consumers moved in and out of curbside parking spaces. Roadside development, then, greatly reduced the capacity of Los Angeles' highways. Conditions became so bad that traffic on some thoroughfares moved at a crawl. As commercial areas began to experience heavy congestion, shoppers searched elsewhere for less crowded developments. Business districts subsequently grew and stagnated shortly thereafter at an alarming rate. "You have only to drive along some of the 'business streets' to see the weather-beaten, deserted shells of what were once the fond hopes of property owners for a productive business section," reported a city official during the early forties.[4]

The central business district, however, suffered the most from this process. The movement of commercial concerns out of the city center and its adjacent industrial area destabilized land values. City officials estimated that commercial properties in the downtown district lost $25,000,000 in assessed value between 1934 and 1939. Although the Depression surely must have caused some of this decline, the City Planning Department attributed it to the effects of decentralization. Residential areas near the city center were also affected by dispersion. The exodus of middle-class residents left those districts near the downtown area to poorer ethnic groups. Poverty and absentee landlords subsequently allowed housing conditions in these sections to deteriorate.

Although most southern California planners argued that decentralization was ultimately "a healthy trend which has been evidenced to a lesser degree in all other large metropolitan centers," they worried that the rapid, premature movement of business into the suburbs would threaten the stability of the area and result in economic loss. The metropolitan region had to maintain the health and vitality of established centers, they contended, "otherwise the entire city will lose tax dollars, civic spirit and enterprise." Social critics worried that "the great distances residents must travel in the course of ordinary business and social engagements have caused incalculable losses of time, money, and energy," while others found the rapid deterioration of recently established shopping centers wasteful.[5]

Decentralization also threatened the efficiency of the automobile, now by far the major means of transportation in the suburbs. "The Los Angeles area has grown up with the automobile," Automobile Club executives wrote. "Motor vehicle transportation has shaped its growth to the extent that the business and social life of the area is today vitally dependent upon the motor vehicle for the major part of its transportation." Although the future orderly growth of the city depended upon the continued use of the automobile, a newspaper reporter in 1938 argued that the city found itself faced with the "peril of stagnation and atrophy." Los Angeles, he claimed, was literally gagging on its own traffic congestion. With at least 80 percent of the city's daily transportation needs being supplied by the privately owned car, Los Angeles once again had to find a way to facilitate its automobile movement. "If the street cars were to stop, life would go on about as usual," the reporter argued. "But if automobiles were to suddenly cease to function, the whole economic and social structure would be disrupted."[6]

Previous efforts to solve the city's traffic congestion focused upon increasing the extent and capacity of the street system. Although the Major Traffic Street Plan had at one time greatly improved circulation, it had not been expanded much since the late twenties. Besides, it had become apparent to transportation experts that street improvements acted as mere palliatives. Los Angeles was now at the point where it could no longer solve its problems by widening or extending the existing roads. The attempt to serve both through and local traffic on the same highway, not the lack in the number or breadth of streets, was at the root of the problem.[7]

In 1937, the Automobile Club of Southern California suggested a solution to the area's crowded traffic conditions. It agreed with others that the region could secure little improvement in congestion by extending the existing highway and street system. Newly opened highways merely attracted commercial use that interfered with vehicular flow. Rather, it proposed a "network of traffic routes for the exclusive use of motor vehicles over which there shall be no crossing at grade and along which there shall be no interference from land use activities." Such a system of roads uninterrupted by traffic signals or intersections would allow high-speed automobile transit throughout the city (see fig. 7). Here was an answer to the decades-long fight with congestion, the club's supporters argued. Residents could live in one area of the city and work in another. These motorways would also end the wasteful deterioration of business centers and preserve land values by providing easy access. They would further allow city officials to plan intelligently for future growth. Most importantly, the parkways would improve the automobile's efficiency as a means of urban transportation.[8]

The Automobile Club's proposal became the initial impetus to the development of what would later be known as the freeways. This was hardly an original suggestion. As early as 1930, city planner Frederick Law Olmsted, Jr., had proposed a system of parkways similar to the one put forth by the club. Other planning agencies soon followed Olmsted in calling for expressways throughout the thirties. None, however, outlined such a network of motorways as boldly or in such detail as the Automobile Club. Its careful collection and analysis of traffic statistics and its fervent report stimulated a lengthy discussion that eventually led to the adoption of a limited-access freeway system as the apparent solution to the region's transportation problem.[9]

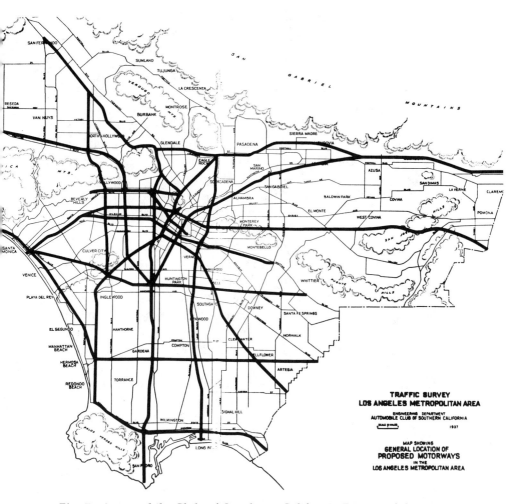

Fig. 7. Automobile Club of Southern California Proposed System of Motorways. *Source*: Automobile Club of Southern California, *Traffic Survey, Los Angeles Metropolitan Area, 1937.* (Courtesy of Automobile Club of Southern California)

The Automobile Club report was inspired by the general agreement that the city needed a traffic study. Los Angeles had recovered from the Depression more quickly than other cities in the United States. By the time the Automobile Club published its findings in 1937, the region had returned to prosperity and once again it became feasible to talk of improving the area's transportation facilities. Almost everyone concerned with civic issues at the time agreed that the region required a government-sponsored transit survey to recommend methods for improving traffic conditions. "The need for the survey becomes more apparent each day as business improves and more people move about," argued the Central Business District Association's annual report.[10] Concern for the region's transit problems finally culminated in a year-long traffic study conducted by the city engineer's office.

The survey emerged out of the Central Business District Association's earlier attempt to secure funding from the federal government's Public Works Administration. Organized in 1924, the association represented business, financial, and property interests in the downtown area. For many years the group had maintained an interest in transportation and traffic matters affecting the city center. Dismayed over the increasing economic dispersion throughout the metropolitan area, the association hoped that a transit study would offer specific solutions to the congestion in the downtown district, and hence the problem of decentralization. After several years of negotiations, city officials working in conjunction with the association convinced the federal government to grant the city $90,000 to pay the salaries of those working for such a survey. The Works Progress Administration, however, insisted that the city contribute an additional $20,000 in materials and engineering costs. After the City Council balked at this final requirement, private citizens and organizations founded the Citizen's Transportation Survey Committee. Led by its president P. G. Winnett, a prominent Los Angeles businessman, the committee raised the necessary money from the local industrial and retail community.[11]

Having secured the required funds, a Transportation Engineering Board appointed by the mayor commenced the study. Engineers from city and county governments and private consulting firms made up the commission. It hoped to develop a progressive transportation plan for the entire metropolitan area. The board sought to serve all interested parties in reaching a consensus, including motorists, street-car patrons, commercial interests, property owners, pedestrians, and the traction companies. Most of all, it wanted a strategy that could begin immediately to improve traffic conditions.[12]

A year later, with the survey completed, the board issued its findings. The study confirmed many of the Automobile Club's conclusions. Travel in Los Angeles was slow and arduous. Streetcars within ten miles of the central business district moved at an average speed of only 11 to 15 miles per hour, while automobiles spent nearly 30 percent of their transit time waiting at intersections. Although the commission believed that the ultimate solution to the problems of urban transportation lay in rapid-rail lines, it concluded that the construction of an expressway system was the only viable solution that the city could immediately put into effect. The board members did not doubt that Los Angeles would eventually have to build a rapid-transit system, but while the region's population density remained low, and the financing of such a system difficult, expressways would serve as a satisfactory solution to the area's transportation problems. The board consequently recommended that the city adopt a freeway plan for the metropolitan region. Since it was unlikely that the city could afford to complete the entire system at once, the plan could guide future development and assure the coordination of a comprehensive network.[13]

The board used the term "express highway" to describe its road system. During the next few years, government officials and others would use several other names, including "parkway" and "expressway," before settling upon the term "freeway." All of these labels were used more or less synonymously. They described a highway free from intersections throughout its length, providing nonstop travel for automobiles and buses. Such roadways would crisscross the county and offer motorists a "continuous flow of traffic, uninterrupted by signal lights or cross traffic and hence make possible sustained speed with safety and high capacity with minimum driving strain." Most important, these express-ways would separate through traffic from local congestion. Recent state legislation allowed government officials to limit access to both the use of these new highways and the land abutting them. The board specifically recommended that the city take advantage of this recent legislation by keeping the shoulders of the parkway free from development. Commer-cial enterprises would not spring up alongside the freeways and impede traffic as in the past because "reasonably rapid transit over substantial distances can be attained only by vehicles operated on routes free from interference of cross-traffic and the resulting delays of traffic signal control."[14]

The board published a map of the proposed express-way routes which later became the basis of today's existing freeway system. Board members believed that their proposal would ameliorate several related problems. First, they ex-pected the freeways to relieve the region's current congestion problems. Second, they felt that their comprehensive plan would tie together existing parkway projects. Two sections of freeways were currently under construction through the Cahuenga Pass and the Arroyo Seco. The State Highway Division had begun building these highways during the late thirties to provide motor routes between the downtown dis-trict and the San Fernando Valley and Pasadena. The board's plan would connect these independent expressways with others in a comprehensive network. Such a system would free the local streets from through traffic and ease congestion in general.

Public transportation also received the board's atten-tion. Viewing rapid transit as an inevitability, the engineers argued that eventually Los Angeles would have to follow eastern cities in constructing subways and elevateds. The metropolitan region's low population density, however, did not at that time warrant the high costs necessitated by rail construction. The PE and the LARY certainly could not afford to erect their own mass transportation system. Nor was the public willing to do so. The board therefore suggested that the city might have to purchase the existing rail lines to create a municipal system even though the public did not want to saddle itself with two failing transit companies. It consequently deemed it inappropriate to recommend rail construction at that time. The board did, however, suggest that buses could use the expressways and in that way provide some measure of rapid transit for the region.

Various civic interests in the metropolitan area coalesced in support of the expressway system, mainly because each group believed it would solve its own problems. Those planners who favored decentralization as a solution to the urban ills of dense, compact cities contended that the freeway network would allow rapid automobile movement between major urban centers. This, they remarked, would solve the two most vexing aspects of decentralization—traffic congestion and unstable land values. The freeways, then, were essential to their vision of a modern, uncrowded metropolis composed of single-family dwellings and pastoral beauty. Planners also saw the parkway network as a future tool of their profession. The freeways would permanently establish the region's transportation routes, they argued. Planners could therefore use the expressways to direct the future development of the metropolitan area along the lines of these corridors. "Opportunity is presented to adjust the entire city pattern to the parkway routes," wrote a city engineer. This would assure "the orderly future development of the City and the stabilization of property values."[15]

E. E. East of the Automobile Club agreed. He noted that transportation technology had greatly affected Los Angeles' urban development. The railways had defined the centralized nature of the city's spatial structure at the turn of the century. The automobile, however, had broken the streetcar's influence over the built environment. Without permanent transportation patterns, the city could not control land use. That lack of control, he insisted, would result in a sprawling, unplanned, and inefficient city. East contended that the freeways could offer a solution by once again establishing the area's transportation lanes, which were "essential to the orderly growth of an efficient and fully satisfying urban community." In his mind, there was no doubt that urban transportation would "shape the pattern of the city of tomorrow."[16]

Ironically, those who disliked decentralization also supported the proposed freeway system. Businessmen and property owners in the downtown district had long worried that their domination of the region's economy was waning. As fewer shoppers traveled into the city center, property values fell there. The Central Business District Association had wrestled with this trend for some time, concluding that consumers would return to their shops if the city could provide the public with ready access to the area. Association members therefore supported any measure that might ease congestion near the downtown region.

In the past, the Central Business District Association had championed rail transit as the way to improve traffic on thoroughfares leading into the commercial district. It never altered its stance. Nevertheless, the organization also realized that at the time it was impossible to finance a fixed-rail system. At $4 million a mile, a rail network was prohibitively expensive. After eight years of the Depression, the public would not even consider subsidizing such a project. Commercial interests in the city center therefore threw their support behind the proposed freeway system. Parkways, they hoped, would free the streets from congestion and allow automobile and streetcar traffic to move more freely in the downtown area. Unencumbered by much of the controversy surrounding the traction companies, it was much more likely that the city could begin erecting the motorways immediately. The public might also agree to subsidize these freeways at the same time that it refused to help the railways. It was still unclear as to how the city would pay for the construction, but at $2 million a mile, freeways would cost half as much as subways. Most important, there seemed to be a consensus building in support of the system. With the automobile supplying 80 percent of the county's transportation needs by this time, it seemed likely that the public would consent to some kind of self-imposed tax to pay for the construction costs of the network.

The Central Business District Association also believed that a freeway system could improve public transportation through the use of buses. The city, it argued, should construct special bus stations along the shoulders of the freeways. Although business interests still hoped to establish a rail system at a later date, rapid transit in Los Angeles after 1940 became largely identified with motor coaches utilizing the freeway network. In the meantime, the downtown merchants could wholeheartedly support the expressway proposal because it seemed the quickest and easiest way to renew the city's centralized spatial structure.[17]

Shortly after the Transportation Engineering Board presented its report, the City Council referred the matter to the City Planning Department for its recommendation. The Planning Department acted as a clearinghouse for all proposals regarding the city's physical development. The State Planning Act of 1929, as amended in 1937, ordered all cities to adopt a master plan "to conserve and promote the public health, safety and general welfare." Los Angeles by that time was well on its way to writing a general program for land use and growth within the city. Naturally, the Planning Department wanted to make certain that the freeway proposal was consistent with the city's master plan.[18] The department approved the report in 1941 with only minor revisions. Noting that the present traffic situation was rapidly approaching stagnation, the department's study argued that the city had a unique transportation problem. The region's widely dispersed population and its unusually high rate of automobile ownership meant that "no mass rail rapid transit system could be financially successful in Los Angeles without a substantial subsidy or increase in fares charged." Nor could it wait for the metropolitan area's population density to increase to the point where it could support mass transit. The city therefore had to design its transportation system differently from other cities. "The problem of transportation has grown so serious," the department insisted, "that it can no longer be ignored."[19]

The department acknowledged that the Major Traffic Street Plan, designed nearly twenty years earlier, had successfully improved the city's streets for a time. By 1940, however, the existing system of roadways failed to handle its traffic load. Designed for slow-moving vehicles, it could not act efficiently as a conduit for modern automobiles. Nor could the city improve the situation by widening or opening streets. Not only would the work prove too costly but also would do little to ameliorate such traffic impediments as intersections and abutting commercial development. Nor would such construction end the constant depreciation of property values along heavily traveled streets or reduce the rising number of fatal accidents on the city's highways. "The phenomenal increase in ownership and use of the motor vehicle . . . ," the report concluded, "has necessitated a radical change in the principles governing the design of highways." Only the separation of grades could solve the city's traffic congestion.[20]

A parkway system, as the department called it, would greatly improve circulation throughout the metropolitan area by eliminating the delays and inconveniences of the present system. The separation of grades would also make automobile travel far safer. Arterial routes would connect the central business district and other commercial centers, while crosstown freeways would tie together the outer suburbs.

Most important, the proposed system would stabilize land values and form a "framework about which the entire structure of the city can be more intelligently planned." The Cahuenga Pass and Arroyo Seco parkways were already in operation by this time and were proving highly satisfactory. The city needed to coordinate these freeways with future development as soon as possible. With the institution of the master parkway plan, Los Angeles would be the first American city with a comprehensive expressway system. The department consequently found the Transportation Engineering Board's proposal a "logical, modern and effective solution for the problems of traffic circulation of this highly motorized community." It approved the plan with only minor revisions to reflect changing transportation conditions.[21]

Because of the comprehensive nature of the freeway plan, the City Council had to coordinate its efforts with other governing bodies throughout the metropolitan district.[22] Once the Planning Department had approved the proposal, the Los Angeles County Regional Planning Commission examined the program. Like their city counterparts, the regional planners adopted the Transportation Engineering Board's study with only a few changes. They decided that the proposed network of parkways fulfilled a need articulated several years earlier by both the County Board of Supervisors and automobile users themselves. "All motorists in Los Angeles, and this means all of us, have for many years felt the need for some superior form of motorway in this region to supplement the existing highways," the planners wrote. "There is no doubt that a system of freeways is a necessity for the Los Angeles region."[23]

The Regional Planning Commission supported the plan for several reasons. Like other organizations, it had long realized the importance of separating different types of traffic. A freeway system coordinated with the existing county and city highway system would ameliorate the congestion caused by the indiscriminate mixing of traffic. The grade separation could also reduce automobile accidents. The cost of collisions in human lives and property was much too high, the commission argued. Many accidents occurred because of poor highway design. Narrow pavement, frequent intersections, cross traffic, and commercial frontage all contributed to the high collision rate. Parkways would free through traffic from these interferences, making driving much safer.[24] The commission also favored the metropolitan area's low population density. By supporting the use of single-family dwellings in the past, it had encouraged population dispersal and later decentralization. Now the regional planners worried that "continued decentralization threatens harmful results unless it is planned." An efficient freeway system, however, could preserve the original promise of suburban development. A well-designed subdivision tied to a network of parkways, remarked the commission, could "provide a better way of living and still preserve the social and economic advantages of the urban center."[25]

Finally, the commission expected freeways to stabilize land prices in business centers throughout the county by providing ready access to the outlying residential areas. Still, once motorists reached these districts they had to find readily available parking facilities. Shoppers would otherwise avoid such centers and thus speed the decline of these business districts. The government should, the commission argued, construct parking structures in conjunction with the freeways. In quoting a national transportation study, the planners insisted that "the provision of parking facilities is a public responsibility, and public action should be taken to assure adequate off-street accommodations as a part of the urban highway plan."[26]

By the time the commissioners had reviewed the freeway proposal, World War II had broken out, halting any further construction.[27] Had the region built a system prior to the war, the federal government could have more efficiently moved men and materiel throughout southern California, now an area with several major defense-related industries. Local governments therefore continued to plan the freeways during the crisis. Although wartime rationing of gasoline and rubber reduced the number of automobiles on the highways during the early forties, the Regional Planning Commission correctly suspected that "the local demands for freeways may soon be more pressing than we have so far dreamed."[28]

Uncertainties surrounding the war also made financial planning for later development impossible. The State Division of Highways in cooperation with city, county, and local governments had undertaken the freeway construction before the war. Although the state's biennial budget allotted gasoline tax monies for special highway projects throughout the state on an ad hoc basis, there was no established funding for parkway construction. The Transportation Engineering Board had suggested toll booths to collect fees from individual users, but other agencies protested that the toll collection would act as a barrier to efficient road use. The regional planners and other officials argued that they had to find a way of establishing a permanent fund for freeway construction because of the large costs involved. The initial development plan of 108 miles of roadways called for a $243,000,000 expenditure. It would take another $160,000,000 to complete the final 103 miles of parkway. Since the government could only build individual sections of the system at a time, it needed a means of raising a continuous stream of income. Without such a fund, the freeways could never be built. Yet local officials could accomplish little until the end of the war.

While local officials and others waxed eloquently over the proposed parkway system, many others continued to support mass transportation. As in the past, the public-transit enthusiasts mainly included downtown businessmen and city officials concerned with the vitality of the central business district. Richard Sachse called for a regional mass-transit plan. Los Angeles, he argued, could not solve its transportation problems by solely relying upon the automobile because of its inefficiency as a means of urban transportation. Still, Sachse recognized that Los Angeles' present rail system was wholly inadequate for the region's transit requirements. The PE and LARY continued to use antiquated cars, which were "noisy, uncomfortable, ugly, and often badly lighted [*sic*] and . . . difficult to use because of the high, steep steps." Public transit's slow speed, indirect routing, and lack of uniform fares, he contended, resulted in extensive patronage losses.[29]

Others agreed that Los Angeles needed improved public transportation. Passenger counts during 1938 noted that each automobile traveling in Los Angeles carried an average of only 1.6 people. Even during the war when gasoline and rubber shortages encouraged car pooling, similar counts recorded a high of only 1.75 persons per car. "This indicates there is great resistance by the motorist to relinquish the freedom of individual movement which he feels is his," commented city officials. Even though streetcars and interurbans could carry more passengers more efficiently, it was becoming apparent that many Angelenos would not use them. "There is sufficient evidence," one report observed, "that any facility to compete with the automobile in Southern California must offer comparable convenience if it is to lighten the burden upon city streets."[30]

By 1940, Sachse believed that the city should assess its property owners to raise funds for a mass-transit system. After all, these homeowners had paid for street construction, why not rapid transit? Sachse noted that the traditional view held that railway passengers themselves should pay for traction service. Now that patronage revenue could never come close to supporting the construction of a rapid-rail system, he felt that the city should subsidize the railways. Here, others disagreed. Even those favoring public transportation realized that they could not equitably finance a rail network.

Property owners had paid for street construction outside their homes because they used those roads. Few of these people would now use a rapid-transit system because of the widespread reliance on the automobile and the lack of correlation between an individual's residence and place of work. Why, they argued, should they subsidize a public-transit system that they would not patronize?[31]

Despite the resistance to financing a rail system, many observers felt that the existing traction companies would continue to operate for some time. The railways, however, had begun to institute major changes including the replacement of streetcars with buses. Railway officials substituted buses for streetcars on many routes because of their greater flexibility and mobility. On crowded streets, motor coaches could move more easily with the flow of automobiles. Buses could also immediately change routes if required to do so; streetcars, of course, required new tracks before they could alter their service. By 1940, the *Times* noted that "the present trend is toward substitution of busses for street cars." Even Sachse believed that buses would "gradually supplant rail lines" in many instances.[32]

This trend was by no means a new one. The PE had begun utilizing motor coaches as early as 1917 to reach newly developed suburbs. The LARY started its bus service in 1923 when it bought 6 motor coaches. By 1930 it had purchased 196 more. In 1925, the LARY and PE jointly established the Los Angeles Motor Coach Company to "meet the emerging demand for more flexible service." Lacking the capital to build new rail lines, the traction companies used buses to serve the areas beyond the reach of their tracks. Buses could also provide public transportation in areas too sparsely populated to justify rail lines. Later, as street congestion worsened in business centers throughout the metropolitan area, the railways began to replace streetcars with buses. Even such champions of mass transit as the Central Business District Association argued that replacing streetcars with buses could make traffic move twice as fast. No longer would mass transit remain tied to tracks in the middle of the street; buses could move from lane to lane and take advantage of their superior mobility. "There is little doubt," the association reported in 1941, "but that the present policy of substituting buses for streetcars will continue in the near future."[33]

Given the movement toward motor coaches and the difficulties of financing a new rapid-rail system, supporters of mass transit found a solution to Los Angeles' transportation problem in the freeways. Public-transit enthusiasts saw little chance of building a rail network in the near future. Buses, however, could begin operating immediately and perhaps stem the tide of decentralization. By the mid-forties, people speaking of rapid transit referred to the use of buses on the expressways. The Central Business District Association, the Traffic Association, and others therefore convinced local and state planners to design the freeways to accommodate high-speed buses. This usually involved constructing special bus lanes and stops along the side of the parkway. Bus service on the freeways, these organizations argued, could more than double the highways' capacity while offering inexpensive rapid transit. One official contended that these buses would "provide rapid transit service for the area at a small fraction of the cost of any type of separate rapid transit system." "Rather than suffer existing difficulties for many years awaiting increased densities," wrote the Central Business District Association in 1945, "the Parkway or Freeway type of facility has been adopted." Such a system would, it believed, make available good service at a low cost.[34]

Despite the widespread support for the proposed freeway system, local officials had yet to find a way to finance it. Residents of the metropolitan district could not afford to pay for the completed network because their local tax dollars went to a variety of other services, including local highway and street maintenance, sewers, flood control, airports, and parks. Nor was present state funding adequate since it

Plate 16. Realizing that a fixed-rail system would be prohibitively expensive, many public transportation advocates favored the establishment of bus service on the freeways. The photograph above shows a bus leaving a bus stop on the Hollywood Freeway. (Courtesy of Los Angeles City Archives)

went towards freeway construction on a piecemeal basis. Shortly after the war a group of representatives from various southern California government municipalities, civic organizations, and the State Division of Highways formed a committee to lobby the state legislature for building funds. The group hoped to convince the state to increase gasoline and highway user taxes and earmark these proceeds specifically for urban and rural freeway construction.

The state had instituted a gasoline tax many years earlier to pay for highway construction and maintenance in the rural parts of the state. During the Depression, urban residents could no longer afford to assess themselves to pay the costs of street construction. The Traffic Association therefore petitioned the state for gasoline tax funds to complete sections of the Major Traffic Street Plan. The association correctly argued that until 1932 the state had used these monies solely for rural highway development even though urban motorists contributed most of the proceeds to the fund. Los Angeles automobile owners alone accounted for 25 percent of the state total. The association consequently asserted that it was time the cities received their fair share. Although it did not secure as much as it would have liked, the organization did convince the state to allocate some money to urban areas throughout California.[35] Later during the thirties, the Automobile Club of Southern California successfully lobbied the state legislature to designate extensions of state routes through urban areas as state highways, making them eligible for state funding. A new law also added many other highways in the cities to the state system, breaking twenty-five years of precedent where the state concerned itself solely with rural highways at the expense of urban areas. It was this action which finally provided state construction funds for the Arroyo Seco Parkway.[36]

Local officials and civic organizations throughout Los Angeles County applauded the efforts of the Automobile Club and Traffic Association in this regard. For years the city motorist had subsidized highways outside of the urban areas. "It is fair and just now that large cities be permitted to use a greater part of the highway tax dollar which they provided in the solution of their own pressing transportation problem," argued one critic. In 1946, local officials hoped to convince the state legislature to finance the proposed freeway system through increased user taxes on gasoline. They succeeded in 1947 when Governor Earl Warren signed the Collier-Burns Act appropriating approximately $76,000,000 a year for the succeeding ten years for state highway construction. Gasoline tax and motor vehicle registration fees would provide the revenue to support this program. Furthermore, these funds were earmarked specifically for highway construction and maintenance. The state would spend 55 percent of the total collections in the thirteen southern counties. The Los Angeles City Planning Commission estimated that the new legislation would make available $300,000,000 for the metropolitan freeway system—enough to build 105 miles of roadway.[37]

The Collier-Burns Act culminated the region's quest to solve its transportation problems by ensuring the construction of an urban freeway system. The city's residents largely approved of this method of finance because it taxed those people who most directly benefited from the network of limited-access roadways. The gasoline tax fairly distributed the costs of the system among those who could best take advantage of it. Once again, urban residents in the Los Angeles metropolitan area agreed to assess themselves to facilitate automobile use. The fact that the Metropolitan Parkway Committee successfully lobbied for the increased user taxes further suggests the power of consensus in urban politics. Urban planners, politicians, property owners, and suburban and downtown commercial concerns all believed that the freeway system could ameliorate their problems. Their collective efforts succeeded in putting forth the freeway network as Los Angeles' answer to twentieth-century urban ills.

Other cities in the United States had similar experiences with freeways. Chicago, for instance, spent heavily between the years of 1915 and 1930 to widen existing streets and open up new thoroughfares. It is not surprising that these activities improved automobile access to the central business district in the short run and thus encouraged more people to commute to the city center by car. Unfortunately, the increased traffic quickly rendered many of these improvements obsolete by jamming them with automobiles. The city government consequently turned to the limited-access superhighway as a way of segregating different kinds of traffic. The onset of the Depression, combined with a voter reaction against corrupt bond issues, however, had put an end to the way Chicago had financed its earlier street construction. The city therefore petitioned the state to release some of its gasoline tax monies to build these expressways connecting the Loop with Chicago's surrounding suburbs. This plan of action received widespread support from the downtown business interests because it promised to open up access to the city center's retail sector. At the same time it shifted the financial burden of facilitating automobile movement from property owners to the motorists themselves. By the late forties and early fifties, other major cities had turned to the freeway as a possible solution to traffic congestion and the deterioration of the inner city. In 1956, the federal government agreed to lend a hand by distributing highway revenues to cities across the United States for the expressed purpose of building urban freeways.[38]

Plate 17. Many organizations hoped that the freeways would reestablish stable transportation patterns in the southern California area. Urban planners believed that the freeways could both engender suburban development and halt the decline of the inner city. This photograph shows the Hollywood Freeway, which connected the downtown area with the San Fernando Valley. (Courtesy of Los Angeles City Archives)

⇐ 9 ⇒

Epilogue

≡

*The fundamental difficulty is that street railways no longer
meet reasonably the transportation needs of modern communities. . . . The basic fault of the street railways is their
fixed track operation on rails. As a result, the service is inflexible and cannot be adjusted to differences and changes in
conditions.*

—John Bauer
1939

*A large segment of our population suspects that what the
public wants to use, and what the public is willing to pay
for . . . is a private automobile and a freeway to drive it on.*

—Lloyd Smith

any sectors within Amer-
ican society believed that freeways could solve the problems
associated with decentralization. The public, however, held
a different view towards mass transit. The split between
suburban and inner-city business interests, combined with
the issue of finance, blocked rapid-rail construction in all but
a handful of cities. Lacking public subsidies, many traction
companies failed. This wave of bankruptcies began immediately following World War I when the high fixed costs
associated with rampant overcapitalization forced many railways into receivership. Those companies surviving the war
soon faced skyrocketing inflation. Although labor and material expenses doubled within four years of the war's end,
most railways found it difficult to raise their fares. The legacy
of mismanagement and poor public relations in the past

made it nearly impossible for traction companies to convince public regulators to increase their rate structures. When public utility commissions did agree to fare increases, the public usually revolted.

Many railways subsequently survived only by merging with larger electric utility holding companies. At a time when the demand for electricity was rapidly expanding, most power companies found that government regulations limited their net income to a fixed percentage of their assets. By purchasing traction companies, electric utilities could augment both their asset base and profits. By 1931, the electric power industry had acquired control of transit companies carrying 80 percent of the nation's urban rail passengers. Altogether, electric utilities owned about one-half of America's electric railways and provided desperately needed capital to the troubled transit industry. The Roosevelt administration, however, sought to restrict the influence of large utility holding companies. In 1935, the president signed the Public Utility Holding Company Act, which required utilities to operate independently of each other. Henceforth, holding companies could no longer own and manage more than one public utility at a time. This forced many electric conglomerates to shed their unprofitable transit operations. Cast aside in the middle of the Depression, many of these railways quickly failed. Those that lasted found that they had to replace their slow, inflexible streetcars with modern buses. Most railway companies, however, found themselves short of both capital and investors.

This opened the way for companies such as National City Lines to buy up urban streetcar networks. With an infusion of cash, the aging trolley companies could complete their conversion to the more efficient buses. The federal government, however, sued National City Lines during the late forties for antitrust violations and eventually forced its corporate stockholders to divest themselves of their ownership in the company. Lacking outside investors, most railway systems either went under or were finally taken over by local municipalities. General Motors did not kill them. Mismanagement, government actions restricting corporate investment in railways, the inflation following World War I, persistent financial problems, and the rise of the automobile all worked together to make streetcars obsolete. By 1941, a survey found that 2,100 urban areas throughout the United States no longer had any fixed-rail transportation system whatsoever. These communities relied upon automobiles and buses to get around.[1]

Los Angeles' railways never fell prey to a public utility holding company. The PE had operated as a subsidiary of the Southern Pacific Railroad since 1910, while the Huntington estate still controlled the LARY. Nevertheless, at the same time that Los Angeles officials pressed forward with their efforts to build a freeway system, the region's railways continued their precipitous decline. The Depression had left the traction companies reeling from heavy patronage and monetary losses. Acting on the recommendation of the state Railroad Commission, railway managers tried to shore up profits and service by replacing streetcars and interurbans with more flexible buses. Unfortunately, this move had little effect and by 1940 both the LARY and the PE had abandoned many of their railway franchises altogether. Only World War II with its rubber and gasoline shortages saved the companies. Although ridership and profits improved dramatically during the war years, the recovery proved temporary. Income and patronage once again fell following the return to normalcy. Angelenos went back to using their cars, while traction executives found themselves stuck with even older and more antiquated equipment.

During the late forties, the PE requested permission to raise its fares to cover rising costs. The California Public Utilities Commission, however, ordered the railway to upgrade its equipment before instituting fee increases. The PE's management, after much thought, eventually decided to eliminate its passenger rail service altogether. Several factors influenced the company's decision. Most important, the railway had suffered a long history of financial losses before and after the war. PE executives also realized that decentralization now occurred in areas far removed from the company's tracks. This, combined with Los Angeles' low population density, made the company question whether the region could ever support rail transit. Ultimately, the PE sold its passenger service in 1953 to the Metropolitan Coach Lines, a company that mainly operated buses in southern California. That corporation ran the PE at a loss for five years before selling out to the state-owned Metropolitan Transit Authority, which formally ended all rail service in 1961. "The rail passenger operations of [the] Pacific Electric," observed a former railway official in 1963, "became obsolete and economically there was no justification for their perpetuation and as a result, like the horse and buggy, dropped from the scene."[2]

The LARY met a similar fate. Its management had hoped to turn its operations around by substituting buses for streetcars on many of its routes. The trolleys, with their tracks running down the middle of the street, were hopelessly mired in heavy automobile traffic. Railway officials believed that the more mobile motor coaches would move with the flow of autos and thus speed traffic. During the late thirties, General Motors perfected a forty-five-seat diesel bus that the president of the LARY hailed as the answer to many of the company's equipment problems. By 1940, the railway had submitted a plan to the Board of Public Utilities which would have replaced all of its streetcars with buses except on the most frequently traveled lines.[3]

Shortages of gasoline and rubber made it impossible for the traction company to implement its plan during the war. Then, in late 1944, the Huntington estate sold the railway to American City Lines. The latter was a subsidiary of National City Lines (NCL), which owned transit systems throughout the United States. The founders of NCL had incorporated their company in 1936 fully realizing that the Public Utility Holding Company Act would lead to a shortage of investment capital available to the railway industry. NCL quickly began to buy streetcar systems cast aside by the power companies. Once the firm had taken over a traction network, it began to modernize it by replacing obsolete trolleys with more mobile buses. When NCL itself began to run short of capital, it turned to its suppliers for additional funds. The company subsequently sold some of its own stock to General Motors and Firestone Tire and Rubber. Investors in NCL's subsidiary, American City Lines, included Phillips Petroleum, Standard Oil of California, and Mack Truck. These resources allowed NCL to purchase failing transit networks in such cities as Miami, San Diego, Baltimore, Oakland, and St. Louis. By 1947, NCL controlled forty-six transit networks.[4]

NCL injected badly needed capital into a dying industry. Some observers have argued that the substitution of buses for streetcars "prevented the financial collapse of the industry." By abandoning streetcars, transit companies could eliminate high fixed costs associated with maintaining rights-of-way, generating electricity, and operating inefficient two-man trolleys. Nevertheless, the United States Justice Department filed an antitrust suit against the corporation to halt its monopolistic practices. The federal government's main objection concerned NCL's supplier contracts. The company refused to purchase its equipment from outside vendors, preferring to rely upon its corporate stockholders. General Motors, the government claimed, controlled a captive market and effectively shut out its competitors. This was the conspiracy the government hoped to halt. During the final disposition held in 1955, Judge Julius Hoffman wrote that the "conspiracy in which the defendants engaged . . . did not involve any attempt to monopolize a whole industry. . . . The only offense . . . was a conspiracy limited to the monopolization of sales to a single corporate system." By the time the case came to trial, NCL had canceled its supplier contracts with its corporate shareholders. In addition, General Motors and the other companies involved divested themselves of NCL's stock. Consequently, the courts decided it was not worthwhile to enjoin NCL from engaging in similar practices in the future. With the last available source of capital cut off, the railway industry went into a dramatic downward spiral. Eventually NCL sold off most of its networks. During the mid-fifties many local governments had to step in to save what was left of their public transportation systems.[5]

Prior to the onset of the antitrust suit, American City Lines had changed the name of the LARY to the Los Angeles Transit Lines. The new management then began to implement the plan outlined by LARY officials before the war. The company hoped that it could reverse the system's financial situation by replacing its antiquated streetcars with buses. The LARY had deferred maintenance on many of its lines for years because of its declining fortune. It had also found it impossible to replace its aging trolleys. American City Lines, however, brought with it the financial wherewithal to purchase modern motor coaches, which not only cost half as much as new streetcars, but could also maneuver more easily in traffic. Unfortunately, the federal antitrust suit encouraged American City Lines to sell the Los Angeles Transit Lines in 1958 before it could complete its modernization program. The Metropolitan Transit Authority subsequently ran the network until the Southern California Rapid Transit system was created during the early sixties.

Bradford Snell later argued that General Motors' actions ruined a healthy streetcar industry. In fact, General Motors, through NCL, provided the capital necessary to improve local transit companies. Trolley networks had been trying to convert to buses for years. Most informed observers agreed with *Fortune* when it wrote in 1936 that motor coaches had become popular because "the faithful electric trolley had sunk into such a state of obsolescence as to be scarcely tolerable."[6] This was something of an overstatement because of the introduction of the modern PCC car. Nevertheless, the crowded traffic conditions in many cities made buses far more practical. This is not to say that General Motors was completely selfless in its actions. It sought to drive its competitors out of business by securing advantageous supplier contracts from its affiliates. Still, the assertion that the General Motors conspiracy led to the decline of the American transit industry is patently absurd. By the time the NCL was founded in 1936, the industry had already suffered two full decades of severe financial problems.

The prospects of providing the Los Angeles area with a rapid-transit system following World War II also faded quickly. Although freeway construction resumed during the late forties, little was done about rapid transportation. This in spite of the fact that the downtown business community renewed its support for an extensive rail network. The partially built freeway system had not done much to help their cause as business retailers in the city center continued to lose customers to suburban business districts. "Traffic congestion along with delays in movement, is making it increasingly inconvenient and costly to transact business in the downtown area," wrote the City Planning Department in 1949. The department hoped to offer downtown merchants some relief by requiring newly constructed buildings to install parking lots, but it would take several years before this effort would begin to help the traffic situation.[7]

In 1948 and 1949, the Rapid Transit Action Group, an organization of businessmen, tried to convince the City Council to establish a metropolitan rapid transit authority. The group wanted the council to give the body the authority to issue bonds with which to finance the construction of rail facilities alongside the Hollywood Freeway. Los Angeles, argued the organization, needed rapid transit to "preserve the integration of the area, and to forestall its imminent unplanned decentralization." Without such lines, the city faced the danger of "disintegration." The City Council, nevertheless, shelved the petition because of the difficulties in financing the project and the public's lack of interest.[8]

Two years later in 1951, the state assembly and senate passed with surprisingly little difficulty an act that founded the Los Angeles Metropolitan Transit Authority. This public entity, among other things, held the right to construct and operate a monorail between the San Fernando Valley and downtown Los Angeles. The new legislation met with the approval of outspoken mass-transit proponents. "There has been a constant cry for improved transit in Los Angeles," claimed Harry Morrison, the general manager of the Downtown Business Men's Association. "The people want it, the community needs it, and business and property interests support it." Another advocate argued that the state had now established a policy of developing "interurban rapid transit systems in the various metropolitan areas within the state for the benefit of the people."[9] Actually, the act that created this authority should have given these proponents of rail transit little to cheer about. The state had allotted the organization no money, nor did it give it the right to levy taxes or issue any kind of debt, save revenue bonds. The authority had to obtain the California Public Utilities Commission's permission before operating any lines and it was not even clear if the body was exempt from corporate income taxes. Although the county supervisors gave the entity some funds to defray administrative costs, the state legislature refused to provide funds with which to build the monorail.[10]

Even more significant were the attitudes of the general public and local officials towards rapid transit. During the mid-fifties, the city government once again proclaimed the impossibility of financing a rail system in Los Angeles. T. M. Chubb, the chief engineer of the city's Public Utilities and Transportation Commission, remarked that although mass-transit facilities were desirable, in fact, "no such system or even nucleus of such a rail system exists at this time, nor can it exist in the very foreseeable future without the expenditure of very substantial sums of money by private investors or by government." Private citizens agreed. "No one, not even the sponsors," one critic wrote, "is willing to say this will not be a financial failure." Even in densely populated cities, he continued, rapid-rail lines had suffered severe losses. With Los Angeles' lightly populated city structure, such a network would prove an even worse investment. Besides, in his opinion only "a small minority will enjoy [its] benefits."[11]

It was also becoming increasingly clear by the mid-fifties that most Angelenos wanted nothing to do with the rapid-transit plans proposed by the downtown business community. A 1954 study showed that few southern California newspaper editors and publishers took the Metropolitan Transit Authority's monorail proposal seriously. Most of those polled opposed the project, while many had not even heard about it. "We have had a tongue-in-cheek attitude towards the Monorail plan . . . ," responded the editor of the Santa Monica *Outlook*, "there seems to be so little interest among our readers." Another editor believed that the monorail was "dreamed up by the business men in downtown Los Angeles" because they were "desperate to concoct some scheme for getting fast transportation into the downtown area." Although Lloyd Smith, the president of the Board of Public Utilities and Transportation, favored rapid-rail construction in the abstract, he realized that "a large segment of our population suspects that what the public wants to use, and what the public is willing to pay for (as long as they can afford it) is a private automobile and a freeway to drive it on—and plenty of 'free' parking lots." With the decentralization of Los Angeles and the advent of the freeway system, most Angelenos turned their backs on the idea of a rapid-rail network. "There now exists a divergence of opinion regarding transportation of such a magnitude as to paralyze action," wrote a committee of local university presidents in 1949. "Opinion in many quarters is against rail rapid transit for Los Angeles." A year later, a government survey found that 74 percent of those using public transit disliked it. They only rode mass transportation because they could not afford any other alternative.[12]

There was little doubt about the place of the automobile in Los Angeles' transportation system. By the fifties, Angelenos had clearly accepted the automobile and the freeway as the major means of transport throughout the region. The freeway, its proponents argued, would solve the problems of decentralization and congestion simultaneously by connecting suburban centers with the central business district and each other. "The proper location and design of urban freeways is the greatest single element in the cure of cities' ills and in directing of their proper and adequate future growth," claimed a nationally renowned planner.[13] The promise of the multinuclear metropolitan area encouraged many residents to embrace the freeway network. Even the rapid-transit advocates could accept the system because they believed the new highways would rid the city center of congestion. Most important, motorists themselves would finance freeway construction by paying gasoline and accessory taxes. Rapid-rail lines could not boast of similar advantages because such networks required extensive public support. Although government subsidies to public transportation would become acceptable by the sixties, during the forties and fifties they were seen as onerous. Why, the public asked, should the municipality support a failing enterprise when motorists were willing and able to finance the freeways?

Freeway construction had commenced again immediately following the war. By 1958 the region had completed nearly one-fifth of the original plan. Although the city built bus facilities along the shoulders of some of the early expressways, the system was almost exclusively utilized by private automobiles and trucks. So popular did the new highways become that they filled to capacity almost upon completion. A state engineer claimed that three times as many cars could travel at twice their previous speed along the new network of limited-access highways while greatly reducing the number of fatal accidents. In addition, the freeways relieved the surface streets of much of their congestion. One observer noted in 1959 that the region's major thoroughfares were experiencing less traffic than at any time since 1939.[14]

During the late fifties, however, some disinterested observers began to worry that the excessive reliance on the automobile would lead to an unbalanced transportation system. "Up to the present time, major freeway links were constructed with a view to relieving overcrowded surface streets," remarked a transportation expert in 1959. "We are now entering a phase in which highway officials are concerned with relieving overcrowded freeways." Like the Major Traffic Street Plan before it, the freeway network rather than solving the area's traffic problems merely forestalled them. By the sixties, the freeways were jammed with cars at rush hour as Angelenos had become almost totally dependent upon their automobiles for transportation. Meanwhile, sales in the central business district continued to decline as the downtown area operated as only one of many regional retail centers. In addition, the reality of suburban life did not always live up to the ideals of the twenties. By continuing to favor single-family dwellings, southern Californians had to distribute themselves over a vast area of countryside, thus eliminating what little was left of the county's rural atmosphere.

Many people today wonder why American cities allowed their extensive railway systems to deteriorate. Not understanding the complex issues associated with early mass transportation, most writers offer one of two ready explanations. Some have implied that the automobile's technological superiority doomed the streetcar to extinction. This argument, however, is far too deterministic. It assumes that technology operates as an autonomous and triumphant force leading to an improved human condition. In fact, scientific advances are powerless to effect significant change if society does not embrace those advances and facilitate their use. The invention of the automobile was perhaps the most significant technological innovation of the twentieth century. Yet American cities could not initially accommodate the car as a major means of urban transportation because of poor roads and narrow streets. It was not until urban dwellers saw the automobile as a democratic alternative to the seemingly corrupt railway companies and the inefficient streetcars that they began to reconstruct their cities' streets. This conscious decision alone allowed the automobile to replace the trolley as America's major mode of urban transport. As Lewis Mumford reminds us, technology and society together "are the result of human choices and aptitudes and strivings. . . . No matter how completely technics relies upon the objective procedures of the sciences, it does not form an independent system . . . it exists as an element in human culture."[15]

The alternative explanation for the automobile's popularity is of course one of the many variations on the conspiracy theory. I have already shown that General Motors' attempt to monopolize the motor coach industry had little to do with the decline of public transit. One third of all streetcar companies went into bankruptcy immediately following World War I. Scores more failed during the Depression. Those remaining knew that they had to convert to buses to have any chance of surviving. National City Lines and General Motors merely satisfied the industry's desperate need for capital to complete this transformation. General Motors did not attempt to destroy mass transportation. Rather, it wanted to save it in order to maintain a market for its buses. The fact that the conglomerate used unsavory and monopolistic business techniques is quite beside the point.

A corollary to this theory is that planners and government officials willfully provided subsidies to the automobile at the same time that they denied public assistance to mass transportation. Historians arguing this point complain that municipalities bowed to the demands of private pressure groups such as real estate brokers, tire manufacturers, and automobile dealers to build an improved street system. Public transportation, these same historians contend, was denied subsidies because of its status as a private industry. These arguments led Kenneth Jackson to conclude that "Americans taxed and harassed public transportation, even while subsidizing the automobile like a pampered child." Lewis Mumford put it even more bluntly. He wrote that "by allowing mass transportation to deteriorate, and by building expressways out of the city and parking garages within, in order to encourage the maximum use of the private car, our highway engineers and city planners have helped to destroy the living tissue of the city."[16]

These arguments, however, ignore the fundamental responsibility of city governments to facilitate the flow of goods and people within urban areas. Consequently, municipalities have long subsidized various forms of transportation within their boundaries.[17] City officials, for example, offered railway corporations exclusive franchises to operate on certain streets. After 1900, urban legislatures also supported the virtual monopoly held by traction companies over public transportation. When jitneys began to provide an alternative to the inefficient streetcars, city councils throughout the United States moved to eliminate the threat. In some instances, city officials tried to protect the traction companies from the automobile by banning parking in their central business districts. The public outcry against such laws indicated that urban dwellers saw the automobile as a substitute for the poorly run and financially troubled transit systems. Furthermore, people were willing to tax themselves to facilitate vehicular movement. Civic leaders, in the meantime, formed broadly based committees to plan better street networks. The improvements themselves required the cooperation of thousands of property owners willing to form assessment districts and finance bond issues. Later, the motorists willingly paid substantial gasoline taxes and registration fees, most of which went towards highway construction.

The point is that America's present urban transportation system largely reflects choices made by the public itself. No one imposed the automobile on the public. Americans embraced the automobile willingly, for they saw it as a liberating and democratic technology. In addition, they pressured their representatives to facilitate what they believed was an important and vital method of transportation. As one might expect, the city officials eventually carried out the public's wishes. After all, that is what one would expect in a democratic society. Nor were municipalities as shortsighted as modern-day critics have indicated. Planners and city councils continued to propose rapid-transit construction. They did, however, face major difficulties in implementing these plans. Rapid-rail systems were extremely expensive, particularly when compared to street improvements. Given a choice, nearly all cities went with the latter because of public pressure and pragmatic concerns about finances. At the same time, it appeared that freeways and expressways could satisfy a variety of interest groups. Mass transit, on the other hand, found its greatest support mainly among the downtown business interests. The public simply was not willing to subsidize a rail system designed to benefit the private railways and central business district concerns when the automobile offered the promise of efficient, individual transport.

It is not clear whether the public's decision to adopt the automobile as its major means of urban transportation was an unwise one. It is obvious that many intellectuals and urban critics despise modern suburbs and the automobile. This bias leaps out at anyone reading their prose. Lewis Mumford long maintained that a decentralized urban structure was not "a new sort of city, but an anti-city." "The anti-city," Mumford concluded, "annihilates the city whenever it collides with it." Kenneth Jackson agrees. "Too late," Jackson laments, "municipal leaders will realize that a slavish duplication of suburbia destroys the urban fabric that makes cities interesting."[18]

Certainly cities such as Los Angeles failed to achieve the suburban utopia that early proponents of deconcentration had promised. Planners and government officials during the twenties and thirties had naively believed that they could create a halcyon urban environment merely by encouraging economic and residential dispersal. But decentralization has not necessarily failed, either. Notwithstanding the prevalence of air pollution, American cities today are far more healthful places to live than their nineteenth-century predecessors. They also offer far more people the opportunity to live in low-density single-family dwellings. Despite the admonition of Mumford and others, Americans seem to prefer this form of housing. That is why condominiums almost universally declined in value during the early eighties. It also explains why young families have continued to flock to new suburban developments well-removed from central cities. In southern California, the San Bernardino–Riverside region is among the fastest growing regions in the country despite its apparent lack of employment opportunities. Young couples with children move into the area because they can buy a detached house for the same price as a condominium in the Los Angeles area. These people are willing to commute as much as two hours each way to work just to obtain an affordable home. Nor does everyone see Los Angeles as "an undifferentiated mass of houses, walled off into sectors by many-laned expressways, with ramps and viaducts that create special bottlenecks of their own."[19] Indeed, at least one critic, architectural historian Reynor Banham, has sensitively portrayed Los Angeles as a region of distinctive architecture and coherent neighborhoods. Banham writes:

For every pedestrian litterateur who finds the place a 'stinking sewer' and stays only long enough to collect the material for a hate-novel, for every visiting academic who never stirs out of his bolt-hole in Westwood and comes back to tell us how the freeways divide communities because he has never experienced how they unite individuals of common interest . . . for these two there will be half a dozen architects, artists, or designers, photographers or musicians who decide to stay because it is possible for them to do their thing with the support of like-minded characters and the resources of a highly diversified body of skills and technologies.[20]

But what about the future of rapid transit in American cities? Unfortunately, the same issues that prevented subway and elevated construction in the past remain with us today. Since the mid-seventies a handful of cities including Los Angeles have begun to plan rapid-rail systems. Financial difficulties, however, have plagued their efforts. Nearly all of the municipalities involved are seeking federal grants to pay for most of their construction costs. The Reagan administration, though, has several times attempted to end federal subsidies to rapid transit. Not only does the White House consider this an issue requiring local solutions, but it is trying to reduce record budget deficits. Unfortunately, individual cities alone cannot afford the heavy expenses associated with modern subway construction.

Although the nation's urban transportation system as a whole is unbalanced, it is not certain that building extensive rapid-rail networks will solve the difficulties. Not only do problems of finance exist, urban transportation patterns have changed dramatically during the past eighty years. Some cities such as San Francisco and Chicago retain a strong central business district. Founded during the early to mid-nineteenth century, these municipalities developed mature, densely built city centers. The Loop in Chicago and San Francisco's financial district still attract sizable numbers of daytime commuters, making these areas natural transportation nodes. Still, both Cook County and the Bay Area have experienced extensive economic and residential dispersion. Unlike the twenties, today there is a substantial peripheral movement making it difficult, if not impossible, to plan an efficient, comprehensive rapid-transit network. The fixed-rail systems in both San Francisco and Chicago have consequently focused on their respective downtown districts, leaving the suburbs to rely upon the automobile. Not surprisingly, each system requires a substantial subsidy. Although there is nothing wrong with public assistance to mass transportation, it is expensive. It is therefore not unusual to hear residents of Bay Area communities not served by BART grumble about paying taxes for a rapid-transit system they do not use.

If rapid-transit lines in older cities have experienced difficulties, then one might imagine the obstacles facing such a system in Los Angeles. I have argued earlier that the decentralization of southern California was not unlike that of other American metropolises. Los Angeles, however, has developed a greater sprawl because it did not emerge as a major urban area until the twentieth century. The electric streetcar and the automobile encouraged deconcentration before the city could create a rigid, densely packed environment, resulting in highly decentralized traffic patterns running throughout the suburbs. In addition, the southern California area has continuously grown throughout the last ninety years to the point where it now rivals New York as the nation's largest metropolis. The region's vast stretches of development therefore make it difficult to plan an efficient public transportation system despite the fact that the city of Los Angeles now ranks as the third most densely populated city in the nation.[21]

Nevertheless, at the time of this writing the city expects to build an eighteen-mile-long subway between the San Fernando Valley and downtown Los Angeles. The project will cost a staggering $100 million a mile. The City Council and mayor have lobbied Congress for years in an attempt to garner federal assistance. City officials know full well that local residents would quickly lose interest in the project if they had to pay for the construction themselves. Even if Congress releases the necessary funds, the subway will probably not do much to solve the city's transportation problems. The system will serve but a tiny fraction of the city's population, as only those living along the route and working in the downtown area or the Wilshire District will be able to take advantage of the innovation. Finally, the initial line will cost so much that it is doubtful that the city will build future extensions.

Some critics have argued that Los Angeles must build the proposed Wilshire subway to protect the city against future traffic gridlocks and oil shortages. I disagree. Urban dwellers throughout the United States have long shown their disdain for public-transit systems, and with good reason. Eighty years ago, railway patrons constantly complained about the quality of streetcar and interurban service. Today, mass transportation for the most part remains slow, crowded, uncomfortable, and relatively inconvenient. During the fifties, a poll found that three-quarters of all those riding buses and streetcars in Los Angeles did so only because they had no alternative. Had they a choice, they would have preferred to drive a car. It is unlikely that these attitudes have changed much in the last thirty years. The point is that most Americans will continue to use their automobiles instead of public conveyances regardless of how much money cities and the federal government spend on rapid-rail construction. It will take astronomical gasoline prices, horrendous traffic congestion, or government fiat to force most people out of their automobiles. If such difficulties do arise, cities may experience some serious short-term transportation problems. But municipalities could quickly adapt their existing infrastructures to the new situation. Possible solutions would include closing down freeways to private vehicles. A coordinated park-and-ride bus system could accommodate a huge influx of riders far more easily than a fixed-rail network. But until some major dislocation occurs, Americans will resist leaving their automobiles at home. It is unrealistic to expect anything else in a society that celebrates individual choice and free-market economics. The public decided several decades ago that it would facilitate automobile usage as an alternative to mass transportation. No matter how much social critics and urban planners push for rapid-rail systems, it is unlikely that urban residents will give up the freedom and convenience afforded by the automobile.

≡ Notes ≡

1 / Introduction

1. See for instance, Kenneth R. Schneider, *Autokind vs. Mankind* (New York: W. W. Norton, 1971); Emma Rothschild, *Paradise Lost: The Decline of the Automobile Age* (New York: Random House, 1973); and B. Bruce-Briggs, *The War Against the Automobile* (New York: E. P. Dutton, 1977).
2. U.S. Congress, Senate Committee on the Judiciary, *The Industrial Reorganization Act: Hearings before a Subcommittee on S. 1167*, 93d Cong., 2d sess., 1974. Part 4A contains "American Ground Transport," by Bradford Snell. Snell's study was, at best, sloppy and poorly researched. The entire diatribe is riddled with factual errors and poorly drawn conclusions. For instance, Snell mistook the Pacific Electric for the Los Angeles Railway Corporation throughout his essay. Snell's most egregious error was in asserting that the antitrust violations committed by General Motors and National City Lines ruined a healthy transit industry. Nothing could be further from the truth.
   Despite Snell's inaccuracies, his testimony was picked up by the press and reprinted in many newspapers. Most others writing about the conspiracy have relied heavily on Snell. See Glenn Yago, "Urban Transportation in the Eighties," *Democracy* 3 (Winter 1983): 45–47; Yago, *The Decline of Transit: Urban Transportation in German and U.S. Cities* (Cambridge: Cambridge University Press, 1984), pp. 56–58 and 245; Robert B. Carson, *Whatever Happened to the Trolleys?* (Washington, D.C.: University Press of America, 1978), pp. 92–95; and James V. Cornehls and Delbert A. Taebel, *The Political Economy of Urban Transportation* (Port Washington, N.Y.: Kennikat Press, 1977), p. 23.
3. Snell, pp. A2–A3 and A31–A35.
4. Ira Swett, "The Los Angeles Railway," *Interurban Specials* 11 (December 1951): 22–23.
5. See, for instance, Sam Bass Warner, *The Urban Wilderness* (New York: Random House, 1972).
6. This point can be illustrated by comparing Los Angeles' population growth with that of other cities in the accompanying table.

Percentage of 1960 Population Level Attained
During Several Eras

	Pre–1830	1830–1870	1870–1920	1920–1960
Los Angeles	0	0+	15	85
Boston	9	18	48	25
Chicago	0	8	47	45
Philadelphia	9	15	38	38
New York	3	11	44	42

Source: John Borchert, "American Metropolitan Evolution."

The table shows increments of population growth for various historical epochs in several cities. For instance, by 1920 Los Angeles had attained only 15 percent of its 1960 population level. Thus, 85 percent of the city's urban growth in terms of population came after 1920. In other words, Los Angeles matured during the automobile age. Boston, on the other hand, experienced most of its growth prior to the introduction of the automobile. It had reached a population level equal to 75 percent of its 1960 figure by 1920.

7. Many technological innovations other than the automobile helped shape the urban environment. See, for example, John G. Clark and Mark H. Rose, "Light, Heat, and Power: Energy Choices in Kansas City, Wichita, and Denver, 1900–1935," *Journal of Urban History* 5 (May 1979): 340–364; Clay McShane, "Transforming the Use of Urban Space: A Look at the Revolution in Street Pavements, 1880–1924," *Journal of Urban History* 5 (May 1979): 279–307; and Stanley K. Schultz and Clay McShane, "To Engineer the Metropolis: Sewers, Sanitation, and City Planning in Late Nineteenth-Century America," *Journal of American History* 65 (September 1978): 389–401.
8. Kenneth T. Jackson, *Crabgrass Frontier: The Suburbanization of the United States* (New York: Oxford University Press, 1985), p. 14. See also Joel A. Tarr, *Transportation Innovation and Changing Spatial Patterns in Pittsburgh, 1850–1934* (Pittsburgh: Public Works Historical Society, 1978), p. 3; and Sam Bass Warner, *Streetcar Suburbs: The Process of Growth in Boston (1870–1900)* (Cambridge: Harvard University Press, 1962), pp. 15–19. Jackson's book is the best introduction to the spatial evolution of the American city.
9. Both quotations cited in Jackson, *Crabgrass Frontier*, pp. 16–17.
10. The literature concerning the social implications of the emerging factory system is voluminous. Paul Johnson, *A Shopkeeper's Millennium: Society and Revivals in Rochester, New York, 1815–1837* (New York: Hill

and Wang, 1978) provides a good introduction, as does Alan Dawley, *Class and Community: The Industrial Revolution in Lynn* (Cambridge: Harvard University Press, 1976).

11. Jackson, *Crabgrass Frontier*, pp. 45–73; Warner, *Streetcar Suburbs*, pp. 11–14; Joel A. Tarr, "From City to Suburb: The 'Moral' Influence of Transportation Technology," in Alexander Callow, ed., *American Urban History*, 2d ed. (New York: Oxford University Press, 1973), pp. 202–212.

12. Quotation cited in Jackson, *Crabgrass Frontier*, p. 34; see also George Rogers Taylor, "The Beginnings of Mass Transportation in Urban America," *Smithsonian Journal of History* 1 (Summer and Autumn 1966): 40–48.

13. Jackson, *Crabgrass Frontier*, pp. 35–39 and 87–102; Taylor, "The Beginnings of Mass Transportation," pp. 31–34. Jackson also describes the importance of steamboats in the suburbanization of Brooklyn; see *Crabgrass Frontier*, pp. 25–33.

14. Jackson, *Crabgrass Frontier*, pp. 20–44. For a history of early modes of transportation in American cities, see Taylor, "The Beginnings of Mass Transportation." See also Warner, *Streetcar Suburbs*; Tarr, *Transportation Innovation*; Tarr, "From City to Suburb"; George Smerk, "The Streetcar: Shaper of American Cities," *Traffic Quarterly* 21 (October 1967): 569–584; Charles Cheape, *Moving the Masses: Urban Public Transit in New York, Boston and Philadelphia, 1880–1912* (Cambridge: Harvard University Press, 1980); and Clay McShane, *Technology and Reform: Street Railways and the Growth of Milwaukee, 1887–1900* (Madison: State Historical Society of Wisconsin, 1974). For a geographic discussion of urban spatial growth see Larry S. Bourne, ed., *Internal Structure of the City* (New York: Oxford University Press, 1971), especially the noteworthy essays by Howard K. Nelson and Homer Hoyt.

  Modern usage dictates that the term "streetcar" be spelled as one word. During the early part of this century, however, it was commonly written as two separate words (i.e., "street car"). With the exception of quotations, I have used the modern spelling.

15. Tarr, *Transportation Innovation*, pp. 17 and 34–35; Jackson, *Crabgrass Frontier*, p. 113; Leon Moses and Harold F. Williamson, "The Location of Economic Activity in Cities," *American Economic Review* 57 (May 1967): 211–222. Tarr notes that some heavy manufacturers moved outside the central business district during the nineteenth century along waterways and near railroad intersections.

16. Tarr, "From City to Suburb," pp. 202–206; Schultz and McShane, "To Engineer the Metropolis," p. 389; Peter Schmitt, *Back to Nature: The Arcadian Myth in America* (New York: Oxford University Press, 1969); Scott Donaldson, *The Suburban Myth* (New York: Columbia University Press, 1969); Kenneth T. Jackson, "The Crabgrass Frontier: 150 Years of Suburban Growth in America," in Raymond A. Mohl and James F. Richardson, eds., *The Urban Experience* (Belmont, California:

Wadsworth Publishing, 1973), pp. 196–221. Alan Anderson's study of Baltimore provides keen insight into the issue of relieving the pressure on the urban infrastructure through improved transportation technology; see Anderson, *The Origin and Resolution of an Urban Crisis: Baltimore, 1890–1930* (Baltimore: The Johns Hopkins University Press, 1977).

17. The best discussions of this issue are in Glen E. Holt, "The Changing Perception of Urban Pathology: An Essay on the Development of Mass Transportation in the United States," in Kenneth T. Jackson and Stanley K. Schultz, eds., *Cities in American History* (New York: Alfred A. Knopf, 1972); and Holt, "Urban Mass Transit History: Where Have We Been and Where Are We Going?" in Jerome Finster, ed., *The National Archives and Urban Research* (Athens, Ohio: Ohio University Press, 1974). See also Ralph Heilman, *Chicago Traction: A Study of the Efforts of the Public to Secure Good Service* (Princeton: American Economic Association, 1908); James Blaine Walker, *Fifty Years of Rapid Transit, 1864–1917* (New York: Law Printing Co., 1918); and Mark S. Foster, "The Automobile and the City," *Michigan Quarterly Review* 19–20 (Fall 1980–Winter 1981): 462–463.

18. For much of this century, historians ignored the impact of the automobile on American society. During the 1970s, however, many scholars turned their attention to the influence of the automobile on the structure of American life. Some, but certainly not all, of these works are listed below: John B. Rae, *The Road and the Car in American Life* (Cambridge: MIT Press, 1971); James J. Flink, *America Adopts the Automobile, 1895–1910* (Cambridge: MIT Press, 1970); Flink, *The Car Culture* (Cambridge: MIT Press, 1975); Flink, "Three Stages of Automobile Consciousness," *American Quarterly* 24 (October 1972): 451–473; Joseph Interrante, "You Can't Go to Town in a Bathtub: Automobile Movement and the Reorganization of Rural Space, 1900–1930," *Radical History Review* 21 (Fall 1979): 151–168; Blaine A. Brownell, "A Symbol of Modernity: Attitudes Toward the Automobile in Southern Cities in the 1920s," *American Quarterly* 24 (March 1972): 20–44; Mark S. Foster, *From Streetcar to Superhighway: American City Planners and Urban Transportation (1900–1940)* (Philadelphia: Temple University Press, 1981); Foster, "The Automobile and the City"; Foster, "The Model-T, the Hard Sell, and Los Angeles' Urban Growth: The Decentralization of Los Angeles During the 1920s," *Pacific Historical Review* 44 (November 1975): 459–484; Paul Barrett, *The Automobile and Urban Transit: The Formation of Public Policy in Chicago, 1900–1930* (Philadelphia: Temple University Press, 1983); Barrett, "Public Policy and Private Choice: Mass Transit and the Automobile in Chicago Between the Wars," *Business History Review* 49 (Winter 1975): 473–497; Howard Preston, *Automobile Age Atlanta* (Athens, Georgia: The University of Georgia Press, 1979); Warren Belasco, *Americans on the Road* (Cambridge: MIT Press, 1979); and Martin Wachs, "Automobiles, Transport, and the

Sprawl of Los Angeles," *Journal of the American Planning Association* 50 (1984): 297–310.

19. Barrett, *The Automobile and Urban Transit.*
20. Jackson, *Crabgrass Frontier*, pp. 181–182; Foster, "The Model-T, the Hard Sell, and Los Angeles' Urban Growth," pp. 476–477.
21. Moses and Williamson, "The Location of Economic Activity in Cities," pp. 211–222; Jackson, *Crabgrass Frontier*, pp. 183–184; Tarr, *Transportation Innovation*, pp. 34–35. Most historians writing about the changing spatial structure of modern cities have not adequately defined the terms "decentralization" and "dispersal." In fact, many have used them synonymously, which only adds to the confusion. In this work I use these words in specific ways. By "dispersal," I mean the movement of residential, commercial, and industrial functions into the suburbs outside of the central business district. This term does not, however, address the issue of transportation patterns within the city. The railways helped disperse urban residents across the countryside, yet Los Angeles maintained a centralized structure because these people continued to ride the railways into the city center on a regular basis. When I talk of "decentralization," I mean the development of a multifocal metropolitan form where the central business district becomes merely one of many commercial districts. In a decentralized city, there is no single prevailing transportation pattern. Rather, there are a multitude of transportation routes. This is what gives cities that grew rapidly during the twentieth century, such as Phoenix and Los Angeles, their seemingly chaotic appearances.
22. City Club of Los Angeles, "Report on Rapid Transit," *City Club Bulletin* (January 30, 1926): supplement.
23. See Foster, *From Streetcar to Superhighway*, pp. 42–43, for a discussion of American urban planners and their attitudes toward decentralization.
24. Even in more densely populated cities, rapid-transit lines could not operate without subsidies.

2 / The Progressive Response

1. Daniel T. Rodgers, "In Search of Progressivism," *Reviews in American History* 10 (December 1982): 114; Arthur S. Link, "What Happened to the Progressive Movement in the 1920's?" *American Historical Review* 64 (July 1959): 836; Peter G. Filene, "An Obituary for 'The Progressive Movement,'" *American Quarterly* 22 (Spring 1970): 20–34; John D. Buenker, "The Progressive Era: A Search for a Synthesis," *Mid-America* 51 (July 1969): 175–193; David P. Thelen, "Social Tensions and the Origins of Progressivism," *Journal of American History* 56 (September 1969): 323–341.
2. Rodgers, "In Search of Progressivism," p. 114. See also Walter Dean

Burnham, *Critical Elections and the Mainsprings of American Politics* (New York: W. W. Norton, 1970); and Richard L. McCormick, "The Discovery that Business Corrupts Politics: A Reappraisal of the Origins of Progressivism," *American Historical Review* 86 (April 1981): 247–274.

3. The following relies heavily upon Rodgers, "In Search of Progressivism," pp. 121–127.

4. Milwaukee tried to control its streetcar companies by offering franchises to several competitors. But these traction companies could not survive the 1894 depression. The lines of these railways were eventually bought up by investors to create a monopoly over Milwaukee's transportation services. See David P. Thelen, *The New Citizenship: Origins of Progressivism in Wisconsin, 1885–1900* (Columbia, Mo.: University of Missouri Press, 1972), pp. 225–228. New York, Boston, and Philadelphia had similar experiences to Milwaukee. See Cheape, *Moving the Masses*, pp. 4–7.

5. On corruption among American railway companies and the angry consumer response, see Thelen, *The New Citizenship*, pp. 254–287; Holt, "The Changing Perception of Urban Pathology," pp. 332–336; Holt, "Urban Mass Transit History," pp. 81–85; Heilman, *Chicago Traction*; Walker, *Fifty Years of Rapid Transit*; Foster, "The Automobile and the City," pp. 459–463; and Cheape, *Moving the Masses*, pp. 15–16 and 65–68.

6. Rodgers, "In Search of Progressivism," pp. 123–124; Thelen, *The New Citizenship*, pp. 2 and 222–226; McCormick, "The Discovery that Business Corrupts Politics," p. 258.

7. James Weinstein, *The Corporate Ideal in the Liberal State, 1900–1918* (Boston: Beacon Press, 1968); Gabriel Kolko, *The Triumph of Conservatism: A Reinterpretation of American History, 1900–1916* (New York: Free Press, 1963).

8. Samuel P. Hays, "The Politics of Reform in Municipal Government in the Progressive Era," *Pacific Northwest Quarterly* 55 (October 1964): 166–168.

9. Hays, "The Politics of Reform"; Hays, "The New Organizational Society," in *American Political History as Social Analysis* (Knoxville: University of Tennessee Press, 1980); Louis Galambos, "The Emerging Organizational Synthesis in Modern American History," *Business History Review* 44 (Fall 1970): 279–290; Robert Weibe, *The Search for Order, 1877–1920* (New York: Hill and Wang, 1967).

10. See, for instance, Weinstein, *The Corporate Ideal in the Liberal State*; and Kolko, *The Triumph of Conservatism*.

11. For further details about the development of early rail transit in Los Angeles, see Spencer Crump, *Ride the Big Red Cars* 5th ed. (Corona Del Mar: Trans-Anglo Books, 1970), pp. 20–34; Robert C. Post, "Street Railways in Los Angeles; Robert Widney to Henry Huntington" (M.A. thesis, University of California, Los Angeles, 1967); and Glenn S. Dumke, "The Growth of the Pacific Electric and Its Influence on the

Development of Southern California" (M.A. thesis, Occidental College, 1939).

12. See Robert M. Fogelson, *The Fragmented Metropolis* (Cambridge: Harvard University Press, 1967); Crump, *Ride the Big Red Cars*; and Judith Powers, "The Absence of Conspiracy: The Effects of Urban Technology on Public Policy in Los Angeles, 1850–1930," (Ph.D. diss., University of California, Los Angeles, 1981).

13. Huntington quoted in Fogelson, *The Fragmented Metropolis*, p. 85. See also Fogelson, pp. 86, 92, 104, 165; Crump, *Ride the Big Red Cars*, pp. 72–75, 91–92, 109–110; passenger totals of the LARY in Box 133, John Randolph Haynes Papers (hereafter cited as JRH); and Ed Ainsworth, *Out of the Noose! Way Pointed for American Cities to Save Themselves From Traffic Strangulation* (Los Angeles: Automobile Club of Southern California, 1939), p. 1. The connection between railway building and real estate promotion in cities throughout the United States is explored in Barrett, *The Automobile and Urban Transit*, p. 12; Jackson, *Crabgrass Frontier*, pp. 120–124; and Holt, "The Changing Perception of Urban Pathology," pp. 328–329.

14. David Ward points out that a transportation innovation must accompany a population influx for that technology to alter significantly the spatial organization of a region. See David Ward, "A Comparative Historical Geography of Streetcar Suburbs in Boston, Massachusetts and Leeds, England: 1850–1920," *Annals of the Association of American Geographers* 54 (December 1964): 477–489.

15. See Taylor, "The Beginnings of Mass Transportation in America"; John Borchert, "American Metropolitan Evolution," *Geographical Review* 57 (July 1967): 301–332; and Warner, *Streetcar Suburbs*. See also Smerk, "The Streetcar"; Tarr, *Transportation Innovation*, pp. 13–18; and Jackson, *Crabgrass Frontier*, pp. 111–117.

16. For an example of nostalgic history see Crump, *Ride the Big Red Cars*, pp. 100–101.

17. Los Angeles *Examiner*, August 22, 1911. See also Bion J. Arnold, "The Transportation Problem in Los Angeles," *California Outlook* 11 (November 4, 1911): special supplement.

18. Los Angeles *Record*, July 18, 1905, September 14, 1906, October 23, 1926; Los Angeles *Herald*, March 16, 1910; Los Angeles *Express*, September 14, 1906, August 26, 1911; Los Angeles *Examiner*, September 30, 1906, December 11, 1906, October 7, 1907, February 5, 1908. See also the numerous newspaper clippings dating from this period in Box 133, JRH. Public utilities in Milwaukee also refused to pay their assessments and taxes; see Thelen, *The New Citizenship*, pp. 231–232 and 259.

19. Los Angeles *Record*, July 18, 1905, September 14, 1906, October 23, 1926; Los Angeles *Herald*, March 16, 1910; Los Angeles *Express*, September 14, 1906, August 26, 1911; Los Angeles *Examiner*, September 30, 1906, December 11, 1906, October 7, 1907, February 5, 1908. On corruption of city officials by New York railway officials, see Cheape,

Moving the Masses, pp. 65–68. For corruption in Milwaukee, see Thelen, *The New Citizenship*, pp. 232–234.

20. Los Angeles *Record*, January 7, 1920; Crump, *Ride the Big Red Cars*, pp. 149–151; Los Angeles *Examiner*, January 31, 1908. See also hundreds of clippings in Boxes 133 and 134, JRH, and a collection of newspaper clippings on transportation and politics in southern California, 1902–1938, in the Henry E. Huntington Library (hereafter cited as HEH). Safety was also an issue in Milwaukee; see Thelen, *The New Citizenship*, pp. 259–260.

21. Newspaper clippings from the Los Angeles *Herald*, Los Angeles *Record*, and the Los Angeles *Examiner*; these clippings (all pre-1910) may be found in Boxes 133 and 134, JRH.

22. Newspaper clippings, pamphlets, and magazine articles in Box 133, JRH. See also Robert C. Post, "The Fair Fare Fight: An Episode in Los Angeles History," *Southern California Quarterly* 52 (September 1970): 275–298.

23. Los Angeles Board of Public Utilities, *7th Annual Report, 1915–1916*, p. 152; Los Angeles *Examiner*, October 2, 1907. See also Board of Public Utilities and Transportation, *18th & 19th Annual Reports, 1926–1928*, p. 5, for a summary of the City Council's fight with the railways.

24. Los Angeles *Times*, August 17, 1913; see also August 6, 1913 and October 17, 1913.

25. Los Angeles *Times*, October 18, 1918, November 28, 1918, May 25, 1920, June 15, 1920, July 16, 1920, August 25, 1920; P. H. Gadsen, "The Readjustment Problems of the Electric Railways" (address to the American Railway Association, March 14, 1919: Box 1, LARY Collection, HEH); Francis Sisson, "Electric Railway and Investors" (typescript of a speech in Box 1, LARY Collection, HEH); Board of Public Utilities, *13th Annual Report, 1921–1922*, pp. 5, 49, and 73; H. M. Titcomb, Untitled speech (typescript in Box 2, LARY Collection, HEH); *Electric Railway Journal* 35 (January 1, 1910): 25 (hereafter cited as *ERJ*).

26. Los Angeles *Herald*, March 16, 1910; Los Angeles *Examiner*, November 21, 1922, November 11, 1913; Los Angeles *Times*, January 27, 1907.

27. Similar complaints were voiced in other cities. The New York *Times* reported that a person riding a streetcar in Manhattan at the turn of the century had to endure "physical discomfort often amounting to little less than real agony." In Chicago, the situation was little better. Historian Paul Barrett writes that "by all reliable accounts, the daily experience of Chicago's mass transit riders was inconviet [*sic*], uncomfortable, and not infrequently, outright dangerous." See Gary A. Tobin, "Suburbanization and the Development of Motor Transportation: Transportation Technology and the Suburbanization Process," in Barry Schwartz, ed., *The Changing Face of the Suburbs* (Chicago: University of Chicago Press, 1976), pp. 101–102; and Barrett, *The Automobile and Urban Transit*, p. 10. For complaints about crowded or inadequate railway conditions in American cities, see Cheape, *Moving the Masses*,

pp. 23–26 and 68; Holt, "The Changing Perception of Urban Pathology," pp. 332–333; and Thelen, *The New Citizenship*, pp. 232–240.

28. *California Outlook* 11 (August 26, 1911): 3–4; Fogelson, *The Fragmented Metropolis*, p. 164. A Chicago city commission wrote in 1900 that Chicago's railways had developed in a "haphazard manner without regard to any well defined and comprehensive plan or policy." New York experienced similar problems with its railways. Charles Cheape quotes one contemporary expert who noted that New York's railways before the turn of the century "were built by independent companies as purely business enterprises; they were built not in accordance with any system, not under the auspices of any authorized commission, not upon any well-devised plan, but rather, as many of our first city sewers were built, namely, in opposition or antagonism to each other." See Barrett, *The Automobile and Urban Transit*, p. 28; and Cheape, *Moving the Masses*, p. 42.

29. Fogelson, *The Fragmented Metropolis*, pp. 164–165. See also George W. Hilton and John F. Due, *The Electric Interurban Railways in America* (Stanford: Stanford University Press, 1960), pp. 208–209; Titcomb, Untitled speech; and Cheape, *Moving the Masses*, pp. 16 and 65–68. Figure 8 illustrates the profitability of the railways.

30. Most of the following discussion concerning progressive politics relies upon Fogelson, *The Fragmented Metropolis*, chap. 10; and George Mowry, *The California Progressives* (New York: Quadrangle, 1951), pp. 38–52. See also Frederic C. Jahar, *The Urban Establishment* (Urbana: University of Illinois Press, 1982), pp. 632–670.

31. Fogelson, *The Fragmented Metropolis*, pp. 211–212.

32. Mowry, *The California Progressives*, pp. 42–52; Fogelson, *The Fragmented Metropolis*, pp. 210–217. The political abuses of railway officials had also unified workers, populists, and progressive Republicans throughout the United States. See Thelen, *The New Citizenship*, p. 275; and McCormick, "The Discovery that Business Corrupts Politics," pp. 260–266.

33. The city government never seriously attempted to purchase the LARY and PE during this period because of the huge costs involved and the unprofitability of the railways. See below.

34. Fogelson, *The Fragmented Metropolis*, pp. 165–166; Los Angeles *Times*, November and December 1909, *passim*; Los Angeles *Examiner*, November and December 1909, *passim*. Cities throughout the United States also concluded that they should force the utility companies to serve the public interest through regulation. See Holt, "Urban Mass Transit History," pp. 81–82; Holt, "The Changing Perception of Urban Pathology," pp. 335–336; and McCormick, "The Discovery that Business Corrupts Politics," pp. 266–272. See also Board of Public Utilities, *1st Annual Report, 1910*, pp. 3–7.

35. Board of Public Utilities, *2nd Annual Report, 1910–1911*, p. 120. New York experienced similar traffic problems long before the general

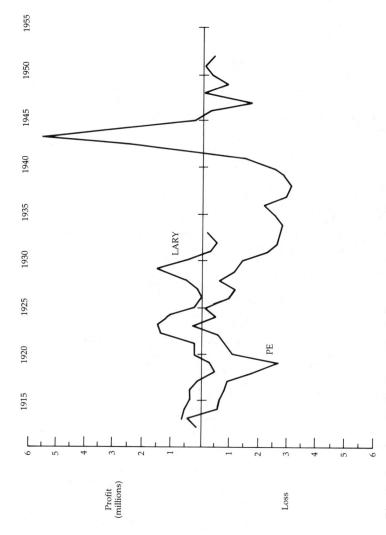

Fig. 8. Los Angeles Railway Profits. *Sources:* Los Angeles Municipal Research Library; Robert Fogelson, *The Fragmented Metropolis;* Spencer Crump, *Ride the Big Red Cars.*

adoption of the automobile as a means of urban transportation. One observer noted during the 1890s that streetcars on Broadway "form an almost unbroken procession from Bowling Green to Madison Square, moving at a snail's pace." See Cheape, *Moving the Masses,* p. 72.

36. Arnold, "The Transportation Problem in Los Angeles," pp. 9–13; *ERJ* 38 (October 21, 1911): 907; "Traffic Congestion in Los Angeles," *Journal of Electricity, Power and Gas* 27 (October 14, 1911): 333–334. See also the newspaper articles in the scrapbooks of the LARY Collection, HEH. Arnold recommended removing interurbans from Main Street and rerouting some local lines as a temporary expedient. He further recommended installing subways and elevateds as a permanent solution to congestion. A year earlier, Arnold found similar problems in Pittsburgh; see Tarr, *Transportation Innovation,* p. 23. Arnold was also heavily involved in planning and regulating Chicago's streetcars. See Barrett, *The Automobile and Urban Transit.*

37. Arnold, "The Transportation Problem in Los Angeles," pp. 9–13; J. R. Haynes to the mayor and City Council, August 3, 1918: Box 133, JRH; Board of Public Utilities, *2nd Annual Report, 1910–1911,* pp. 120–122. See also Board of Public Utilities, *4th Annual Report 1912–1913,* pp. 65–68 and 78; and Los Angeles *Express,* March 1, 1911.

38. Board of Public Utilities, *6th Annual Report, 1914–1915,* p. 50. The centralizing tendencies of Chicago's railways are described in Barrett, *The Automobile and Urban Transit,* pp. 12–17.

39. The board also noted that this would ease congestion in the central business district. Board of Public Utilities, *6th Annual Report, 1914–1915,* p. 50; *2nd Annual Report, 1910–1911.* See also *1st Annual Report, 1910,* pp. 128–129; Arnold, "The Transportation Problem in Los Angeles," p. 13; and *ERJ* 38 (October 21, 1911).

40. Fogelson, *The Fragmented Metropolis,* pp. 232–233. On the financial problems of other railways and their inability to expand services after 1910, see Barrett, *The Automobile and Urban Transit,* pp. 173–183; Cheape, *Moving the Masses,* p. 16; and Hilton and Due, *The Electric Interurban Railways in America,* pp. 208–209.

41. Figure 9 illustrates the dramatic decline in per capita ridership during the teens and late twenties. Glenn Yago in *The Decline of Transit,* pp. 56–57, argues that the railway industry was more resilient than many realized because streetcar patronage in cities with more than one million residents fell only 4 percent during the twenties. Yago ignores the fact that this was a time of extremely high urban growth. One must therefore examine ridership on a per capita basis. This latter method would show a very rapid decline in streetcar usage.

42. *ERJ* 46 (September 11, 1915): 500; Edwin Lewis, "Street Railway Development in Los Angeles and Environs, 1895–1938" (typescript in the LARY Collection, HEH), p. 52. See also volume I of a series of scrapbooks on transportation and politics in southern California at the

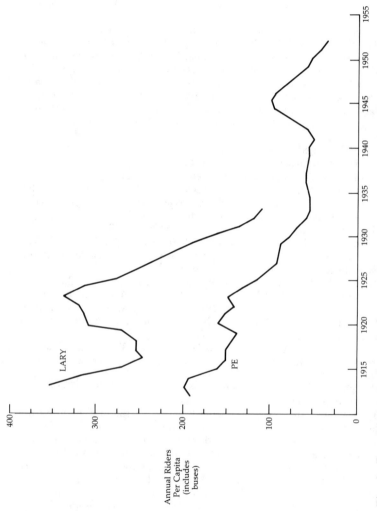

Fig. 9. Per Capita Railway Usage in Los Angeles. *Sources:* Los Angeles Municipal Research Library; Robert Fogelson, *The Fragmented Metropolis;* Spencer Crump, *Ride the Big Red Cars.*

HEH; Board of Public Utilities, *5th Annual Report, 1913–1914*, pp. 122–123; *6th Annual Report, 1914–1915*; and Fogelson, *The Fragmented Metropolis*, pp. 166–167.

43. *ERJ* 46 (September 11, 1915): 505. Another LARY official wrote in the same issue that "with everything in its favor the 5-cent automobile can injure but not succeed the electric railway as the chief means of city transportation." See also *ERJ* 45 (January 16, 1915): 156; *ERJ* (September 11, 1915): 503–505; Lewis, "Street Railway Development," pp. 126–128; and Los Angeles *Record*, November 21, 1916, June 8, 1917, October 3, 1917.

44. *ERJ* 45 (January 2, 1915): 76–77; Board of Public Utilities, *8th Annual Report, 1916–1917*, pp. 166–167. Two vigorous initiative campaigns in 1915 and 1917 confirmed and extended this legislation by bare majorities. See *ERJ* 45 (June 5, 1915): 1094; *ERJ* 46 (September 11, 1915): 501; and *ERJ* 49 (June 16, 1917): 1115. See also Ross D. Eckert and George Hilton, "The Jitneys," *Journal of Law and Economics* 15 (October 1972): 293–325.

45. Los Angeles *Record*, November 21, 1916.

46. Eckert and Hilton, "The Jitneys," p. 295. Eckert and Hilton argued that the jitneys became popular because of a natural economic reaction to the incentives presented by the streetcar monopolies. The monopolies artificially set the price of short-haul passenger transportation too high. The jitneys took advantage of this situation by providing superior service at the same price. This argument is only partially correct because it ignores the political and social ramifications of the controversy. See also Preston, *Automobile Age Atlanta*, pp. 57 and 72.

47. Quoted in Brownell, "A Symbol of Modernity," pp. 33–34.

3 / The Democratic Impulse and the Automobile

1. Weinstein, *The Corporate Ideal in the Liberal State*; Kolko, *The Triumph of Conservatism*.

2. Weibe, *The Search for Order*; Hays, "The Politics of Reform"; Galambos, "The Emerging Organizational Synthesis." See also Rodgers, "In Search of Progressivism," pp. 117–120; and McCormick, "The Discovery that Business Corrupts Politics," pp. 247–250.

3. On this point I am indebted to Richard McCormick's fine article, "The Discovery that Business Corrupts Politics."

4. Flink, *America Adopts the Automobile*, pp. 31 and 278; Los Angeles *Examiner* quoted in Fogelson, *The Fragmented Metropolis*, p. 164. For an account of recreational automobile use see Warren Belasco, *Americans on the Road*. Flink's book is an excellent study of the influence of the early automobile on American society.

5. Board of Public Utilities, *9th Annual Report, 1917–1918*, p. 54; *10th Annual Report, 1918–1919*, pp. 52–56; Los Angeles *Examiner*, November 21, 1911; Los Angeles *Times*, March 16, 1913.

6. Figure 10 shows per capita automobile registration versus railway patronage.

7. Los Angeles *Times*, January 1, 1920.

8. Los Angeles *Times*, August 31, 1919. The "ancient" Ford he refers to was probably only twelve years old.

9. Los Angeles *Times*, August 24,1919; Flink, *America Adopts the Automobile*, p. 202. See also Rae, *The Road and the Car in American Life*, for more on the nationwide "Good Roads" movement.

10. Los Angeles Engineering Department, *Annual Report, 1912–1913*, p. 76; *Annual Report, 1914–1915*, p. 8; Los Angeles *Times*, August 6, 1913.

11. Fogelson, *The Fragmented Metropolis*, p. 95; Engineering Department, *Annual Report, 1916–1917*, p. 68.

12. Los Angeles *Times*, January 1, 1920, September 14, 1919.

13. Engineering Department, *Annual Report, 1921–1922*, p. 39; Automobile Club of Southern California, *The Los Angeles Traffic Problem* (Los Angeles: By the Club, 1922), p. 9 (hereafter cited as ACSC, 1922); Los Angeles *Times*, April 20, 1919.

14. Los Angeles *Times*, May 4, 1919.

15. Ibid. See also "Pictorial Report: Overcrowded Condition of Los Angeles Street Car System, 1919" (typescript in the Los Angeles City Archives); and Los Angeles *Times*, September 7, 1919, August 31, 1919.

16. See Los Angeles *Times*, May 25, 1919, October 1, 1919.

17. Los Angeles *Times*, October 5, 1919.

18. Los Angeles *Times*, September 3, 1919, November 16, 1919, December 21, 1919.

19. Board of Public Utilities and California Railroad Commission Engineering Departments, "Report on Service, Operating and Financial Conditions of the Los Angeles Railway Corporation, 1919" (unpublished report in the Los Angeles City Archives); Board of Public Utilities, *11th Annual Report, 1919–1920*, pp. 61–88; Edwin Lewis (?), Speech to the Rotary Club, March 19, 1920 (typescript in Box 1, LARY Collection, HEH); Titcomb, Untitled speech; Gadsen, "The Readjustment Problems of Electric Railways"; Los Angeles Street Traffic Bureau, "Report on Los Angeles Traffic Conditions" (typescript in JRH); Los Angeles *Times*, November 11, 1919.

20. Los Angeles *Times*, October 12, 1919.

21. Los Angeles City Council, *Minutes* (December 23, 1919), v. 116, p. 389 (Los Angeles City Archives; hereafter cited as *Minutes*). Fred Very to City Council, December 20, 1919, City Council File 3065 (1919) (Los Angeles City Archives; hereafter cited as CF); Los Angeles *Times*, September 7, 1919. For the City Council's Public Utilities Committee recommendations, see CF 2771 (1919).

22. Los Angeles *Times*, December 2, 1919; CF 2771 (1919) and 2581 (1919).

23. Los Angeles *Times*, December 2, 1919, December 7, 1919, December 23, 1919; Wholesale Dry Goods Association to the City Council, October 24, 1919 and November 19, 1919, CF 2554 (1919); Donald Faries to the City Council, November 15, 1919, CF 2771 (1919).

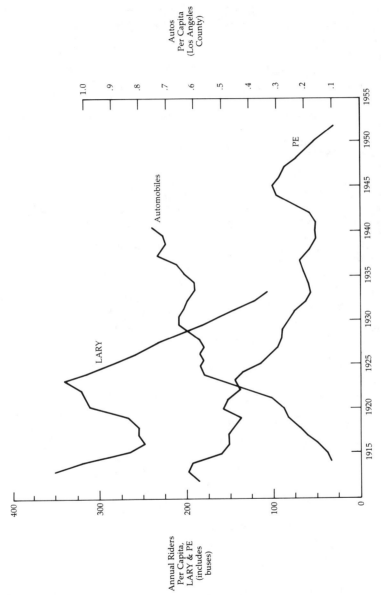

Fig. 10. Per Capita Automobile Registration Versus Per Capita Railway Usage in Los Angeles. *Sources*: Los Angeles Municipal Research Library; Regional Planning Commission; Robert Fogelson, *The Fragmented Metropolis*; Spencer Crump, *Ride the Big Red Cars*.

24. Los Angeles *Times*, December 23, 1919. A January editorial from the *Times* compared the parking crisis to the Battle at Gettysburg. See the *Times*, January 3, 1920.

25. Los Angeles *Times*, December 23, 1919, December 24, 1919; *Minutes* (December 26, 1919), v. 116, p. 405; CF 3076 (1919).

26. *Minutes* (December 26, 1919), v. 116, p. 405; CF 3076 (1919); Los Angeles *Times*, December 21, 1919, December 23, 1919, December 24, 1919.

27. Los Angeles *Times*, December 24, 1919, December 25, 1919, December 26, 1919.

28. *Minutes* (November 24, 1919), v. 116, p. 126; (December 15, 1919), v. 116, p. 315; Los Angeles *Times*, December 24, 1919; December 25, 1919, December 26, 1919.

29. Los Angeles *Times*, December 21, 1919, December 24, 1919, December 26, 1919; Fred Very to the City Council, CF 3065 (1919); *Minutes* (December 23, 1919), v. 116, p. 389. Paul Barrett discusses this issue in reference to Chicago; see Barrett, "Public Policy and Private Choice," p. 480.

30. Business Men's Co-Operative Association to the City Council, December 23, 1919, CF 3081 (1919); *Minutes* (December 26, 1919), v. 116, p. 406; Los Angeles *Examiner*, January 5, 1920; W. F. Thorne to the City Council, December 23, 1919, CF 3080 (1919).

31. Business Men's Co-Operative Association to the City Council, January 12, 1920, CF 128 (1920); see also Committee as a Whole Report, January 5, 1920, CF 2771 (1919); Los Angeles *Times*, January 3, 1920; Los Angeles *Examiner*, January 3, 1920.

32. Los Angeles *Record*, January 7, 1920; see also Los Angeles *Examiner*, January 10, 1920.

33. Los Angeles *Record*, January 7, 1920.

34. Ibid. See the *Record*, January 8, 1920, for the LARY's defense of itself. For earlier complaints about the poor railway service of the strike-breaking operators, see the numerous letters sent to the City Council by irate citizens during the previous fall: CF 2147; CF 2195; CF 2238; CF 2262; CF 2325 (all series 1919).

35. United Improvement Federation to the City Council, undated, CF 73 (1920); *Minutes* (January 8, 1920), v. 116, p. 500; Los Angeles *Record*, January 8, 1920.

36. Los Angeles *Record*, January 9, 1920; the *Record* reported that southern California patrons even criticized the Public Utilities commissioners for being too lenient on the railways.

37. Los Angeles *Record*, January 8, 1920.

38. Los Angeles *Record*, January 12, 1920.

39. Ibid.

40. Ibid. See also Los Angeles *Record*, January 13, 1920.

41. Los Angeles *Record*, January 22, 1920.

42. Los Angeles *Times*, January 14, 1920; see also Los Angeles *Times*, January 3, 1920.
43. Board of Public Utilities, *11th Annual Report, 1919–1920*, p. 89.
44. H. Z. Osborne to the City Council, January 10, 1920, CF 73 (1920); see also Los Angeles *Times*, January 14, 1920 and January 3, 1920.
45. Los Angeles *Times*, January 22, 1920, January 20, 1920, January 14, 1920; Los Angeles *Record*, January 21, 1920.
46. Los Angeles *Times*, January 29, 1920, January 20, 1920.
47. Los Angeles *Times*, January 22, 1920, January 23, 1920; Los Angeles *Examiner*, January 24, 1920; Los Angeles *Record*, January 23, 1920.
48. Los Angeles *Record*, January 22, 1920. The *Record* later admitted that the general public was hesitant about starting a municipal bus line. But the paper insisted that the public was interested in seeing what buses had to offer. See the *Record*, February 17, 1920. For citizens' views of buses see the *Record*, January 20, 1920, March 5, 1920, February 24, 1920, February 16, 1920. The paper argued in one of its editorials that "if motor buses can put the Pacific Electric out of business, then the Pacific Electric deserves to be put out of business."
49. *Minutes* (February 2, 1920), v. 116, pp. 707–708; CF 2771 (1920); Los Angeles *Times*, January 24, 1920; Los Angeles *Record*, January 23, 1920. On pedestrians see the *Examiner* and the *Times*, January 3, 1920. The Automobile Club argued that the ordinance was a "gross injustice" because it allowed trucks and delivery wagons to park on the street to make deliveries. The club threatened the City Council with litigation. See the Los Angeles *Times*, January 23, 1920.
50. *Minutes* (February 3, 1920), v. 116, p. 718; Los Angeles City Council, *Ordinances*, v. 1042, no. 39791 (hereafter cited as *Ordinances*); Los Angeles *Times*, February 4, 1920; Los Angeles *Examiner*, February 4, 1920; Los Angeles *Record*, February 3, 1920; *ERJ* 55 (March 1920): 623. The council eliminated a proposal that would have regulated pedestrians, but agreed to reinstate it should it prove necessary.
51. Los Angeles *Times*, February 8, 1920, February 24, 1920, February 29, 1920; Los Angeles *Record*, February 12, 1920, February 14, 1920, February 16, 1920.
52. Los Angeles *Times*, February 29, 1920.
53. Ibid. The only good the *Times* saw in the ordinance was that it would encourage the construction of parking lots in the central business district.
54. *Minutes* (March 11, 1920), v. 117, pp. 230–231; Los Angeles *Times*, March 12, 1920; Los Angeles *Record*, March 12, 1920.
55. Los Angeles *Times*, April 11, 1920, April 14, 1920; Los Angeles *Record*, April 12, 1920; Los Angeles *Examiner*, April 11, 1920.
56. Los Angeles *Examiner*, April 11, 1920, April 12, 1920, April 13, 1920; Los Angeles *Times*, April 11, 1920, April 12, 1920, April 13, 1920; Los Angeles *Record*, April 12, 1920.

57. L. Boyd to the City Council, April 12, 1920, CF 898 (1920); *Minutes* (April 14, 1920), v. 117, p. 565; Hoyt Lesher to the City Council, April 21, 1920, CF 1002 (1920); Los Angeles *Record*, April 12, 1920; Los Angeles *Examiner*, April 11, 1920; Los Angeles *Times*, April 18, 1920, April 13, 1920, April 14, 1920.

58. Los Angeles *Times*, April 18, 1920, April 20, 1920.

59. *Minutes* (April 21, 1920), v. 117, p. 629; (April 23, 1920), v. 117, p. 678; Los Angeles *Times*, April 21, 1920; Los Angeles *Record*, April 20, 1920; Los Angeles *Examiner*, April 21, 1920, April 22, 1920; P. E. Woods et al. to the City Council, April 20, 1920, CF 963 (1920).

60. Los Angeles *Times*, April 21, 1920, April 22, 1920; Los Angeles *Record*, April 21, 1920, April 22, 1920; Los Angeles *Examiner*, April 18, 1920; *Minutes* (April 14, 1920), v. 117, p. 565; L. Boyd to the City Council, April 12, 1920, CF 898 (1920).

61. Los Angeles *Examiner*, April 21, 1920.

62. Los Angeles *Record*, April 14, 1920, April 23, 1920. The original quotations were oddly capitalized; I have chosen to regularize the capitalization in these quotations.

63. Los Angeles *Times*, April 25, 1920. See also the Los Angeles *Record*, April 22, 1920; and the Los Angeles *Examiner*, April 23, 1920.

64. President Edgerton (of the Railroad Commission) wrote to the City Council that "the Railroad Commission cannot give weight to the contentions or interests of any particular group of citizens as against the interests of the citizens or street car riders as a whole." Edwin Edgerton to the City Council, April 23, 1920, CF 997 (1920); *Minutes* (April 23, 1920), v. 117, pp. 676–677; (April 26, 1920), v. 117, p. 693; *Ordinances*, v. 1046, no. 40199; South Park Improvement Association to the City Council, undated, CF 968 (1920); Chas. Fox et al. to the City Council, undated, 1003 (1920); Joseph Williams to the City Council, undated, CF 1005 (1920); H. Z. Osborne and Richard Sachse to the City Council, April 26, 1920, CF 1025 (1920); Los Angeles *Examiner*, April 24, 1920, April 25, 1920; Los Angeles *Times*, April 27, 1920; Los Angeles *Record*, April 22, 1920.

65. Geographer A. J. Scott recently argued that city governments in capitalist societies formulate transportation policies in an attempt to facilitate economic transactions. See A. J. Scott, *The Urban Land Nexus and the State* (London: Pion Limited, 1980).

66. A survey done in 1939 would reveal that more than 80 percent of those Angelenos working in factories outside of the central business district used automobiles for their daily transportation needs. See chapter 7.

67. Arthur S. Link notes this point in "What Happened to the Progressive Movement in the 1920's?" pp. 833–851.

68. Holt, "Urban Mass Transit History," pp. 81–97. See also Foster, *From Streetcar to Superhighway*, pp. 6–7; and Foster, "The Automobile and The City," pp. 462–463.

69. Philip Nichols, "The Massachusetts Law of Planning and Zoning," in

American Transit Association, ed., *Postwar Patterns of City Growth* (New York: By the Association, 1944), p. 25.
70. Barrett, *The Automobile and Urban Transit*, pp. 134–135.
71. Quoted in Brownell, "A Symbol of Modernity," pp. 20–44.
72. Barrett, *The Automobile and Urban Transit*, pp. 159–160. Several years after its aborted attempt in 1920, the Chicago City Council passed another parking ban.
73. Spencer Miller, Jr., "History of the Modern Highway in the United States," in Jean Labatut and Wheaton J. Lane, eds., *Highways in Our National Life* (Princeton: Princeton University Press, 1950), p. 88.

4 / The Power of Consensus

1. Frederick Law Olmsted, Jr. et al., *A Major Traffic Street Plan for Los Angeles* (Los Angeles: Committee on Los Angeles Plan of Major Highways of the Traffic Commission of the City and County of Los Angeles, 1924), pp. 11–12 (hereafter cited as *Major Traffic Street Plan*).
2. *Major Traffic Street Plan*, pp. 11–12; Barrett, *The Automobile and Urban Transit*, p. 161; Tarr, *Transportation Innovation*, p. 36; Jackson, *Crabgrass Frontier*, p. 182.
3. Quotation from David Owen Wise and Marguerite Dupree, "The Choice of the Automobile for Urban Passenger Transportation: Baltimore in the 1920's," in Jack R. Censer et al., eds., *South Atlantic Urban Studies* Vol. II (Columbia: University of South Carolina Press, 1978), p. 174. See also the footnote in Barrett, "Public Policy and Private Choice," p. 475; Barrett, *The Automobile and Urban Transit*, p. 132; Tarr, *Transportation Innovation*, pp. 27–28; and Brownell, "A Symbol of Modernity," p. 28.
4. Both passages quoted in Brownell, "A Symbol of Modernity," p. 28; see also Jackson, *Crabgrass Frontier*, p. 174.
5. For contemporary comments on the aftermath of the parking crisis, see Los Angeles *Times*, October 31, 1920; *ERJ* 56 (August 7, 1920): 292; *Traffic* (September 1925).
6. Engineering Department, *Annual Report, 1920–1921*, p. 3; and *Annual Report, 1921–1922*, p. 39.
7. See Engineering Department, *Annual Report, 1919–1920*, p. 83; Los Angeles *Times*, December 21, 1919. Street opening and widening occurred in other cities also; see Joseph Barnett, "The Highway in Urban and Suburban Areas," in Labatut and Lane, eds., *Highways in Our National Life*, pp. 145–146.
8. Engineering Department, *Annual Report, 1919–1920*, p. 3.
9. Los Angeles *Times*, August 27, 1922. The Chamber of Commerce had argued earlier that prevailing practices in the past had seen subdividers "ignore the continuity of streets already open, and . . . disregard the general public interest in the proper location of streets in new tracts." See the Los Angeles *Times*, June 18, 1922.

10. ACSC, 1922, pp. 3–9; see also, Los Angeles *Times*, October 31, 1920, July 16, 1922. Mark Foster has argued that planners held little power to effect change during the twenties. See Foster, *From Streetcar to Superhighway*, pp. 6–32.
11. ACSC, 1922, p. 17.
12. Ibid.
13. Ibid., p. 18.
14. Ibid., pp. 29–32.
15. *Minutes* (February 20, 1922), v. 126, p. 640; H. Z. Osborne to the Board of Public Utilities Commissioners, undated, CF 725 (1922); Los Angeles *Times*, December 13, 1921; Los Angeles *Herald*, June 9, 1922.
16. Los Angeles Traffic Commission, *The Los Angeles Plan* (Los Angeles: By the Commission, 1922), p. 3; ACSC, 1922, p. 9; Los Angeles *Times*, December 13, 1921; Traffic Commission, *President's Annual Report, 1924* (Los Angeles: By the Commission), p. 3 (hereafter cited as Traffic Commission, *Annual Report*); Board of Public Utilities, *13th Annual Report, 1921–1922*, p. 111. Elected officials were prohibited from participating in the Traffic Commission because the organization deemed it inappropriate for these officials to take sides on issues where public opinion was divided.
17. Los Angeles *Times*, August 13, 1922.
18. Traffic Commission, *The Los Angeles Plan*, pp. 6–9 and 23. The Traffic Commission grandiloquently spoke of the Automobile Club report as "one of the greatest civic contributions ever made to the City of Los Angeles."
19. Ibid., pp. 6–7.
20. Ibid., pp. 7–9.
21. *Minutes* (August 2, 1923), v. 138, p. 308; "Public Works Report," CF 3888 (1923). See also Los Angeles *Times*, June 28, 1924, August 3, 1923, August 14, 1923, August 23, 1923; *Minutes* (August 14, 1923), v. 138, p. 499; (November 5, 1923), v. 140, p. 339.
22. Engineering Department, *Annual Report, 1924–1925*, p. 85; Traffic Commission, *Annual Report, 1924*, p. 10; *Major Traffic Street Plan*, p. 5.
23. *Major Traffic Street Plan*, p. 7.
24. Ibid., pp. 9–11. Despite these claims there is much data to indicate that traffic congestion in such cities as Chicago, Boston, New York, and Philadelphia was just as bad as in Los Angeles.
25. Ibid., p. 11. These new suburban dwellers demanded paved streets for their automobiles. The city engineer wrote in 1924 that "the work of the surveying department for the past year has been carried on under constantly increasing pressure. Orders for street improvements have been received faster than the necessary surveys could be turned out and the demand of the public for speed has been insistent." See the Engineering Department, *Annual Report, 1923–1924*, p. 68.
26. *Major Traffic Street Plan*, pp. 11–12.
27. These planning commissions did not have much power to effect

change anyway. See Mark S. Foster, "The Decentralization of Los Angeles during the 1920s" (Ph.D. diss., University of Southern California, 1972).

28. *Major Traffic Street Plan,* p. 12; see also Engineering Department, *Annual Report, 1921–1922,* p. 43.
29. *Major Traffic Street Plan,* pp. 12–16.
30. Ibid., pp. 16–49. Bartholomew completed thirty-two comprehensive street plans for cities throughout the United States during the twenties. The fundamental element in all of these plans was an improved street system providing wide thoroughfares radiating from the city center. See Blaine Brownell, "The Commercial-Civic Elite and City Planning in Atlanta, Memphis, and New Orleans in the 1920s," *Journal of Southern History* 41 (August 1975): 354–355.
31. *Major Traffic Street Plan,* pp. 16–19.
32. Los Angeles *Times,* October 3, 1924, October 4, 1924, January 12, 1925, June 24, 1925; see also Traffic Commission, *Annual Report, 1924,* pp. 10–11.
33. Los Angeles *Times,* October 7, 1924, August 17, 1924, October 19, 1924, October 26, 1924. See also Los Angeles *Record,* October 31, 1924; and Los Angeles *Examiner,* October 31, 1924.
34. Traffic Commission, *Annual Report, 1924,* p. 3.
35. Los Angeles *Times,* June 29, 1925.
36. Traffic Commission, *Annual Report, 1927,* p. 29. Even before the passage of the Major Traffic Street Plan, city residents were eager to see improvements made. See Engineering Department, *Annual Report, 1923–1924,* p. 50.
37. Los Angeles *Times,* January 1, 1925, April 13, 1924, December 29, 1924; Engineering Department, *Annual Report, 1925–1926,* p. 71; Traffic Commission, *Annual Report, 1927,* pp. 19–29.
38. Traffic Commission, *Annual Report, 1926,* pp. 15–17; *1927,* p. 19; *1928,* p. 12.
39. More than a hundred members contributed $500 each to belong to the committee.
40. Traffic Commission, *Annual Report, 1924,* pp. 7–8; *1925,* pp. 3 and 15; *1926,* pp. 3–18; *1928,* p. 3; *1929,* p. 6.
41. Traffic Commission, *Annual Report, 1925,* p. 10; *1927,* pp. 17–19; Los Angeles *Times,* June 25, 1925, June 28, 1925.
42. McClintock proudly announced that "Los Angeles from one of the worst has become one of the best traffic regulated cities in the world." See the Los Angeles *Times,* July 3, 1927, and August 20, 1927. See also *Minutes* (July 2, 1924), v. 146, p. 654; (July 10, 1924), v. 147, p. 79; Traffic Commission, *Annual Report, 1924,* pp. 4–5; *1926,* pp. 3–4; Los Angeles *Times,* October 9, 1924, November 13, 1925. The new laws banned horse-drawn vehicles in the central business district between 7 A.M. and 6:15 P.M. They also finally forced pedestrians to obey traffic signals. Before this, pedestrians could cross streets on red lights and

cross intersections at diagonals rather than at right angles. The commission also worked hard to install timed traffic signals to improve traffic flow. See Traffic Commission, *Annual Report 1924*, p. 6; *1927*, p. 9; *1928*, pp. 8–29; and *1930*, p. 18. See also Miller McClintock, *Street Traffic Control* (Los Angeles: Los Angeles City Council, 1925).

43. Traffic Commission, *Annual Report, 1927*, pp. 19–35.
44. Traffic Commission, "Major Traffic Street Plan" (map in Box 137, JRH); Los Angeles *Times*, October 25, 1931, October 18, 1931. Judith Powers has argued that only when private interests can rally around a common cause can a city government aggressively pursue community-wide planning. See Powers, "The Absence of Conspiracy," p. 16.
45. Traffic Commission, *Annual Report, 1929*, p. 15.
46. Brownell, "A Symbol of Modernity," pp. 25–41; see also Brownell, "The Commercial-Civic Elite," pp. 339–368.
47. Barrett, *The Automobile and Urban Transit*, pp. 129–161; Barnett, "The Highway in Urban and Suburban Areas," pp. 145–146; Tarr, *Transportation Innovation*, p. 27. Southern cities also advocated the construction of new thoroughfares, the widening of existing streets, and comprehensive urban planning. See Brownell, "A Symbol of Modernity," p. 41. For a look at street pavements and their role in responding to modern autos, see Clay McShane, "Transforming the Use of Urban Space," pp. 279–307.
48. See Scott, *The Urban Land Nexus*.
49. Barrett argues that street planning in Chicago was never politicized. It seems to me, however, that street planning in both Chicago and Los Angeles was highly political in nature. But unlike transit planning, street improvements were supported by many politically active interest groups, which made it easier to pass legislation and programs favorable to the automobile.

5 / The Union Station Controversy

1. See, for instance, Link, "What Happened to the Progressive Movement in the 1920's?" pp. 833–851.
2. Paul Barrett discusses this issue extensively in *The Automobile and Urban Transit*, pp. 85–88.
3. Foster, *From Streetcar to Superhighway*, pp. 72–78; Barrett, *The Automobile and Urban Transit*, pp. 99–103; Richard Wade, "Urbanization," in C. Vann Woodward, ed., *The Comparative Approach to American History* (New York: Basic Books, 1968), pp. 191–200.
4. Los Angeles *Times*, May 13, 1923; see also the Los Angeles *Citizen*, November 16, 1923.
5. *Major Traffic Street Plan*.
6. See H. Z. Osborne's remarks about subways in the Los Angeles *Times*, February 14, 1922.

7. I have used the terms "rapid transit," "rapid transportation," and "rapid rail" throughout this work to describe subway and elevated plans. I have used the term "mass transportation" to mean any form of public transportation.
8. Engineering Department, *Annual Report, 1925–1926*, p. 71; Los Angeles *Times*, August 13, 1925.
9. Traffic Commission to City Council, December 17, 1923, CF 6749 (1923); Traffic Commission, *Annual Report, 1924*, p. 13.
10. F. A. Lorentz to E. F. Bogardus, undated, and E. F. Bogardus to City Council, undated, CF 6749 (1923).
11. *Minutes* (February 14, 1924), v. 142, p. 697; (February 15, 1924), v. 142, p. 772; (February 25, 1924), v. 143, p. 125.
12. The Traffic Commission was a major proponent of this alteration.
13. Los Angeles *Times*, April 22, 1925; Kelker, De Leuw & Company, *Report and Recommendations on a Comprehensive Rapid Transit Plan for the City and County of Los Angeles* (Chicago: Kelker, De Leuw & Co., 1925), pp. xv–xvi, and 1 (hereafter cited as Kelker–De Leuw); for a summary of the plan see Traffic Commission, "A Synopsis of the Kelker–De Leuw Transit Report" (pamphlet in Box 135, JRH).
14. Kelker–De Leuw, pp. 1–2.
15. Ibid., pp. 1–2 and 38.
16. Ibid., pp. 2–6.
17. Ibid., pp. 2–7 and 171–182.
18. Los Angeles *Times*, November 27, 1925, April 22, 1925.
19. Los Angeles *Times*, September 11, 1925; see also the following City Council Files for original copies of the petitions: 5612, 5934, 6358, 7005, 7054, 7133, 7961 (all series 1925). See also A. F. Southwick, "The Kelker L.A. Traffic Plan," *Municipal League of Los Angeles Bulletin* 3 (September 25, 1925): 7–8.
20. Los Angeles *Times*, September 30, 1925, April 22, 1925, September 27, 1925; Traffic Commission, *Annual Report, 1926*, p. 28; *Minutes* (September 16, 1925), v. 160, p. 414; (November 27, 1925), v. 162, p. 647; George W. Scott, "More Light on the Kelker–De Leuw Traffic Survey," *Municipal League of Los Angeles Bulletin* 3 (November 25, 1925): 1.
21. The League wanted the Traffic Commission heavily represented on the committee because of its experience with the Major Traffic Street Plan; see *Minutes* (September 28, 1925), v. 160, p. 637; Municipal League to the City Council, undated, CF 5891 (1925); "The League's Approach to the Kelker Plan," *Municipal League of Los Angeles Bulletin* 3 (October 28, 1925): 12–13.
22. The riders had been fighting fare increases for years; see chapter 2.
23. Los Angeles *Times*, December 17, 1925.
24. For a general history of the controversy see Marshall Stimson, "The Battle for a Union Station in Los Angeles," *Historical Society of Southern California Quarterly* 21 (March 1939): 37–44; *ERJ* (August 21, 1926); "The Truth About Municipal Grade Crossings and Union Stations" (pam-

phlet in Box 133, JRH); Boyle Workman, *The City That Grew* (Los Angeles: By the Author, 1931).

25. Arnold, "The Transportation Problem in Los Angeles," pp. 5–6, 17; Los Angeles *Times*, February 9, 1926; *Minutes* (August 31, 1925), v. 160, p. 79; (September 3, 1925), v. 160, pp. 173–174; CF 5333 (1925); Los Angeles *Examiner*, March 12, 1925; "A Symposium on the L.A. Grade Crossing and Union Terminal Problems," *Municipal League of Los Angeles Bulletin* 3 (January 30, 1926): 1–2; *ERJ* 67 (February 6, 1926): 260.

26. The City Council asked the city's newspapers to unite in an effort to pressure the railroads into accepting the council's position. *Minutes* (August 31, 1925), v. 160, p. 79; (September 3, 1925), v. 160, pp. 173–174; CF 5333 (1925). The City Planning Commission argued that the uncertainty surrounding the union station was making it difficult to complete the Major Traffic Street Plan projects in that area. The commission asked the railroads to cooperate with the city in resolving this issue. *Minutes* (December 23, 1925), v. 163, p. 635; City Planning Commission to City Council, December 8, 1925, CF 8352 (1925).

27. The railroads would continue using Alameda for industrial switching at night. Los Angeles *Times*, January 5, 1926, January 6, 1926; Los Angeles *Record*, January 5, 1926, January 6, 1926; Los Angeles *Examiner*, January 5, 1926, January 6, 1926; *Minutes* (January 6, 1926), v. 164, pp. 83–86; Pacific Electric Railway Corporation to City Council, undated, CF 83 (1926); Southern Pacific Railroad to City Council, undated, CF 84 (1926); "A Symposium," p. 10.

28. *Minutes* (January 6, 1926), v. 164, pp. 83–84; Pacific Electric Railway Corporation to City Council, undated, CF 83 (1926).

29. Los Angeles *Examiner*, January 3, 1926, January 5, 1926.

30. Los Angeles *Examiner*, January 8, 1926.

31. Los Angeles Chamber of Commerce to City Council, January 6, 1926, CF 120 (1926); *Minutes* (January 7, 1926), v. 164, p. 118; Los Angeles *Examiner*, January 6, 1926; Los Angeles *Times*, January 8, 1926.

32. Board of Public Utilities and Transportation Commissioners to City Council, January 26, 1926, CF 531 (1926); *Minutes* (January 27, 1926), v. 164, pp. 604–605; Los Angeles *Examiner*, January 27, 1926; Los Angeles *Record*, January 27, 1926; Los Angeles *Times*, January 31, 1926.

33. Los Angeles *Examiner*, January 13, 1926, January 15, 1926, January 21, 1926, January 25, 1926, January 29, 1926.

34. The *Times* argued that the Southern Pacific Railroad financed this advertising campaign, using the association's name as an attempt to hide its own interest in the matter. See Los Angeles *Times*, April 12, 1926.

35. See the advertisements in the Los Angeles *Examiner*, January 4, 1926, January 12, 1926, January 14, 1926, January 19, 1926; Los Angeles *Record*, January 7, 1926, January 13, 1926, January 16, 1926, January 23, 1926. See also the advertisement signed by William Sproule, presi-

dent of the Southern Pacific Railroad in the Los Angeles *Examiner*, January 17, 1926; and in the Los Angeles *Record*, January 18, 1926.

36. Traffic Commission to City Council, January 29, 1926, CF 628 (1926); Traffic Commission, *Annual Report, 1926*, p. 28; Kelker–De Leuw, p. 1; Los Angeles *Record*, January 7, 1926; Los Angeles *Examiner*, January 22, 1926.

37. Los Angeles *Record*, January 22, 1926, February 3, 1926.

38. Traffic Commission Rapid Transit Committee to City Council, January 29, 1926, CF 628 (1926); Los Angeles *Times*, January 30, 1926; Los Angeles *Examiner*, January 30, 1926. The *Times* reported that the meeting was packed with railroad officials and Business Men's Association members, which allowed them to push the resolution through. Their action was highly irregular because it had not been reviewed by the commission's executive committee. See the Los Angeles *Times*, April 13, 1926.

39. Los Angeles *Times*, January 29, 1926, January 31, 1926.

40. Los Angeles *Times*, January 30, 1926, February 2, 1926, February 9, 1926; Los Angeles *Examiner*, February 2, 1926.

41. Los Angeles *Times*, February 4, 1926, February 9, 1926, February 16, 1926; Lincoln Heights Commercial and Industrial Association to the City Council, February 5, 1926, CF 784 (1926); The South Huntington Drive Improvement Association also favored the removal of the board because it was "influenced by the corporations." See the Los Angeles *Times*, February 16, 1926.

42. Los Angeles *Times*, April 12, 1926.

43. Los Angeles *Times*, February 8, 1926, February 9, 1926; E. M. Schwartz to the City Council, January 30, 1926, CF 650 (1926).

44. Los Angeles *Record*, February 26, 1926; Los Angeles *Times*, February 26, 1926; Los Angeles *Examiner*, February 26, 1926; *Minutes* (February 19, 1926), v. 165, p. 413; (March 12, 1926), v. 166, p. 228; (April 16, 1926), v. 167, pp. 387–388; CF 885 and 1155 (both series 1926). See also Los Angeles *Record*, January 28, 1926, February 3, 1926, February 9, 1926; Los Angeles *Examiner*, January 28, 1926, January 29, 1926, February 4, 1926; Los Angeles *Times*, February 2, 1926, February 10, 1926; *Minutes* (February 9, 1926), v. 165, p. 161; (February 19, 1926), v. 165, p. 413; (February 26, 1926), v. 165, p. 607; CF 1555, 887, 1155 (all series 1926). Seven other issues were already on the ballot.

45. Los Angeles *Examiner*, January 29, 1926, February 4, 1926, February 10, 1926, February 23, 1926, March 2, 1926. This tactic did not always work. The Harbor District Chambers of Commerce continued to favor the union station despite the railroads' efforts to persuade them otherwise. See Lawndale Chamber of Commerce to the City Council, February 24, 1926, CF 1372 (1926).

46. Los Angeles *Examiner*, February 2, 1926, February 10, 1926. The *Times* argued that its land holdings were in a different area of the city; see February 9, 1926. See also Los Angeles *Examiner*, February 21, 1926.

47. Los Angeles *Examiner*, February 23, 1926; Los Angeles *Record*, February 23, 1926.
48. The committee also felt a union station was not needed because only three railroads entered Los Angeles and the city was a terminus not a transfer point. *Minutes* (February 15, 1926), v. 165, p. 265; Mayor George Cryer to the City Council, February 15, 1926, and M. McAdoo et al. to Mayor George Cryer, February 13, 1926, CF 989 (1926); Los Angeles *Examiner*, February 16, 1926; Los Angeles *Times*, February 16, 1926; Los Angeles *Record*, February 15, 1926.
49. McAdoo et al. to Mayor George Cryer, February 13, 1926, CF 989 (1926); see also the Los Angeles *Record*, February 15, 1926.
50. Los Angeles *Times*, February 9, 1926, February 10, 1926.
51. Los Angeles *Times*, February 10, 1926, February 16, 1926, February 18, 1926; "A Symposium," p. 3.
52. Taxpayer's Anti-Elevated League to the City Council, February 20, 1926, CF 1305 (1926); Taxpayer's Anti-Elevated League to the City Council, February 25, 1926, CF 1510 (1926); see also the Los Angeles *Times*, February 20, 1926. The *Times* quoted a Chicago traction company president who said that elevateds were disastrous for property values. Los Angeles *Times*, February 16, 1926.
53. James Cordray to the City Council, February 7, 1926, CF 994 (1926).
54. Los Angeles *Times*, February 21, 1926; Los Feliz Improvement Association to the City Council, February 24, 1926, CF 1370 (1926).
55. Los Angeles *Times*, March 4, 1926, March 5, 1926, March 10, 1926.
56. Los Angeles *Times*, March 6, 1926, March 12, 1926.
57. Los Angeles *Examiner*, March 30, 1926.
58. Los Angeles *Examiner*, March 30, 1926, April 8, 1926, April 12, 1926, April 20, 1926.
59. Los Angeles *Times*, April 13, 1926.
60. Ibid. See also "A Symposium," p. 12; and D. W. Pontius, "The Plan of the Railroads for Station Facilities in Los Angeles," *Southwestern Purchasing Agent* (February 1926): 20.
61. Los Angeles *Times*, April 13, 1926, April 21, 1926; Los Angeles *Examiner*, April 21, 1926.
62. Los Angeles *Times*, April 14, 1926, April 16, 1926.
63. Los Angeles *Times*, April 19, 1926, April 20, 1926, April 21, 1926, April 22, 1926, April 23, 1926, April 25, 1926.
64. This analysis depends upon petitions sent to the City Council (as found in the City Archives), newspaper reports, campaign literature, and advertisements.
65. Not surprisingly, the *Times* and the *Examiner* gave different reports on how the council members aligned themselves. The *Times* reported that eight of the fifteen members opposed dropping the city's fight for a union station, one favored ending the fight, and the others were uncommitted. The paper also claimed that five members explicitly

opposed granting the forty-year franchises to the PE and Southern Pacific Railroad, while none favored the issue. The *Examiner* argued that only three members favored the Plaza terminal, while one opposed it, with the rest leaning in the direction of the railroads. See the Los Angeles *Times*, February 2, 1926; and the Los Angeles *Examiner*, January 29, 1926.

66. Los Angeles *Examiner*, February 4, 1926.
67. Lincoln Heights Commercial and Industrial Association to the City Council, February 5, 1926, CF 784 (1926); Los Angeles *Times*, February 4, 1926. See also Hollywood Junction Business Men's Association to the City Council, February 3, 1926, CF 745 (1926).
68. After failing to convince the larger body, railroad officials tried to coerce the individual chambers to relent. One local group wrote to the City Council declaring that they were "as a unit in oposition [*sic*] to the railroads [*sic*] plan and favor the central station at the Plaza." Lawndale Chamber of Commerce to the City Council, February 24, 1926, CF 1372 (1926).
69. This plan sought to build a union station at a different site. Two other union station plans had been proposed by others but none were considered very carefully. The election remained a campaign between the Plaza terminal and the railroads' elevated system. For a description of the three alternatives, see "A Symposium"; and the Los Angeles *Examiner*, March 4, 1926, April 9, 1926.
70. City Club of Los Angeles, "Report on Rapid Transit"; Los Angeles *Times*, January 30, 1926. Fogelson argues that the City Club's opposition to decentralization was indicative of a citywide consensus against rapid transit. This interpretation is misleading, however, since the City Club stood alone on this issue. Angelenos generally continued to recognize the importance of rapid transit and favored a centralized city at the time of the election. It was not until after the election that large numbers of residents turned against the idea of a centralized city. See Fogelson, *The Fragmented Metropolis*, p. 178.
71. Los Angeles *Times*, February 4, 1926, February 14, 1926, March 10, 1926, March 13, 1926. See the following City Council Files at the City Archives: 721, 759, 774, 981, 982, 983, 1057, 1114, 1115, 1370, 2146 (all series 1926). Two days before the election, the *Examiner* reported that representatives from fifty Los Angeles improvement associations unanimously voted to back the railroads in opposition to the union station, but I have not been able to verify this, making me suspicious that the *Examiner* made up this statistic. See the Los Angeles *Examiner*, April 28, 1926.
72. Los Angeles *Times*, May 1, 1926, May 2, 1926. See also Los Angeles *Record*, May 1, 1926, May 2, 1926; Los Angeles *Examiner*, May 1, 1926, May 2, 1926; "Los Angeles Voters Approve Union Depot at Plaza Site," *Engineering News-Record* 96 (May 13, 1926): 786. Those who

feared the railroads would further delay the construction of the union station through litigation were correct. The union station was not completed until 1939, thirteen years after the election.

73. See, for instance, the Los Angeles *Record* proudly acknowledging the improved automobile traffic resulting from the partial completion of the Major Traffic Street Plan, December 31, 1925. PE officials during the campaign had dubbed subways "gopher holes." See Los Angeles *Times*, March 13, 1926. The Traffic Commission's *Annual Report* for 1927 and 1928 reported little activity in rapid-transit planning.

6 / A Lack of Consensus

1. City Club, "Report on Rapid Transit," p. 3.
2. Ibid., pp. 4–9.
3. Clarence A. Dykstra, "Congestion De Luxe—Do We Want It?" *National Municipal Review* 15 (July 1926): 395–398.
4. John Ihdler, "The Automobile and Community Planning," *Annals of the American Academy of Political and Social Sciences* 116 (November 1924): 200.
5. Donald M. Baker, "What Shall We Do With Our Next Million People?" (speech before the Downtown Business Association of Los Angeles, 1936, JRH); Los Angeles Board of City Planning Commissioners, *Second Conference on Mass Transportation* (Los Angeles: By the Commission, 1930), p. 6 (hereafter cited as *Second Conference*); Los Angeles County Regional Planning Commission, *Business Districts* (Los Angeles: By the Commission, 1944), p. 1.
6. For streetcar conditions, see the Los Angeles *Record*, March 15, 1929. On the lack of government activity regarding rail service see Traffic Commission, *Annual Report, 1928*, p. 13; and *1929*, pp. 45–46.
7. Los Angeles Board of City Planning Commissioners, *Conference on the Rapid Transit Question* (Los Angeles: By the Commission, 1930), pp. 18–19 (hereafter cited as *Conference*). The Board of Public Utilities changed its name to the Board of Public Utilities and Transportation after 1924.
8. Ibid. p. 7. See also Traffic Commission, *Annual Report, 1929*, p. 46.
9. *Conference*, pp. 40 and 62.
10. Ibid., pp. 8, 19, and 21.
11. Ibid., pp. 33, 44, and 51–58.
12. Ibid, pp. 32–42.
13. *Second Conference*, p. 15.
14. Ibid., pp. 8–13.
15. Ibid., pp. 9–11 and 33. See the Los Angeles *Record*, January 9, 1926, on the burden of assessments for property owners; see also Los Angeles Board of City Planning Commissioners, *Annual Report, 1929–1930*, p. 20.

16. *Second Conference*, pp. 5–18.
17. City Planning Commissioners, *Annual Report, 1929–1930*, p. 19.
18. *Second Conference*, p. 18.
19. Committee to Accomplish Mass Transportation, *Report* (pamphlet in Los Angeles Municipal Research Library), p. 20. Paul Barrett argues that the commonly held attitude that rapid transit should pay for itself crippled the railways in Chicago. See Barrett, "Public Policy and Private Choice," p. 491; and *The Automobile and Urban Transit*, p. 6.
20. Donald Baker, *Report on Rapid Transit System* (Los Angeles: Central Business District Association, 1933); "Report on Rapid Transit Meeting of the Central Business District Association," December 14, 1933 (Box 135, JRH). Baker's report engendered a new series of arguments and criticisms. Several people contended at public meetings that Baker's rail system would benefit the downtown business community at the expense of merchants located in the suburbs. Others expressed their preference for a decentralized city structure over a centralized one. See the Los Angeles *News-Journal*, February 9, 1934.
21. Los Angeles *Examiner*, August 14, 1933; see also September 7, 1933, October 11, 1934, October 12, 1934. More complaints can be found in the following: Los Angeles *Herald & Express*, February 9, 1934, October 11, 1934, April 20, 1934; Los Angeles *Illustrated Daily News*, October 12, 1934; Los Angeles *Times*, October 12, 1934; California Railroad Commission, *Case No. 4002. Report on the Local Public Transportation Requirements of Los Angeles* (San Francisco: By the Commission, 1935). See also a typescript relating to the case in Box 135, JRH; Baker, *Report on Rapid Transit System*, p. 23; Los Angeles Board of Public Utilities and Transportation Commissioners, *General Conclusions and Recommendations Concerning Mass Transportation in the Los Angeles Area* (Los Angeles: By the Board, 1940), p. 3; and Los Angeles Traffic Survey Committee, *Street Traffic Management for Los Angeles* (Los Angeles: By the Committee, 1948), p. 19.
22. Los Angeles Transportation Engineering Board, *Report of Traffic and Transportation Survey* (Los Angeles: Citizens' Transportation Survey Committee, 1940), pp. 14–27; Milton Breivogel, "Transportation Characteristics of the Los Angeles Metropolitan Area" (unpublished typescript in the Los Angeles Municipal Research Library, dated 1941).
23. Committee to Accomplish Mass Transportation *Report*, p. 17; City Planning Commissioners, *Annual Report, 1937–1938*, p. 5; Transportation Engineering Board, *Report of Traffic and Transportation Survey*, p. 69; Los Angeles Department of City Planning, *A Parkway Plan for the City of Los Angeles and the Metropolitan Area* (Los Angeles: By the Department, 1941), p. 21; Baker, *Report on Rapid Transit System*, pp. 44–45.
24. Barrett, *The Automobile and Urban Transit*, pp. 67–68 and 93–103.
25. Foster, *From Streetcar to Superhighway*, pp. 80–86.
26. Barrett, *The Automobile and Urban Transit*, pp. 2–8 and 81.
27. Several historians have suggested that an understanding of this split

between downtown and suburban interests is vital to explaining twentieth-century urban politics. See Wade, "Urbanization," pp. 187–205; Samuel P. Hays, "The Changing Political Structure of the City in Industrial America," *Journal of Urban History* 1 (November 1974): 6–38; Zane L. Miller, *Box Cox's Cincinnati: Urban Politics in the Progressive Era* (New York: Oxford University Press, 1968); and Carl Abbott, *The New Urban America: Growth and Politics in Sunbelt Cities* (Chapel Hill: The University of North Carolina Press, 1981).

28. John A. Beeler and Walden E. Sweet quoted in Foster, *From Streetcar to Superhighway*, pp. 70–71.

7 / Reshaping the Modern City

1. Davenport quoted in Cheape, *Moving the Masses*, pp. 27–28; Charles Horton Cooley quoted in Tarr, "From City to Suburb," p. 202.
2. Cooley again quoted in Tarr, "From City to Suburb," p. 202. See also Jackson, *Crabgrass Frontier*, pp. 68–69; Scott Donaldson, *The Suburban Myth*; and Peter Schmitt, *Back to Nature: The Arcadian Myth in America*.
3. Both quotations cited in Jackson, *Crabgrass Frontier*, pp. 50 and 45. I am indebted to Jackson for the ideas contained in this paragraph.
4. For more on balloon frame construction, see Jackson, *Crabgrass Frontier*, pp. 124–128; and Christopher Tunnard and Henry Hope Reed, *American Skyline: The Growth and Form of Our Cities and Towns* (New York: New American Library, 1956), p. 69.
5. *Conference*, p. 20; Baker, "What Shall We Do With Our Next Million People?"
6. Baker, "What Shall We Do With Our Next Million People?"; *Conference*, pp. 6 and 59; Miscellaneous items in Box 2, LARY Collection, HEH; City Planning Commissioners, *Annual Report, 1929–30*, p. 49. See also Foster, *From Streetcar to Superhighway*, for a discussion of American planners and their favorable attitudes towards decentralization. Several years earlier, Foster argued that Los Angeles planners consciously promoted decentralization in Los Angeles. See Foster, "The Model-T, the Hard Sell, and Los Angeles' Urban Growth" pp. 459–484. Blaine Brownell discusses city planners in the South and their support of decentralization in "The Commercial-Civic Elite," pp. 359–360.
7. E. E. East, "Streets," in George W. Robbins and L. Deming Tilton, eds., *A Preface to a Master Plan* (Los Angeles: The Pacific Southwest Academy, 1941), p. 97; Regional Planning Commission, *Business Districts*. See also Regional Planning Commission, *Master Plan and Land Use Inventory and Classification* (Los Angeles: By the Commission, 1941), pp. 23–29; Robert O. Thomas, "Transportation Problems in the Los Angeles Metropolitan Area," *Civic Affairs* 7 (March 1940): 4; Traffic Survey Committee, *Street Traffic Management*, pp. 23–27; Los Angeles City Planning Commission, *Mass Transit Facilities and the Master Plan*

of Parkways, p. 8; Richard Sachse, "Transit," in Robbins and Tilton, *Preface to a Master Plan,* p. 103.

It is important to realize that Angelenos moved into the suburbs because of this aesthetic ideal and not because developers were running out of room in the area near the central business district. The city center and its peripheral areas had an abnormally high proportion of vacant lots at the time decentralization began. See Earl Hanson and Paul Beckett, *Los Angeles: Its People and Its Homes* (Los Angeles: The Haynes Foundation, 1944). Kenneth T. Jackson has shown that federal officials also favored suburban single-family dwelling construction through their implementation of FHA housing legislation. See Jackson, "Federal Subsidy and the Suburban Dream: The First Quarter-Century of Government Intervention in the Housing Market," *Records of the Columbia Historical Society, Washington, D.C.* 50 (1980): 421–451. Mark Foster discusses the attitudes of planners towards decentralization. See Foster, *From Streetcar to Superhighway,* p. 159. The automobile and the suburban ideal is discussed in Preston, *Automobile Age Atlanta,* p. 74.

8. Lawrence B. De Graaf, "The City of Black Angels: Emergence of the Los Angeles Ghetto, 1890–1930," *Pacific Historical Review* 39 (Summer 1970): 323–352; see also De Graaf, "Negro Migration to Los Angeles, 1930–1950" (Ph.D. diss., University of California, Los Angeles, 1962). For information regarding spatial segregation in other cities see, Brownell, "A Symbol of Modernity," pp. 34–35; Brownell, "The Commercial-Civic Elite," pp. 358–359; Jackson, *Crabgrass Frontier,* pp. 133 and 190–230; and Preston, *Automobile Age Atlanta,* pp. 74–75.

9. Ricardo Romo, *East Los Angeles: History of a Barrio* (Austin: University of Texas Press, 1983).

10. This phenomenon occurred in other cities as well. As late as 1925, 98.3 percent of those residing in Baltimore lived within one-quarter mile of a streetcar line. See Wise and Dupree, "The Choice of the Automobile," p. 154.

11. Wise and Dupree note this same economic incentive as a possible reason behind the adoption of the automobile in Baltimore. See "The Choice of the Automobile."

12. Spot Maps, LARY Collection, HEH. See also Foster, "The Model-T, the Hard Sell, and Los Angeles' Urban Growth," p. 476.

13. Hanson and Beckett, *Los Angeles,* pp. 4–5 and 28–30; Edwin A. Cottrel and Helen Jones, *Metropolitan Los Angeles: Characteristics of the Population* (Los Angeles: The Haynes Foundation, 1952), p. 48; Federal Housing Administration, *Housing Market Analysis: Los Angeles, California* (Washington: Government Printing Office, 1938).

14. Kenneth Jackson provides a good analysis of how suburban development responded to the automobile in cities other than Los Angeles; see *Crabgrass Frontier,* pp. 157–272. Also see Abbott, *The New Urban America,* pp. 168–171; Leo Schnore, "The Timing of Metropolitan De-

centralization: A Contribution to the Debate," in Schnore, ed., *The Urban Scene: Human Ecology and Demography* (New York: The Free Press, 1967), pp. 98–113; Foster, *From Streetcar to Superhighway*, pp. 47–48; and Tobin, "Suburbanization and the Development of Motor Transportation," pp. 103–106.

15. Sachse, "Transit," p. 104; East, "Streets," p. 94; Baker, *Report on Rapid Transit System,* pp. 46–47.

16. The accompanying table shows the increase in parking spaces in the central business district over a twenty-six-year period.

Increase of Parking Spaces in the CBD

Year	Off-Street Parking Spaces
1912	128
1923	12,500
1925	30,350
1928	32,257
1929	42,752
1931	45,727
1937	56,442
1938	65,000

Source: Central Business District Association, *Activities, 1940.*

CBD = Central Business District

17. Baker, "What Shall We Do With Our Next Million People?"; *Conference,* p. 6; Traffic Commission, *Annual Report, 1929,* p. 5; Ralph Hancock, *Fabulous Boulevard* (New York: Funk & Wagnalls, Co., 1949), p. 170; Reynor Banham, *Los Angeles: The Architecture of Four Ecologies* (New York: Pelican Books, 1973), p. 87; Central Business District Association, *Activities, 1940;* Automobile Club of Southern California, *Traffic Survey, Los Angeles Metropolitan Area, Nineteen Hundred Thirty-Seven* (Los Angeles: By the Club, 1937), p. 21 (hereafter cited as ACSC, 1937); Department of City Planning, *A Parkway Plan,* p. 23; Traffic Survey Committee, *Street Traffic Management,* p. 19; Metropolitan Parkway Engineering Committee, *Interregional, Regional, Metropolitan Parkways* (Los Angeles: By the Committee, 1946), p. 21; Baker, *Report on Rapid Transit System,* pp. 39–40; Los Angeles *Times,* January 17, 1941; City Planning Commissioners, *Activities, 1947,* p. 34; *1948,* pp. 19–29. Parking was a problem common to all large metropolitan areas at the time; see the American Transit Association, *Postwar Patterns of City Growth,* pp. 27–28. For a discussion of declining retail sales in American cities

after the adoption of the automobile, see Howard K. Nelson, "The Form and Structure of Cities," in Larry S. Bourne, ed., *Internal Structure of the City*, p. 81; and Homer Hoyt, "Recent Distortions of the Classical Models of Urban Structure," also in Bourne, pp. 87–89.

18. East, "Streets," p. 94; Donald M. Baker, "Traffic Problems in Los Angeles Today and Tomorrow," *Western City* 9 (December 1933): 20; Citizens' Traffic and Transportation Committee for the Extended Los Angeles Area, *Transportation in the Los Angeles Area* (Los Angeles: By the Committee, 1957).

19. Arthur G. Coons, *An Economic and Industrial Survey of the Los Angeles and San Diego Areas* (Sacramento: California State Planning Board, 1941), pp. 14–23: Warner, *The Urban Wilderness*, p. 117; Rae, *The Road and the Car*, p. 111; Dudley F. Pegrum, *Urban Transport and the Location of Industry in Metropolitan Los Angeles* (Los Angeles: Bureau of Business and Economic Research, University of California, Los Angeles, 1963); William A. Bresnahan, "Freight Transportation on the Highway," in Labatut and Lane, eds., *Highways in Our National Life*, pp. 248–249. Traffic Survey Committee, *Street Traffic Management*, p. 8; Moses and Williamson, "The Location of Economic Activity in Cities," pp. 211–222; Tarr, *Transportation Innovation*, pp. 34–35; Jackson, *Crabgrass Frontier*, pp. 183–184; Brian J. L. Berry and Yehoshua S. Cohen, "Decentralization of Commerce and Industry: The Restructuring of Metropolitan America," in Louis H. Masotti and Jeffrey K. Hadden, eds., *The Urbanization of the Suburbs* (Beverly Hills: Sage Publications, 1973), pp. 431–455.

20. Moses and Williamson, "The Location of Economic Activity in Cities," pp. 213–214; Bresnahan, "Freight Transportation on the Highway," pp. 248–249; Board of Public Utilities, *10th Annual Report, 1918–1919*, p. 83; Los Angeles *Times*, May 4, 1919, August 31, 1919, October 5, 1919, November 16, 1919.

21. United States Department of Commerce, *Historical Statistics of the United States, Colonial Times to 1970*, v. 2 (Washington, D.C.: Government Printing Office, 1975), p. 716; Los Angeles *Times*, May 4, 1919, August 31, 1919, October 12, 1919, February 22, 1920.

22. Fogelson, *The Fragmented Metropolis*, pp. 120–134.

23. Los Angeles Transportation Engineering Board, *Report of Traffic and Transportation Survey* (Los Angeles: Citizens' Transportation Survey Committee, 1940), pp. 66–67; Rae, *The Road and the Car*, pp. 249–255.

24. Fred W. Viehe, "Black Gold Suburbs: The Influence of the Extractive Industry on the Suburbanization of Los Angeles, 1890–1930," *Journal of Urban History* (November 1981): 3–26. Viehe argues that the development of an extensive oil industry was the primary factor in the suburbanization of Los Angeles. He notes that the discovery of oil in southern Los Angeles and northern Orange Counties led to the rise of several cities outside of Los Angeles' central business district. He therefore concludes that the oil industry and not transportation was

responsible for the early decentralization of southern California. Viehe's argument unfortunately is far too simplistic and deterministic.

First, these outlying areas were basically isolated from Los Angeles and did not act so much as suburbs as independent towns. True, places such as Fullerton and Whittier did have residential functions as early as the 1880s, but the people living there worked in the oil fields and not in Los Angeles. Nor did they have much interaction with Los Angeles because of the lack of adequate transportation. Viehe also completely ignores the importance of the suburban ideal, racial prejudice, population growth, and technological innovation on the suburbanization of southern California. What Viehe calls suburbanization then was really town building in rural areas. Without transportation, which later arrived in the form of interurbans and the automobile, these communities would have had little of the interchange with a major urban center that is characteristic of suburbs.

Like the other industries moving into the suburbs, the oil refineries and drilling fields had an important influence on the decentralization of Los Angeles. But this was only one factor in the general trend.

25. Tobin, "Suburbanization and the Development of Motor Transportation," p. 107; Pegrum, *Urban Transport*, pp. 12–38. In 1960, 62 percent of the factories in Los Angeles employing more than 500 people were directly serviced by the railroads. Far fewer than half of all other manufacturing facilities and all service companies (regardless of size) were connected with the carriers. Pegrum argues, however, that the proximity of most large factories in Los Angeles to rail lines in 1960 indicates that the truck and automobile did not greatly influence the location of industrial concerns. But this assertion is flawed.

First, Pegrum's own figures show that few factories regardless of size were actually linked to rail lines. Second, major boulevards paralleled many railroad and PE freight tracks. Therefore, the correlation between the location of plants and railroad routes does not naturally imply causation. The Transportation Engineering Board's 1938 survey further demonstrated the importance of the automobile to manufacturers by showing that most of their employees relied upon their cars as a means of getting to work. More than 70 percent of all workers in factories outside of the central business district in 1938 drove cars to their places of employment. Finally, Pegrum attempts to make a historical argument based upon modern data. He did not examine the evolution of industrial decentralization over time. Rather, almost his entire argument rests upon material from the 1960 census.

26. Traffic Commission, *Annual Report, 1929*, p. 5; *1930*, p. 14; Regional Planning Commission, *Business Districts*, p. 19; Transportation Engineering Board, *Traffic and Transportation Survey*. Automobile congestion and decentralization in Atlanta is discussed in Preston, *Automobile Age Atlanta*, pp. 113–115.

27. Baker, *Report on Rapid Transit System*, p. 37–d; Committee to Accomplish Mass Transportation, *Report*, p. 21; *Conference*, p. 6.
28. Sachse, "Transit," p. 104; Transportation Engineering Board, *Traffic and Transportation Survey*. See also East, "Streets," p. 94; City Planning Commissioners, *A Parkway Plan*, p. 16.
29. East, "Streets," pp. 95–96; Los Angeles County Regional Planning Commission, *Freeways for the Region* (Los Angeles: By the Commission, 1943), p. 26; ACSC, 1937, pp. 20–21; Dudley Pegrum, *Residential Population and Urban Transport Facilities in the Los Angeles Metropolitan Area* (Berkeley and Los Angeles: Bureau of Business and Economic Research, University of California, 1964), p. 24.
30. Jackson, *Crabgrass Frontier*, pp. 172–189.
31. Tarr, *Transportation Innovation*, p. 36. Another 2 percent rode commuter trains.
32. In a few cities, the number of commuters using their autos on a daily basis matched or exceeded that in Los Angeles. By 1929, more than half of all those entering Kansas City's central business district drove their own cars, while fully 66 percent of those arriving in the downtown area of Washington, D.C., did so by automobile. See Tobin, "Suburbanization and the Development of Motor Transportation," pp. 105–109. See also, Abbott, *The New Urban America*, pp. 57–63 and 161–189.
33. Jackson, *Crabgrass Frontier*, pp. 287–296. See also Gary R. Hovinen, "Suburbanization in Greater Philadelphia, 1880–1941," *Journal of Historical Geography* 11 (April 1985): 174–195.

8 / The Road to Autopia

1. Quoted in Foster, *From Streetcar to Superhighway*, p. 143; see also pp. 38–45; and Foster, "City Planners and Urban Transportation: The American Response, 1900–1940," *Journal of Urban History* 5 (May 1979). I rely heavily upon Foster for the next few paragraphs.
2. All quotations appear in Foster, *From Streetcar to Superhighway*, pp. 147, 102, 149. Emphasis in original.
3. For more on freeways, see Foster, *From Streetcar to Superhighway*, pp. 162–165; Barrett, *The Automobile and Urban Transit*, pp. 142–150; David Brodsly, *L.A. Freeway. An Appreciative Essay* (Berkeley, Los Angeles, London: University of California Press, 1981).
4. Regional Planning Commission, *Business Districts*, p. 2; Regional Planning Commission, *Freeways*, p. 26; Traffic Survey Committee, *Street Traffic Management*, p. 24; East, "Streets," p. 97; City Planning Commissioners, *A Parkway Plan*, p. 16.
5. De Leuw, Cather & Company et al., *City of Los Angeles Recommended Program for Improvement of Transportation and Traffic Facilities* (Los

Angeles: By the Consultants, 1945), p. 22; E. E. East, "Los Angeles' Street Traffic Problem," *Civil Engineering* 12 (August 1942): 436; Traffic Survey Committee, *Street Traffic Management*, p. 30; Cottrel and Jones, *Metropolitan Los Angeles*, p. 67.

6. Ainsworth, *Out of the Noose!*; Los Angeles County Regional Planning Commission, *A Comprehensive Report on the Master Plan of Highways for the Los Angeles County Regional Planning District* (Los Angeles: By the Commission, 1941), p. 33; Metropolitan Parkway Engineering Committee, *Interregional, Regional, Metropolitan Parkways* (Los Angeles: By the Committee, 1946), p. 4; ACSC, 1937, pp. 5–12. Passenger miles traveled in the late thirties were as follows: Buses—3%; Street railways—17%; Automobiles—80%.

7. Ainsworth, *Out of the Noose!*; ACSC, 1937, pp. 5 and 30; Baker, "Traffic Problems in Los Angeles," p. 20. Ihdler noted that widening streets was a temporary expedient as early as 1924; see Ihdler, "The Automobile and Community Planning," p. 201.

8. ACSC, 1937, p. 30; Ainsworth, *Out of the Noose!*

9. For examples and lists of earlier freeway proposals see Regional Planning Commission, *Freeways*, p. 8. See also Olmsted Brothers and Bartholomew and Associates, *Parks, Playgrounds, and Beaches for the Los Angeles Region* (Los Angeles: Citizens' Committee on Parks, Playgrounds, and Beaches, 1930), p. 13; City Planning Commissioners, *Annual Report, 1931–1932*, p. 17; *1937–1938*, p. 8; Traffic Commission, *Annual Report, 1937*, p. 1; Los Angeles County Regional Planning Commission, *Report of a Highway Traffic Survey in the County of Los Angeles, 1937* (Los Angeles: By the Commission, 1937), p. 18.

10. Central Business District Association, *Activities, 1937*, p. 2; Fred L. Mowder to Ella Stolman, September 8, 1938, Box 133, JRH; Coons, *An Economic and Industrial Survey*, p. 26.

11. Central Business District Association, *Activities, 1949*, p. 23; *1937*, p. 2; *1938*, p. 2; Traffic Commission, *Annual Report, 1937*; Lloyd Aldrich to Fred L. Mowder and Walter R. Lindersmit, January 6, 1938, Box 133, JRH; Los Angeles *Times*, March 19, 1939. The committee was composed of representatives from the Traffic Association, the Central Business District Association, and representatives from eight areas of the metropolis and eighteen cities in the area.

12. Los Angeles Transportation Engineering Board, *A Transit Program for the Los Angeles Metropolitan Area* (Los Angeles: Citizens' Transportation Survey Committee, 1939); Central Business District Association, *Activities, 1938*, p. 3.

13. Transportation Engineering Board, *A Transit Plan*, IV.

14. Ibid., pp. 4–6; see also the Arroyo Seco Parkway Dedication Committee, *The Arroyo Seco Parkway, the West's First Freeway* (pamphlet commemorating dedication ceremonies, December 30, 1940, JRH).

15. Central Business District Association, *Activities, 1942*; Transportation Engineering Board, *A Transit Program*, pp. 4–6.

16. East, "Streets," pp. 91–97.
17. Ainsworth, *Out of the Noose!*; Los Angeles Board of Public Utilities and Transportation Commissioners, *General Conclusions and Recommendations Concerning Mass Transportation in the Los Angeles Area* (Los Angeles: By the Commission, 1940), p. 5; Traffic Survey Committee, *Street Traffic Management*, p. 8; Robert O. Thomas, "Transportation Problems in the Los Angeles Metropolitan Area," p. 6; Central Business District Association, *Activities, 1949*, p. 6. The Transportation Engineering Board proposed reserving a strip down the middle of the freeways to later accommodate rapid-transit tracks.
18. Department of City Planning, *A Parkway Plan*, pp. 3–6; Central Business District Association, *Activities, 1941*, p. 4.
19. Department of City Planning, *A Parkway Plan*, pp. 8–12.
20. Ibid.
21. Ibid., pp. 3, 27, and 41–45. Chicago and New York had by this time built individual expressways with great success but did not as yet have a system of freeways planned.
22. The Citizens' Transportation Committee had already addressed this problem by accepting representatives from different areas in the county.
23. Regional Planning Commission, *Freeways*, pp. 1–3 and 20.
24. Ibid., pp. 3–6, and 32. Los Angeles during the thirties had the reputation as the least safe American city for pedestrians and motorists. See Traffic Survey Committee, *Street Traffic Management*, p. 21.
25. Regional Planning Commission, *Freeways*, p. 13.
26. Ibid.
27. The Ramona (later the San Bernardino Freeway) and the Santa Ana freeways were under construction when the war broke out.
28. Regional Planning Commission, *Freeways*, p. 9.
29. Sachse, "Transit," pp. 101–113.
30. Traffic Survey Committee, *Street Traffic Management*, pp. 27–30; Central Business District Association, *Activities, 1942*, p. 9.
31. Sachse, "Transit," p. 109; Central Business District Association, *Activities, 1944–1945*. See also Regional Planning Commission, *Business Districts*, p. 4; Lloyd Aldrich to Fred L. Mowder, November 18, 1946 (Xerox copy found loose inside Central Business District Association, *Los Angeles Parkway and Transit System* [Los Angeles: By the Association, 1946], JRH).
32. Sachse, "Transit," pp. 102–104; Los Angeles *Times*, October 3, 1940; East, "Los Angeles' Street Traffic Problem," p. 438.
33. Central Business District Association, *Activities, 1941*, p. 10; Baker, *Report on Rapid Transit System*, pp. 22a–d; Sachse, "Transit," pp. 104–105; Transportation Engineering Board, *Traffic and Transportation Survey*, p. 14; Los Angeles Board of Public Utilities and Transportation Commissioners, *A Study of the Feasibility and Desirability of a City Wide Motor Coach System to Replace Existing Local Transportation Systems in the*

City of Los Angeles (Los Angeles: By the Commission, 1935); *Los Angeles Times*, December 2, 1940, March 15, 1941, March 30, 1941; East, "Los Angeles' Street Traffic Problem," p. 438; Regional Planning Commission, *Business Districts*, p. 4.

34. Central Business District Association, *Activities, 1944–1945*; see also 1941 and 1942 reports. Parkway Engineering Committee, *Metropolitan Parkways*, p. 5; Lloyd Aldrich to Fred L. Mowder, November 18, 1946; Central Business District Association, *Parkway Transit Lines in the Central Business District* (Los Angeles: By the Association, 1945), pp. 13–16; Central Business District Association, *Transit Study, 1944: Los Angeles Metropolitan Area* (Los Angeles: By the Association, 1944), Letter of Transmittal and p. 21; Lloyd Aldrich to Fred L. Mowder, (May 9, 1945), reprinted in Central Business District Association, *Activities, 1944–1945*. The association expected the buses would converge on the central business district, thus creating a centralizing influence. The Traffic Commission changed its name to the Traffic Association during the thirties.

35. Traffic Commission, *Annual Report, 1932*, p. 11; *1933*, pp. 4–11.

36. Arroyo Seco Parkway Dedication Committee, *The Arroyo Seco Parkway*.

37. East, "Streets," pp. 99–100; American Transit Association, *Postwar Patterns of City Growth*, p. 22; City Planning Commissioners, *Annual Report, 1947*, p. 28; Brodsly, *L.A. Freeway*, pp. 115–116. See also an unsigned, untitled typescript in Box 15 of the John Anson Ford Papers, HEH, which talks about the inequities of the state allocation of gas tax funds prior to 1947. See also Paul T. McElhiney, "The Freeways of Metropolitan Los Angeles: An Evaluation in Terms of Their Objectives," (Ph.D. diss., University of California, Los Angeles, 1959), p. 212.

38. Barrett, *The Automobile and Urban Transit*, pp. 141–153; Richard Davies, *Age of Asphalt: The Automobile, the Freeway, and the Condition of Metropolitan America* (Philadelphia: Lippincott, 1975). See also Jackson, *Crabgrass Frontier*, pp. 248–251.

9 / Epilogue

1. The foregoing relies heavily upon James Ortner and Martin Wachs, "The Cost-Revenue Squeeze in American Public Transit," *Journal of the American Planning Association* 45 (January 1979): 11–12; and Richard J. Solomon and Arthur Saltzman, "History of Transit and Innovative Systems," Report No. USL TR–70–20 (1971), Urban Systems Laboratory, Massachusetts Institute of Technology. See also Jackson, *Crabgrass Frontier*, p. 189.

2. D. R. Lewis, "The Pacific Electric" (typescript in Box 64, Fletcher Bowron Papers, HEH); Crump, *Ride the Big Red Cars*, pp. 208–210.

3. Eli Bail, "From Railway to Freeway: The Pacific Electric and the Motor

Coach," *Interurbans Special* 90 (1984); Ira Swett, "The Los Angeles Railway," *Interurbans Special* 11 (December 1951). Some authors have argued that buses could operate at half the cost of streetcars; see, for instance, John Bauer, "The Street Railways Struggle against Traffic Losses," *Public Utilities Fortnightly* 23 (1939): 209–217. More recently, David St. Clair has contended that streetcars were less expensive to run than buses; see "The Motorization and Decline of Urban Public Transit, 1935–1950," *Journal of Economic History* 41 (September 1981). Regardless of which interpretation is correct, railway officials realized that streetcars could no longer operate efficiently in traffic. They believed that only buses with their increased mobility could recapture lost patrons.

4. This and the following paragraphs rely heavily upon Solomon and Saltzman, "History of Transit and Innovative Systems," pp. 1–18 to 1–29.

5. The antitrust case against General Motors continued into the sixties. The government accused the company of conspiring to monopolize the manufacturing of buses in the United States. In 1965 GM signed an agreement that restricted its ability to curb its competitors. See Solomon and Saltzman, "History of Transit and Innovative Systems," pp. 1–26 to 1–29.

6. Quoted in Solomon and Saltzman, "History of Transit and Innovative Systems," p. 2–9.

7. City Planning Commissioners, *Activities, 1949*, pp. 28–32; Lettergram, December 7, 1956, Box 14, John Anson Ford Papers, HEH; Typescript dated March 1954, Box 15, John Anson Ford Papers, HEH; Traffic Survey Committee, *Street Traffic Management*, p. 19.

8. Lloyd M. Smith, "An Introduction to the Study of Public Transportation in the Los Angeles Metropolitan Area" (typescript in Box 64, Fletcher Bowron Papers, HEH), pp. 5–8 and 16.

9. Typescript dated March 1954, Box 15, John Anson Ford Papers, HEH; Lloyd Smith, pp. 9–10; "Presentation Before Mass Rapid Transit Subcommittee of Legislative Joint Committee on Transportation, January 17, 18, 19, and 20, 1956" (typescript, Box 15, John Anson Ford Papers, HEH).

10. Lloyd Smith, pp. 9–10.

11. Ibid., pp. 7–8 and 15.

12. Ibid., pp. 10–17; "Monorail" (typescript in Box 15, John Anson Ford Papers, HEH); see also a memo and attached letter dated September 4, 1956, Box 14, John Anson Ford Papers, HEH; and Brodsly, *L.A. Freeway*, p. 160.

13. Frank H. Malley in American Transit Association, *Postwar Patterns of City Growth*, p. 18.

14. McElhiney, "The Freeways of Metropolitan Los Angeles," pp. 217–223; Traffic Survey Committee, *Street Traffic Management*, p. 27; De Leuw, Cather & Co., *Recommended Program for Improvement of Transportation*,

p. 22; "Do People Like Freeways?" *California Highways and Public Works* (November and December, 1955); "Citizens' Traffic and Transportation Committee Recommendations for Development of Transportation Program for Los Angeles Basin Area" (typescript, Box 14, John Anson Ford Papers, HEH).

15. Lewis Mumford, *Technics and Civilization* (New York: Harcourt, Brace, Jovanovich, 1963), p. 6.
16. Jackson, *Crabgrass Frontier*, p. 170; Lewis Mumford, *The City in History* (New York: Harcourt, Brace & World, 1961), p. 510. See also Barrett, *The Automobile and Urban Transit*, for a similar perspective.
17. Scott, *The Urban Land Nexus*. See also George Rogers Taylor, *The Transportation Revolution* (New York: Reinhart and Company, 1951), for information on transportation subsidies in the nineteenth century.
18. Mumford, *The City in History*, p. 505; Jackson, *Crabgrass Frontier*, p. 271.
19. Mumford, *The City in History*, p. 510.
20. Banham, *Los Angeles: The Architecture of Four Ecologies*, p. 243.
21. Larry Long and Diana DeAre, "The Slowing of Urbanization in the United States," *Scientific American* 249 (July 1983): 39. Some advocates of public transportation have argued that the construction of fixed rail lines will encourage denser population clusters and centralized transportation patterns. Recent planning studies, however, have generally dismissed this argument. See, for example, David Harrison, Jr., "Transportation and the Dynamics of Urban Land Use" (Harvard University Department of City and Regional Planning, Discussion Paper D78–22, December 1978); and Harrison, Jr., "Simulating the Impacts of Transportation Policies on Urban Land Use Patterns" (Harvard University Department of City and Regional Planning, Discussion Paper D78–32, December 1979).

≡ Index ≡

40, 118, 167, 191; commercial development of, 40, 81, 167, 198–200, 287–288 n. 24; congestion in, 15–16, 18, 45, 55–56, 59–63, 95, 97–99, 101–103, 105–106, 108, 114, 130, 161, 193–194, 201–202, 206, 213–215, 219, 242; and decentralization, 14, 32–33, 167, 176, 206–207, 246; development of, 14, 31–33, 56, 58, 95, 129, 176–207, 252; and ethnic neighborhoods, 181–182; and freeways, 213, 216–234; inadequacy of streets in, 16, 59–60, 95–98, 107–109, 194, 215–216; low population density of, 177, 187–189; and street improvements, 16, 58, 95–97, 101, 105, 114–115; and parking ban, 15–16, 64–71, 76–89; progressivism in, 41–44, 89
Los Angeles Board of Public Utilities Commissioners, 45, 46–47, 55, 60, 101, 244; founding of, 44; and Los Angeles traction companies, 44–48, 54, 63–64, 77–79, 125; and parking ban, 64–66, 76–79, 87, 89; and rapid transit, 127–129, 132–133, 161; and union station controversy, 139, 154
Los Angeles Chamber of Commerce, 138–139
Los Angeles City Engineering Department, 55, 154
Los Angeles City Planning Commission, 98, 108, 146, 161, 164
Los Angeles City Planning Department, 214, 242; criticizes traction companies in Los Angeles, 170; duties of, 223; recommends freeway system, 223–225; supports union station, 154
Los Angeles County Board of Supervisors, 129
Los Angeles Examiner, 33, 155; and automobile, 55; complains about traction companies in Los Ange-

les, 34–35, 38–39; and parking ban, 83, 85; and union station controversy, 139, 144–145
Los Angeles Metropolitan Transit Authority, 239, 241, 243–244
Los Angeles Motor Coach Company, 229
Los Angeles Railway Company, 31, 35, 36, 63, 238, 241; declining patronage of, 49, 56; defends self against public criticism, 72, 74; and development of Los Angeles, 31–33, 183; financial problems of, 16–17, 40–41, 127, 169, 238–239; inadequate service of, 40, 221, 228; and jitneys, 50; and parking ban, 65; public attempts to limit fares of, 33–34, 36; public criticism of, 33–40, 45–46, 68, 71–76, 125, 166, 168; and real estate development, 39–40; sold to American City Lines, 2, 239; usage of, 31, 33, 170; and use of buses, 3, 186, 229, 239, 241
Los Angeles Rate Association, 37
Los Angeles Record, 50–51, 74, 75, 143–144; complains about poor railway service, 34–36, 71–76, 79, 86; and parking ban, 74–75, 79–80, 85–86; supports alternative transportation to streetcars, 74–76, 79
Los Angeles Regional Planning Commission, 225–227
Los Angeles Times, 42–43, 58, 79, 197; and automobile, 59, 70; and fear of decentralization, 67–68, 81; notes congestion in Los Angeles, 55, 59, 61–62; opposes elevated railways, 141, 152–153; and parking ban, 67, 70, 81–82, 83–85; and railways, 81–82, 125, 229; supports Major Traffic Street Plan, 113–114; and union station controversy, 142–143, 156
Los Angeles Traffic Commission,

Designer:	David Lunn
Compositor:	Prestige Typography
Text:	11/13 Palatino
Display:	Bauhaus Light
Printer:	Vail-Ballou Press
Binder:	Vail-Ballou Press

LOS ANGELES CHAMBER OF COMMERCE MAP / 1929

Los Angeles County and Southern California constitute a paradise for the motorist. The hundreds of miles of excellent paved highways link together the various communities of the County and make accessible to the motorist all the various points of interest such as mountains, desert and